GILES GORDON has a particul~~ar~~ ... ...he short story. He has edited a n~~umber of~~ collections including *Modern Scottish Short Stories* (with Fred Urquhart), *Shakespeare Stories* and *English Short Stories: 1900 to the present* (published in Everyman in 1988). He has published six novels and three collections of his own stories.

MODERN SHORT STORIES 2
1940-1980

Edited by Giles Gordon

J.M. Dent & Sons Ltd: London
EVERYMAN'S LIBRARY

First published in Everyman in 1982. Reissued 1991
Selection, Introduction and Notes © Giles Gordon 1982

Printed and bound in Great Britain by
The Guernsey Press Co. Ltd., Guernsey, C.I.
for J.M. Dent & Sons Ltd.
91 Clapham High Street
London SW4 7TA

British Library Cataloguing in Publication Data

Modern Short Stories 2, 1940-80
1. Short stories, English
I. Gordon, Giles
823'.01'08[F]   PR1309.S5

ISBN 0 460 87058 0

CONTENTS

CONTENTS

CONTENTS

Acknowledgements

Acknowledgements are due to the following for permission to include the stories which appear in this book: the author's literary estate and Chatto & Windus Ltd for 'The Fifth of November' from *A Spirit Rises* by Sylvia Townsend Warner (Chatto & Windus, 1962); the author's literary estate and Anthony Sheil Associates Ltd for 'Let them Call it Jazz' from *Tigers are Better-Looking* by Jean Rhys (Andre Deutsch, 1968); the executors of the author's estate and Hamish Hamilton Ltd for 'Someone in the Lift' from *Two for the River* by L. P. Hartley (Hamish Hamilton, 1961); the author's estate and Jonathan Cape Ltd for 'Sunday Afternoon' from *The Demon Lover* by Elizabeth Bowen (Jonathan Cape, 1945); the author and Constable Publishers for 'The Woman Who Married Clark Gable' from *Teresa and Other Stories* by Sean O'Faolain (Jonathan Cape, 1947); the author and Longman Paul Ltd for 'Old Man's Story' from *A Man and His Wife* by Frank Sargeson (Caxton Press, Christchurch, 1940); the author and Harold Matson Company Inc for 'A Very Merry Christmas' from *Stories 2* by Morley Callaghan (MacGibbon & Kee, 1962); the author's estate and Curtis Brown Ltd for 'Gents Only' from *Collected Stories* by Rhys Davies (Heinemann, 1955); the author and Laurence Pollinger Ltd for 'The Blue Film' from *Twenty-One Stories* by Graham Greene (William Heinemann, 1954); the author and John Calder (Publishers) Ltd for 'Still' from *For to End Yet Again and other Fizzles* by Samuel Beckett (John Calder, 1976); the author and Anthony Sheil Associates Ltd for 'An Astrologer's Day' from *An Astrologer's Day and Other Stories* by R. K. Narayan (Eyre & Spottiswoode, 1947); Elaine Greene Ltd for 'Difficulty with a

Bouquet' from *Fireman Flower* by William Sansom (The Hogarth Press, 1944); the author and Curtis Brown (Aust) Pty Ltd for 'Willy-Wagtails by Moonlight' from *The Burnt Ones* by Patrick White (Eyre & Spottiswoode, 1964); the author and Constable Publishers for 'Sarah' from *The Stories of Mary Lavin, Volume II* (Constable, 1974); the author's estate and Virago Ltd for 'The Fly-paper' from *The Devastating Boys* by Elizabeth Taylor (Chatto & Windus, 1972); the author and Anthony Sheil Associates Ltd for 'But German Girls Walk Different' from *The Last GI Bride Wore Tartan* by Fred Urquhart (Serif Books, Edinburgh, 1947); the author and Curtis Brown Ltd for 'A Visit in Bad Taste' from *The Wrong Set* by Angus Wilson (Secker & Warburg, 1949); the author and Murray Pollinger for 'The Hitch-hiker' from *The Wonderful Story of Henry Sugar and Six More* by Roald Dahl (Jonathan Cape and Penguin Books, 1977); the author and Harold Ober Associates Inc for 'The Ormolu Clock' from *Voices at Play* by Muriel Spark (Macmillan, 1961); the author and Curtis Brown Ltd for 'Flight' from *The Habit of Loving* by Doris Lessing (MacGibbon & Kee, 1957); the author and Anthony Sheil Associates Ltd for 'Pedestrian' from *The Night of the Funny Hats* by Elspeth Davie (Hamish Hamilton, 1980); the author's estate and Victor Gollancz Ltd for 'Who Killed Baker?' by Edmund Crispin and Geoffrey Bush from *Fen Country* by Edmund Crispin (Victor Gollancz, 1979); the author and The Hogarth Press Ltd for 'The Wireless Set' from *A Time to Keep* by George Mackay Brown (The Hogarth Press, 1969); the author and A. M. Heath & Co Ltd for 'The Puppets' from *The Japanese Umbrella* by Francis King (Longmans, 1964); the author, Jonathan Cape Ltd and Viking Penguin Inc for 'Happy Event' from *Six Feet of the Country* by Nadine Gordimer (Victor Gollancz, 1956); the author and John Farquharson Ltd for 'The General Danced at Dawn' from *The General Danced at Dawn* by George MacDonald Fraser (Barrie & Jenkins, 1970); the author and John Murray (Publishers) Ltd for 'Desecration' from *How I Became a Holy Mother* by R. Prawer Jhabvala (John Murray, 1976); the

ACKNOWLEDGEMENTS

author and Rosica Colin Ltd for 'Mr Raynor the School-teacher' from *The Loneliness of the Long-Distance Runner* by Alan Sillitoe (W. H. Allen, 1959); the author and A. D. Peters & Co Ltd for 'Broken Homes' from *Lovers of Their Time* by William Trevor (Bodley Head, 1978); the author and C. & J. Wolfers Ltd for 'Venus Smiles' from *Vermilion Sands* by J. G. Ballard (Jonathan Cape, 1973); and the author and Faber and Faber Ltd for 'Lavin' from *Nightlines* by John McGahern (Faber and Faber, 1970).

The copyright in the individual stories is as follows: 'The Fifth of November' © Sylvia Townsend Warner 1962; 'Let them Call it Jazz' © Jean Rhys 1962; 'Someone in the Lift' from *The Complete Short Stories of L. P. Hartley* © 1973 the executors of the estate of the late L. P. Hartley; 'Sunday Afternoon' © Elizabeth Bowen 1945; 'The Woman Who Married Clark Gable' © Sean O'Faolain 1947; 'Old Man's Story' © Frank Sargeson 1940; 'A Very Merry Christmas' © Morley Callaghan 1959; 'Gents Only' © Rhys Davies 1955; 'The Blue Film' © Graham Greene 1972; 'Still' © Samuel Beckett 1976; 'An Astrologer's Day' © R. K. Narayan 1947; 'Difficulty with a Bouquet' © William Sansom 1963; 'Willy-Wagtails by Moonlight' © Patrick White 1964; 'Sarah' © Mary Lavin 1974; 'The Fly-paper' © Elizabeth Taylor 1972; 'But German Girls Walk Different' © Fred Urquhart 1947; 'A Visit in Bad Taste' © Angus Wilson 1949; 'The Hitch-hiker' © Roald Dahl 1977; 'The Ormolu Clock' © Muriel Spark 1960; 'Flight' © Doris Lessing 1957; 'Pedestrian' © Elspeth Davie 1980; 'Who Killed Baker?' © Barbara Montgomery 1979; 'The Wireless Set' © George Mackay Brown 1969; 'The Puppets' © Francis King 1964; 'Happy Event' © Nadine Gordimer 1956; 'The General Danced at Dawn' © George MacDonald Fraser 1970; 'Desecration' © R. Prawer Jhabvala 1976; 'Mr Raynor the School-teacher' © Alan Sillitoe 1959; 'Broken Homes' © William Trevor 1976; 'Venus Smiles' © J. G. Ballard 1957; 'Lavin' © John McGahern 1970.

Introduction

It is fashionable to assert various things about the short story. First, that it is dying (although never that it is dead). Second, that as a literary form it is closer to poetry than to the novel. Third, that it is at its best when depicting a single incident or character. These ideas, like other generalizations about short stories, are to such a degree but a part of the truth that they are, as an attempt at definition, almost meaningless, certainly misleading. As the South African novelist, short story writer and critic Dan Jacobson has stated: '. . . all that one can say with absolute veracity, in attempting to distinguish between the short story, the novella and the novel, is that some works of fiction are shorter (or longer) than others'.

The somewhat puritanical suggestion that the short story is more akin to poetry than to the novel bears with it the implication that poetry is tightly written and ordered, that language, craft and form are paramount, whereas the novel is a gutsy ragbag, a portmanteau of experience, emotional and intellectual sloppiness allied to linguistic imprecision. This seems to me demeaning both of the art of the novelist, and of the power and effect of prose fiction used beguilingly at shorter length. After all, when a piece of writing is described today as a prose poem a compliment is not normally intended.

A further platitude is that the short story is an impoverished relative of the novel, of interest primarily to readers – not to mention writers – lacking in stamina; which is analogous to stating that the mile or the marathon is more significant than the one hundred metres or the high jump.

Were this anthology to have been edited five or ten or fifteen years ago it would have been a very different compilation from what it is, even if it had comprised stories of the previous forty years and the same editor had made the selection. This is not because stories which have been written and published change their shape and form (at least not usually: authors have been known in their later and perhaps grander years to tinker with their younger and more rough-shod if spontaneous work) but that our ideas of what are or are not 'good' short stories change more according to the times in which we live and the vagaries of literary fashion than is the case with substantial novels.

Short stories, to purloin the brilliant title of a collection by B. S. Johnson and Zulfikar Ghose, are statements against corpses; an affirmation of living. Being statements of interpretation, they are highly susceptible to shifting critical attitudes, as are, for instance, drawings and paintings. This has as much to do with the form of the short story – what technically can and cannot be done with it – as with its subject matter, assuming form and content can be divorced in this way. Relatively few words have to do the trick, achieve the purpose, establish the required resonance, ambiguity and depth, and – somewhere, somehow – deliver the body blow (which isn't, these days, necessarily a punch line, a crack of the whip in the final sentence).

To me, short stories explore, crystallize and interpret singular incidents, emotions, attitudes, places, characters, relationships, concepts. The thirty-one stories in this book, all written out of the English (as opposed to American) tradition of literature, differ marvellously in style and content from one another, not least where they contrast and complement: Patrick White's Australia – the place manipulating the people – as against Frank Sargeson's New Zealand, individuals destroying themselves, whatever the country; the very English Sylvia Townsend Warner and the very Canadian Morley Callaghan exploring the influence of the church in local communities in different continents; jealousies,

loves and self-determination in the South Africa of Doris
Lessing as against the pathetic inevitability of Black lives and
deaths as seen by Nadine Gordimer.

Above all, I have tried to present a showcase of the range,
possibilities and achievements of a most variegated literary
form since 1940. (Is it a coincidence that the three stories
written about the Second World War are all by Celts, as is a
fourth about soldiers?) The collection, in terms of the years it
spans, is a sequel and companion to the Everyman *Modern
Short Stories* edited by John Hadfield, published in 1939 and
still in print. That anthology contained stories written during the first forty-odd years of the century, and of the twenty
authors represented therein half were still alive and most of
them writing when the war broke out. Because of the quan-
tity and quality of short stories and their authors in the last
four decades I have reluctantly but inevitably had to omit
pieces by any of those ten – I particularly regret having to
exclude W. Somerset Maugham, P. G. Wodehouse, V. S.
Pritchett and H. E. Bates. (Of my thirty-one authors, all but
nine are alive as I write.)

It is a commonplace that there are infinitely fewer outlets
for the commercial publication of short stories today than in
the heyday of periodical publishing, both in the nineteenth
century and in the years leading up to the Second World
War. I've seen it stated less often that the thinner appetites of
publishers (although not, judging by public library lendings,
of readers) for short stories means first, that the standard of
those published is more consistent and higher than in previous years; and second, that there is less compulsion upon
the writer to make his or her short stories long, if you will
allow the paradox. Consequently, the best short story
writers in the language today – but not always those in
America, to whom the number of pages too often seems
more important than the quality of the prose – have learned
to their artistic benefit to compress, to be more exact, to say
as much as possible and precisely what they want to say in as
few words as are compatible with their intentions, and

ambitions. (Thus in a similar number of total words to John Hadfield I am able to include thirty-one stories whereas he had room only for twenty.)

Elspeth Davie's 'modernist' story is a superb example of this: she evokes in a few pages much about the lust affair of the twentieth century between man and motor car. By way of contrast, Roald Dahl glamorizes ironically some of our fantasies about speed and the fast life. Mr Dahl, in the traditional sense, tells a story, narrates an anecdote compulsively. Mrs Davie projects, as did Chekhov and Kafka, a world.

The collection excludes stories by Americans (John Hadfield included three) although it embraces writers from five continents. R. K. Narayan and Ruth Prawer Jhabvala delineate two Indias, the first 'native' and poignant, the second seedy and exotic, both stories about a people and a country which cannot resolve its love-hate relationship with the British going back to the days when that part of the sub-continent was painted red on the map. Patrick White, like Moses in Israel, has to represent Australia, though in his story here he writes in less epic, more suburban vein than often; yet this Australia comes across as positively raw and vulnerable in comparison with Frank Sargeson's New Zealand love affair, or so it seems at the beginning of this too little known writer's *tour de force*.

The short story, as we understand it in its widest sense, derives from what Fred Urquhart has described as 'unbridled imagination' and, more specifically, the ballad tradition. People, individuals, have always told stories, and 'telling tales' doesn't only mean telling lies. Nevertheless, the best inventions of the imagination are frequently preferable to a more literal and mundane sort of truth. The Border Ballads led to the tales of Sir Walter Scott and Robert Louis Stevenson, although in the nineteenth century the form, as practised and published in the British Isles, was often closer to journalism than to literature. Plot and narrative pace were more fundamental than character and psychology.

But in Europe the art of the short story was being transformed by, among others, Chekhov and Tolstoy, Maupassant and Turgenev. In 1900 Freud published *The Interpretation of Dreams*, then in 1914 James Joyce's *Dubliners* arrived in the world. (Oscar Wilde had published his superb fairy tales less than three decades before.) After *Dubliners* (and John McGahern's story here is very much in that tradition) the short story in English was never again to feel inferior. It could attempt anything, and did. Samuel Beckett, once Joyce's secretary, has extended, even revolutionized, the possibilities of short fiction as well as of the theatre and the novel. Whether his piece in this collection is closer to the conventional short story or the conventional novel is not a question that occurs.

The Irish, along with the other Celtic nations, have always excelled in the form. It was, for me, a case of who to leave out. Unlike Wilde, Sean O'Faolain sets his fairy tales in the contemporary world but whether his story here is romantic or anti-romantic is for the individual reader to decide. Mary Lavin's humanity is in her gentle humour as much as in her imagination, and yet she is as lyrical as Yeats. Elizabeth Bowen straddles, slightly stiffly but powerfully, the Irish and English traditions. As for William Trevor, like no one else writing today, he combines compassion and wry humour in his poignant, marvellously observed stories that explore the depths of the human heart.

Likewise, although Muriel Spark is Scottish, her coruscating prose and exemplary fables have as much to do with the Renaissance, a time when anything and everything was possible, as with our greyer era: her characters aspire. George Mackay Brown's northern Scots go back even further in history: tradition and the past are what shape the present. It's a delightful surprise that one of too few writers who employ the short story as a vehicle for revelation of character through humour should be a Scot, a race not usually associated with jokes or wit, George MacDonald Fraser. The same applies to Fred Urquhart, whose humour is rooted in day-to-day drudgery, his working-class characters knowing that they might as well make the most of today because tomorrow almost definitely will be worse.

As an influence on his fellow-countrymen as writers, Dylan Thomas has a lot to answer for. Rhys Davies, in his touching (and anti-feminist?) story here, completely eschews the purple and realizes his poetry by narrating the ordinary.

It has always seemed to me that much of the best work in the short story in English has been in so-called 'genre' fiction: ghost stories, detective stories, romances and science fiction or fantasy, and I scoured the shelves for one outstanding example in each category. I failed only with romance: no 'genre' story I could discover compared for poignancy and secret passion with William Sansom's miniature. Much of L. P. Hartley's best work is in the ghost story, and his incident here, ethereal though its image is, does not easily leave the mind. Edmund Crispin and J. G. Ballard are, I believe, undervalued because they write, respectively, detective stories and science fiction, yet each is a considerable writer. Crispin's story reprinted in these pages is, for me, the perfect crime story, totally accomplished. And Mr Ballard acknowledges that science and mankind have to co-habit on Earth – if survival is to be possible.

Which leaves the other English contributors to the book. One of the Irish writers represented herein confided to me that the English cannot write short stories because they will never understand the form, its literary antecedents and traditions. I would not go quite as far as that but it has to be noted that relatively few of the best short story writers are English. Certainly the English tend to be quite conventional in their approach to the form (to declare that my parentage is Scottish and Irish is, I suppose, to reveal my prejudice). Nevertheless, there is more than gentle irony and satire in Angus Wilson's barbed indictment of middle-class English cosiness. As to Graham Greene, his story may, by his standards, be minor work but it reveals beautifully what the guilty English male thinks he can get away with, even with his wife in tow. Alan Sillitoe's working-class reports are still the exception, younger working-class writers tending to special-ize in *grand guignol* or surrealism.

Francis King and Elizabeth Taylor somehow represent the art of the English story at its most typical, employing almost outrageous understatement: the former seeing the British (or rather, in this case, two English speaking Americans), intrepid yet assertive but not unaware of alien cultures, abroad; the latter portraying what T. S. Eliot called the weasel underneath the cocktail cabinet. Yet of all the writers here it is surely Jean Rhys who endows her story – all her work – with the weight and gravitas of a lifetime. Her story is as world-weary and worldly-wise, as understanding and compassionate and tragic as any in the language that is ten or twenty times its length.

What, above all, appeals to me about the short story is that both writer and reader can indulge themselves and each other: the commitment is not (for the writer) to a year or more of hard labour as it may be with a novel, or (to the reader) of evening after evening, week after week of reading the same book. Thus both writer and reader may be daring and imaginative in the infinite pastures of the short story, and constantly be surprised and stimulated. The world may, and frequently is, being made wondrously new.

Giles Gordon 1982

SYLVIA TOWNSEND WARNER

The Fifth of November

Feeling the need for a little repose and luxury, Ellie, on her way back from the carpet factory where she worked, turned aside into the church of St Mary Ragmarket. She had done so before at various times, and could enter without feeling constrained to put on any particular behaviour, to bow the knee and adapt the heart to the presence of a ciborium that, wrapped in a striped veil, presented a rather Turkish appearance, to avoid the melancholy stare of the figure on the cross, to admire the architecture, or to apprehend interruption. The church stood in the old part of the town, whose venerable slums were in process of being cleared away and replaced by industrial buildings. The fairground from which it took its name was now occupied by a bus depot, and the remaining streets and alleyways did not house a churchgoing population. Though St Mary Ragmarket had been the parish church of one of the Pilgrim Fathers, whose ancestors knelt among the emblazoned figures in its armorial east window, and as such was visited by a certain number of pilgrim Americans, the proportion of American visitors in a town like Thorpe is small at any time, smaller still in November; and at 6 p.m. on a November evening any American visitor would be pursuing livelier interests. Ellie could feel pretty sure of having the church to herself.

The door closed behind her, and the noises of traffic, though still audible, passed into a different dimension of sound. Her sense of hearing relaxed. Her eyes recovered from the joggle of dark streets and devouring headlights. She saw instead the composed clear-obscure of the dimly lit interior, where, as if she were a fish in a pool, the dark pews, the glimmering effigies, the blackness of the glass in the traceried windows surrounded her like rocks and fronded waterweeds. But when she sighed with relief, no bubble rose to the surface. Nothing corroborated her sigh.

As she expected, the church was pleasantly warm. Warmth is one of the outward signs of the variety of English churchmanship known as High – an atmosphere in which ciboriums, images of the Blessed Virgin, sanctuary lamps, stands for holding votive candles, and shallow wadded mats referred to as 'kneelers' are in their natural clime. In churches known as Low one finds, instead of kneelers, hassocks, which themselves are high. It varies inversely. Ellie knew all this, not because she was religiously inclined but because, in the days before calamity forced her down in the world, she had been on the fringe of the class called educated, with a mind sufficiently at leisure to enjoy noticing things, and speculating over them, and reading books from the public library in order to learn more exactly about them. But this was a long time ago, and the scraps of knowledge she had then accumulated lay like a heap of dead leaves, broomed away into an unfrequented corner of her mind and only stirring now and then, and only the lightest and least significant of them stirring, at that. The Reformation of the English Church had come about, men had burned at the stake and a faith as fiery had blown the flames, Jesuit missionaries had been disembowelled at Tyburn, Laud's hands had fluttered in blessing through the prison grate, Quakers had been whipped through the streets, Newman had torn himself weeping from the mother he abjured, and as a result of all this anguish and altercation Ellie knew that St Mary Ragmarket could be relied on to provide warmth, repose, and a sense of luxury.

They were being provided as usual, and with them the amplitude of the nave, the remoteness of the roof, a serene faint smell of wax polish and candle wax, an uncluttered spaciousness; but to-night, for some reason, the quiet and the solitude had taken on a different quality, and were silence and emptiness. No building had ever been so totally silent so totally uninhabited. It was as if the fabric had grown up, and endured through the centuries, without anyone ever knowing about it or ever coming here. It was as though it were unvisitable, like a place in a dream, a dream into which she had got by mistake and out of which she would never pass. Perhaps the difference lay in herself. For to-night, though her body was relaxing like a cat on a familiar hearth, her mind would not relax. It was as though she were waiting, helplessly, ignorantly, rigidly waiting – as during the air-raid winters one had waited – for some dreadful thing that was about to declare itself, some inevitable, shattering recognition that would presently explode from within her. She ransacked her memory for a possible cause – a tap left running, a bill unpaid. She ran through the familiar rota of familiar dreads – Mother dying, herself taken ill and carted off to hospital, the rent raised, her job lost, another war, a purely hypothetical illegitimate son of Father's, specious and bullying, turning up to prey on them. There was no quiver of response. It must be nerves. For everything was just as usual. Her day had been no more tiring or uncongenial than usual. She was going home, as usual, where as usual she would get supper and serve it to Mother in her wheelchair, talk for a while, put her to bed, wash up, set things to rights, and go to bed herself, with the door ajar, so that she would wake up at any call from the adjoining room. Other women led lives quite as restricted, and much sadder, having no one to love. She had her mother, who, together with the habit of love, had survived thirty years of poverty and had been, till only a short time ago, a supporting and even a reviving person to go home to. For it was only in these last few years – four years, six years? – when deafness had closed her in, and given her the stunned, inattentive expression it was so painful to see, that acquaintances had begun to say she was wonderful for her age, and quite a character, and that Ellie would feel quite lost when she passed on.

This was the sort of acquaintance they were now reduced to – people who thirty years ago would only have been deserving old dears for Mother to give port wine and blankets to, people to whom it would be inconceivable that thirty years ago Mother walked on three-inch heels with the gait of a queen, subjugated everyone she met, and could kiss the wall behind her. Then, too, she was wonderful for her age – but no one would have dared say so. This was the being whom Father deserted, going off with a smug slut whose petticoats dangled below her skirts. 'I can do without him,' Mother had declared. 'Alimony is as good as matrimony at my age.' It was a brave boast, and while the alimony lasted, it held. Then, during the slump, he died, penniless. She mourned him briefly and tempestuously, and afterward began to pick holes in him.

Poor Mother!

It was time to think of getting back to her. Pauses for repose and luxury in St Mary Ragmarket seldom exceeded ten minutes, and tonight, since St Mary Ragmarket was not living up to Ellie's expectations, there was the less reason to linger there. Yet she wanted to linger; or rather, she was reluctant to quit it for streets where she would certainly encounter more of those horrible Guys. It was the Fifth of November, and at every turn she had met groups of children bearing their dummy towards the bonfire, on a chair or in a handcart, and assailing her with, 'Penny for the Guy'. It was curiously shocking to be confronted with these effigies, stuffed with straw, bedizened in human rags, sagging forward over the string that fastened them by the waist to their conveyance. It was mortifying not to be able to spare the penny. As she walked on, the chant pursued her like a hail of pebbles:

> *'Guy, Guy, hit him in the eye!*
> *Hang him on a lamp-post and never let him die.'*

Nevertheless, she rose and went to the door. As she opened it, she heard a spurt of sound, the sizzling uprush of a rocket, an outburst of young yells. Then a voice said, 'Now for the squibs!' Remembering the squib that had burned a hole in her stocking, she drew back into the church; and to kill time and combat the sense of silence and emptiness, she began a tour of examination. Presently she came to the stand for votive candles. It was an iron frame supporting three tiers of branching sockets. All were empty. Only a few had remnants of candle grease in them, and in these, as she discovered by poking, the grease was hardened and quite cold. Below was a platform, and on it were candles in a container, a box of matches, a few match ends, and a slotted box fastened to the stand by a chain and lettered 'CANDLES FOURPENCE EACH.' Fourpence apiece for such puny specimens! No wonder the sockets were empty.

Even while this reflection was passing through her mind, she had dropped four pennies into the box and taken a candle.

Though what does one burn a candle for, and to whom, and why? What deity or demiurge did she think to invoke? Certainly not that presiding white plaster Virgin near by, to which she had taken an instant dislike because its expression of pigheaded meekness recalled the woman Father had gone off with. Not God, that Maker and Manager of all things visible and invisible, of whom it is declared by the Prophets that He is above the heavens, and who is therefore, presumably, above bribes. And on whose behalf – her luckless own, her irremediable mother's? And why? Out of all the things that can be done for fourpence – still, in spite of the rise in the cost of living, quite a considerable number – why pick on this?

Meanwhile, she was painstakingly fixing the candle to stand firm and upright. When it was settled to her satisfaction, she struck a match and held the flame to the wick, which after a momentary halfheartedness took fire and began to burn independently. Oh, no need to ask why! The answer was in the act. The dated confident little flame, the minute dated warmth, the wax gently yielding – by bringing this about she had brought a new light and a new warmth into the cavernous world. She had created an impersonal good, a good that would benefit no one and harm no one, impose no obligation and fulfil no duty. Looking at her candle, now burning so diligently and composedly, she felt a kind of delighting trust in it. How far it spread its beams! How pleased it looked! How bravely it burned, the phoenix of its kind, among those yawning empty sockets! She had another four pennies; and although eightpence is two-thirds of a shilling, which is the economic unit of a slot meter, yet, if only out of gratitude – gratitude for having experienced a purity of gratitude such as she had not felt since childhood – she must light a second candle, a votive candle to the first. She tried it in one socket and another, to see where it looked best. When this was decided on, and the candle firmly established, she struck a match. As if she had provoked an echo, there came from outside an answering spurt, a rushing sizzle as the rocket tore upwards, a thud.

The match burned unheeded in her hand. Only when it scorched her finger did she throw it down.

With a spurt and a sizzle and a thud, a realization had exploded in her mind. Those dummies, those frightful pitiable dummies! They were exhibitions to her of what her mother was becoming, had almost become. The horror they aroused in her only corroborated and proclaimed an abhorrence she had not dared to admit. It was with abhorrence that she now looked at her mother. Abhorrence must have been there for months, disguised as a flinching pity. And now, knowing the truth, she must go home and experience it.

She lit the second candle, stared at its magicless flame, and went to the back of the church, where it was darkest and sternest, to sit for a while longer. She would be late. Mother, clutching at her last pleasure, a nice hot supper with something tasty, would be angry at having been kept waiting. She would scold, in her flat voice, and afterwards she would weep. She was eighty-four; hunger, suspicion, and self-pity was all that was left to spice her dreary days. Ellie, telling herself that she must somehow scratch up a handful of courage – or if not courage, compassion, and if not compassion, common sense – sat waiting for the candles to burn out. The first died easily. The second flared and struggled. After this, there was no excuse to remain. She remained, sitting bolt upright, her head gradually drooping forward.

She became conscious of a stir of cold air, and heard footsteps approaching. She did not move. The footsteps slowed, drew level with her, and halted, creaking slightly. She did not look up, but out of the corner of her eye she saw a straight black garment reaching to the floor – a cassock, no doubt, a rector. He coughed, drew breath to speak, thought better of it, coughed again, again drew a breath.

'Good evening! Jolly of you to come in like this.'

She made no reply. After a moment or two, he moved on. She stumbled to her feet and hurried out of the building, knowing that never again would she set foot in it.

When the door had closed behind her, he gave a movement of the shoulders that could have been a shrug if habit had not made it an acknowledgement of a burden. Once again he had done the wrong thing. He had spoken when he should have kept silence. Surely, there had never been a visitor more patently in need of a kind word than this poor old girl, so gaunt and derelict, her bony, coarsened hands clamped on her shabby handbag. But it had been the wrong thing. He had offended her, and she had fluttered away like some ungainly bird. Perhaps a notice in the porch saying, as much to him as to others, 'Persons entering this Church will not be spoken to' . . . Better phrased, of course. If by some extraordinary chance – a forgotten glove (but had those hands ever been gloved?), a change of heart – she were to return . . . But she did not return.

His purpose resumed him. He went to the altar rail, knelt down, and began to pray for the soul of Guy Fawkes.

Let them Call it Jazz

One bright Sunday morning in July I have trouble with my Notting Hill landlord because he ask for a month's rent in advance. He tell me this after I live there since winter, settling up every week without fail. I have no job at the time, and if I give the money he want there's not much left. So I refuse. The man drunk already at that early hour, and he abuse me – all talk, he can't frighten me. But his wife is a bad one – now she walk in my room and say she must have cash. When I tell her no, she give my suitcase one kick and it burst open. My best dress fall out, then she laugh and give another kick. She say month in advance is usual, and if I can't pay find somewhere else.

Don't talk to me about London. Plenty people there have heart like stone. Any complaint – the answer is 'prove it'. But if nobody see and bear witness for me, how to prove anything? So I pack up and leave, I think better not have dealings with that woman. She too cunning, and Satan don't lie worse.

I walk about till a place nearby is open where I can have coffee and a sandwich. There I start talking to a man at my table. He talk to me already, I know him, but I don't know his name. After a while he ask, 'What's the matter? Anything wrong?' and when I tell him my trouble he say I can use an empty flat he own till I have time to look around.

This man is not at all like most English people. He see very quick, and he decide very quick. English people take long time to decide – you three-quarter dead before they make up their mind about you. Too besides, he speak very matter of fact, as if it's nothing. He speak as if he realize well what it is to live like I do – that's why I accept and go.

He tell me somebody occupy the flat till last week, so I find everything all right, and he tell me how to get there – three-quarters of an hour from Victoria Station, up a steep hill, turn left, and I can't mistake the house. He give me the keys and an envelope with a telephone number on the back. Underneath is written 'After 6 p.m. ask for Mr Sims'.

In the train that evening I think myself lucky, for to walk about London on a Sunday with nowhere to go – that take the heart out of you.

I find the place and the bedroom of the downstairs flat is nicely furnished – two looking glass, wardrobe, chest of drawers, sheets, everything. It smell of jasmine scent, but it smell strong of damp too.

I open the door opposite and there's a table, a couple chairs, a gas stove and a cupboard, but this room so big it look empty. When I pull the blind up I notice the paper peeling off and mushrooms growing on the walls – you never see such a thing.

The bathroom the same, all the taps rusty. I leave the two other rooms and make up the bed. Then I listen, but I can't hear one sound. Nobody come in, nobody go out of that house. I lie awake for a long time, then I decide not to stay and in the morning I start to get ready quickly before I change my mind. I want to wear my best dress, but it's a funny thing – when I take up that dress and remember how my landlady kick it I cry. I cry and I can't stop. When I stop I feel tired to my bones, tired like old woman. I don't want to move again – I have to force myself. But in the end I get out in the passage and there's a postcard for me. 'Stay as long as you like. I'll be seeing you soon – Friday probably. Not to worry.' It isn't signed, but I don't feel so sad and I think, 'All right, I wait here till he come. Perhaps he knows of a job for me.'

Nobody else live in the house but a couple on the top floor – quiet people and they don't trouble me. I have no word to say against them.

First time I meet the lady she's opening the front door and she give me a very inquisitive look. But next time she smile a bit and I smile back – once she talk to me. She tell me the house very old, hundred and fifty year old, and she and her husband live there since long time. 'Valuable property,' she says, 'it could have been saved, but nothing done of course.' Then she tells me that as to the present owner – if he is the owner – well he have to deal with local authorities and she believe they make difficulties. 'These people are determined to pull down all the lovely old houses – it's shameful.'

So I agree that many things shameful. But what to do? What to do? I say it have an elegant shape, it make the other houses in the street look cheap trash, and she seem pleased. That's true too. The house sad and out of place, especially at night. But it have style. The second floor shut up, and as for my flat, I go in the two empty rooms once, but never again.

Underneath was the cellar, full of old boards and broken-up furniture – I see a big rat there one day. It was no place to be alone in I tell you, and I get the habit of buying a bottle of wine most evenings, for I don't like whisky and the rum here no good. It don't even *taste* like rum. You wonder what they do to it.

After I drink a glass or two I can sing and when I sing all the misery goes from my heart. Sometimes I make up songs but next morning I forget them, so other times I sing the old ones like *Tantalizin'* or *Don't Trouble Me Now*.

I think I go but I don't go. Instead I wait for the evening and the wine and that's all. Everywhere else I live – well, it doesn't matter to me, but this house is different – empty and no noise and full of shadows, so that sometimes you ask yourself what make all those shadows in an empty room.

I eat in the kitchen, then I clean up everything nice and have a bath for coolness. Afterwards I lean my elbows on the windowsill and look at the garden. Red and blue flowers mix up with the weeds and there are five–six apple trees. But the fruit drop and lie in the grass, so sour nobody want it. At the back, near the wall, is a bigger tree – this garden certainly take up a lot of room, perhaps that's why they want to pull the place down.

Not much rain all the summer, but not much sunshine either. More of a glare. The grass get brown and dry, the weeds grow tall, the leaves on the trees hang down. Only the red flowers – the poppies – stand up to that light, everything else look weary.

I don't trouble about money, but what with wine and shillings for the slot-meters, it go quickly; so I don't waste much on food. In the evening I walk outside – not by the apple trees but near the street – it's not so lonely.

There's no wall here and I can see the woman next door looking at me over the hedge. At first I say good evening, but she turn away her head, so afterwards I don't speak. A man is often with her, he wear a straw hat with a black ribbon and goldrim spectacles. His suit hang on him like it's too big. He's the husband it seems and he stare at me worse than his wife – he stare as if I'm wild animal let loose. Once I laugh in his face because why these people have to be like that? I don't bother them. In the end I get that I don't even give them one single glance. I have plenty other things to worry about.

To show you how I felt. I don't remember exactly. But I believe it's the second Saturday after I come that when I'm at the window just before I go for my wine I feel somebody's hand on my shoulder and it's Mr Sims. He must walk very quiet because I don't know a thing till he touch me.

He says hullo, then he tells me I've got terrible thin, do I ever eat. I say of course I eat but he goes on that it doesn't suit me at all to be so thin and he'll buy some food in the village. (That's the way he talk. There's no village here. You don't get away from London so quick.)

It don't seem to me he look very well himself, but I just say bring a drink instead; as I am not hungry.

He come back with three bottles – vermouth, gin and red wine. Then he ask if the little devil who was here last smash all the glasses and I tell him she smash some, I find the pieces. But not all. 'You fight with her, eh?'

He laugh, and he don't answer. He pour out the drinks then he says, 'Now, you eat up those sandwiches.'

Some men when they are there you don't worry so much. These sort of men you do all they tell you blindfold because they can take the trouble from your heart and make you think you're safe. It's nothing they say or do. It's a feeling they can give you. So I don't talk with him seriously – I don't want to spoil that evening. But I ask about the house and why it's so empty and he says:

'Has the old trout upstairs been gossiping?'

I tell him, 'She suppose they make difficulties for you.'

'It was a damn bad buy,' he says and talks about selling the lease or something. I don't listen much.

We were standing by the window then and the sun low. No more glare. He puts his hand over my eyes. 'Too big – much too big for your face,' he says and kisses me like you kiss a baby. When he takes his hand away I see he's looking out at the garden and he says this – 'It gets you. My God it does.'

I know very well it's not me he means, so I ask him, 'Why sell it then? If you like it, keep it.'

'Sell what?' he says. 'I'm not talking about this damned house.'

I ask what he's talking about. 'Money,' he says. 'Money. That's what I'm talking about. Ways of making it.'

'I don't think so much of money. It don't like me and what do I care?' I was joking, but he turns around, his face quite pale and he tells me I'm a fool. He tells me I'll get push around all my life and die like a dog, only worse because they'd finish off a dog, but they'll let me live till I'm a caricature of myself. That's what he say, 'Caricature of yourself.' He say I'll curse the day I was born and everything and everybody in this bloody world before I'm done.

I tell him, 'No I'll never feel like that,' and he smiles, if you can call it a smile, and says he's glad I'm content with my lot. 'I'm disappointed in you, Selina. I thought you had more spirit.'

'If I contented that's all right,' I answer him, 'I don't see very many looking contented over here.' We're standing staring at each other when the door bell rings. 'That's a friend of mine,' he says. 'I'll let him in.'

As to the friend, he's all dressed up in stripe pants and a black jacket and he's carrying a brief-case. Very ordinary looking but with a soft kind of voice.

'Maurice, this is Selina Davis,' says Mr Sims, and Maurice smiles very kind but it don't mean much, then he looks at his watch and says they ought to be getting along.

At the door Mr Sims tells me he'll see me next week and I answer straight out, 'I won't be here next week because I want a job and I won't get one in this place.'

'Just what I'm going to talk about. Give it a week longer, Selina.'

I say, 'Perhaps I stay a few more days. Then I go. Perhaps I go before.'

'Oh no you won't go,' he says.

They walk to the gates quickly and drive off in a yellow car. Then I feel eyes on me and it's the woman and her husband in the next door garden. The man make some remark and she look at me so hateful, so hating I shut the front door quick.

I don't want more wine. I want to go to bed early because I must think. I must think about money. It's true I don't care for it. Even when somebody steal my savings – this happen soon after I get to the Notting Hill house – I forget it soon. About thirty pounds they steal. I keep it roll up in a pair of stockings, but I go to the drawer one day, and no money. In the end I have to tell the police. They ask me exact sum and I say I don't count it lately, about thirty pounds. 'You don't know how much?' they say. 'When did you count it last? Do you remember? Was it before you move or after?'

I get confuse, and I keep saying, 'I don't remember,' though I remember well I see it two days before. They don't believe me and when a policeman come to the house I hear the landlady tell him, 'She certainly had no money when she came here. She wasn't able to pay a month's rent in advance for her room though it's a rule in this house.' 'These people terrible liars,' she say and I think 'it's you a terrible liar, because when I come you tell me weekly or monthly as you like.' It's from that time she don't speak to me and perhaps it's she take it. All I know is I never see one penny of my savings again, all I know is they pretend I never have any, but as it's gone, no use to cry about it. Then my mind goes to my father, for my father is a white man and I think a lot about him. If I could see him only once, for I too small to remember when he was there. My mother is fair coloured woman, fairer than I am they say, and she don't stay long with me either. She have a chance to go to Venezuela when I three-four year old and she never come back. She send money instead. It's my grandmother take care of me. She's quite dark and what we call 'country-cookie' but she's the best I know.

She save up all the money my mother send, she don't keep one penny for herself – that's how I get to England. I was a bit late in going to school regular, getting on for twelve years, but I can sew very beautiful, excellent – so I think I get a good job – in London perhaps.

However here they tell me all this fine handsewing take too long. Waste of time – too slow. They want somebody to work quick and to hell with the small stitches. Altogether it don't look so good for me, I must say, and I wish I could see my father. I have his name – Davis. But my grandmother tell me, 'Every word that come out of that man's mouth a damn lie. He is certainly first class liar, though no class otherwise.' So perhaps I have not even his real name.

Last thing I see before I put the light out is the postcard on the dressing table. 'Not to worry.'

Not to worry! Next day is Sunday, and it's on the Monday the people next door complain about me to the police. That evening the woman is by the hedge, and when I pass her she says in very sweet quiet voice, *'Must* you stay? *Can't* you go?' I don't answer. I walk out in the street to get rid of her. But she run inside her house to the window, she can still see me. Then I start to sing, so she can understand I'm not afraid of her. The husband call out: 'If you don't stop that noise I'll send for the police.' I answer them quite short. I say, 'You go to hell and take your wife with you.' And I sing louder.

The police come pretty quick – two of them. Maybe they just round the corner. All I can say about police, and how they behave is I think it all depend who they dealing with. Of my own free will I don't want to mix up with police. No.

One man says, you can't cause this disturbance here. But the other asks a lot of questions. What is my name? Am I tenant of a flat in No. 17? How long have I lived there? Last address and so on. I get vexed the way he speak and I tell him, 'I come here because somebody steal my savings. Why you don't look for my money instead of bawling at me? I work hard for my money. All-you don't do one single thing to find it.'

'What's she talking about?' the first one says, and the other one tells me, 'You can't make that noise here. Get along home. You've been drinking.'

I see that woman looking at me and smiling, and other people at their windows, and I'm so angry I bawl at them too. I say, 'I have absolute and perfect right to be in the street same as anybody else, and I have absolute and perfect right to ask the police why they don't even look for my money when it disappear. It's because a dam' English thief take it you don't look,' I say. The end of all this is that I have to go before a magistrate, and he fine me five pounds for drunk and disorderly, and he give me two weeks to pay.

When I get back from the court I walk up and down the kitchen, up and down, waiting for six o'clock because I have no five pounds left, and I don't know what to do. I telephone at six and a woman answers me very short and sharp, then Mr Sims comes along and he don't sound too pleased either when I tell him what happen. 'Oh Lord!' he says, and I say I'm sorry. 'Well don't panic,' he says, 'I'll pay the fine. But look, I don't think. . . .' Then he breaks off and talk to some other person in the room. He goes on, 'Perhaps better not stay at No. 17. I think I can arrange something else. I'll call for you Wednesday – Saturday latest. Now behave till then.' And he hang up before I can answer that I don't want to wait till Wednesday, much less Saturday. I want to get out of that house double quick and with no delay. First I think I ring back, then I think better not as he sound so vex.

I get ready, but Wednesday he don't come, and Saturday he don't come. All the week I stay in the flat. Only once I go out and arrange for bread, milk and eggs to be left at the door, and seems to me I meet up with a lot of policemen. They don't look at me, but they see me all right. I don't want to drink – I'm all the time listening, listening and thinking, how can I leave before I know if my fine is paid? I tell myself the police let me know, that's certain. But I don't trust them. What they care? The answer is Nothing. Nobody care. One afternoon I knock at the old lady's flat upstairs, because I get the idea she give me good advice. I can hear her moving about and talking, but she don't answer and I never try again.

Nearly two weeks pass like that, then I telephone. It's the woman speaking and she say, 'Mr Sims is not in London at present.' I ask, 'When will he be back – it's urgent,' and she hang up. I'm not surprised. Not at all. I knew that would happen. All the same I feel heavy like lead. Near the phone box is a chemist's shop, so I ask him for something to make me sleep, the day is bad enough, but to lie awake all night – Ah no! He gives me a little bottle marked *One or two tablets only* and I take three when I go to bed because more and more I think that sleeping is better than no matter what else. However, I lie there, eyes wide open as usual, so I take three more. Next thing I know the room is full of sunlight, so it must be late afternoon, but the lamp is still on. My head turn around and I can't think well at all. At first I ask myself how I get to the place. Then it comes to me, but in pictures – like the landlady kicking my dress, and when I take my ticket at Victoria Station, and Mr Sims telling me to eat the sandwiches, but I can't remember everything clear, and I feel very giddy and sick. I take in the milk and eggs at the door, go in the kitchen, and try to eat but the food hard to swallow.

It's when I'm putting the things away that I see the bottles – pushed back on the lowest shelf in the cupboard.

There's a lot of drink left, and I'm glad I tell you. Because I can't bear the way I feel. Not any more. I mix a gin and vermouth and I drink it quick, then I mix another and drink it slow by the window. The garden looks different, like I never see it before. I know quite well what I must do, but it's late now – tomorrow. I have one more drink, of wine this time, and then a song come in my head, I sing it and I dance it, and more I sing, more I am sure this is the best tune that has ever come to me in all my life.

The sunset light from the window is gold colour. My shoes sound loud on the boards. So I take them off, my stockings too and go dancing but the room feel shut in, I can't breathe, and I go outside still singing. Maybe I dance a bit too. I forget all about that woman till I hear her saying, 'Henry, look at this.' I turn around and I see her at the window. 'Oh yes, I wanted to speak with you,' I say, 'Why bring the police and get me in bad trouble? Tell me that.'

'And you tell *me* what you're doing here at all,' she says. 'This is a respectable neighbourhood.'

Then the man come along. 'Now young woman, take yourself off. You ought to be ashamed of this behaviour.'

'It's disgraceful,' he says, talking to his wife, but loud so I can hear, and she speaks loud too – for once. 'At least the other tarts that crook installed here were *white* girls,' she says.

'You a dam' fouti liar,' I say. 'Plenty of those girls in your country already. Numberless as the sands on the shore. You don't need me for that.'

'You're not a howling success at it certainly.' Her voice sweet sugar again. 'And you won't be seeing much more of your friend Mr Sims. He's in trouble too. Try somewhere else. Find somebody else. If you can, of course.' When she say that my arm moves of itself. I pick up a stone and bam! through the window. Not the one they are standing at but the next, which is of coloured glass, green and purple and yellow.

I never see a woman look so surprise. Her mouth fall open she so full of surprise. I start to laugh, louder and louder – I laugh like my grandmother, with my hands on my hips and my head back. (When she laugh like that you can hear her to the end of our street.) At last I say, 'Well, I'm sorry. An accident. I get it fixed tomorrow early.' 'That glass is irreplaceable,' the man says. 'Irreplaceable.' 'Good thing,' I say, 'those colours look like they sea-sick to me. I buy you a better windowglass.'

He shake his fist at me. 'You won't be let off with a fine this time,' he says. Then they draw the curtains. I call out at them. 'You run away. Always you run away. Ever since I come here you hunt me down because I don't answer back. It's you shameless.' I try to sing 'Don't trouble me now'.

> Don't trouble me now
> You without honour.
> Don't walk in my footstep
> You without shame.

But my voice don't sound right, so I get back indoors and drink one more glass of wine – still wanting to laugh, and still thinking of my grandmother for that is one of her songs.

It's about a man whose doudou give him the go-by when she find somebody rich and he sail away to Panama. Plenty people die there of fever when they make that Panama canal so long ago. But he don't die. He come back with dollars and the girl meet him on the jetty, all dressed up and smiling. Then he sing to her, 'You without honour, you without shame.' It sound good in Martinique patois too: 'Sans honte'.

Afterwards I ask myself, 'Why I do that? It's not like me. But if they treat you wrong over and over again the hour strike when you burst out that's what.'

Too besides, Mr Sims can't tell me now I have no spirit. I don't care, I sleep quickly and I'm glad I break the woman's ugly window. But as to my own song it go *right* away and it never come back. A pity.

Next morning the doorbell ringing wake me up. The people upstairs don't come down, and the bell keeps on like fury self. So I go to look, and there is a policeman and a policewoman outside. As soon as I open the door the woman put her foot in it. She wear sandals and thick stockings and I never see a foot so big or so bad. It look like it want to mash up the whole world. Then she come in after the foot, and her face not so pretty either. The policeman tell me my fine is not paid and people make serious complaints about me, so they're taking me back to the magistrate. He show me a paper and I look at it, but I don't read it. The woman push me in the bedroom, and tell me to get dress quickly, but I just stare at her, because I think perhaps I wake up soon. Then I ask her what I must wear. She say she suppose I had some clothes on yesterday. Or not? 'What's it matter, wear anything,' she says. But I find clean underclothes and stockings and my shoes with high heels and I comb my hair. I start to file my nails, because I think they too long for magistrate's court but she get angry. 'Are you coming quietly or aren't you?' she says. So I go with them and we get in a car outside.

I wait for a long time in a room full of policemen. They come in, they go out, they telephone, they talk in low voices. Then it's my turn, and first thing I notice in the court room is a man with frowning black eyebrows. He sit below the magistrate, he dressed in black and he so handsome I can't take my eyes off him. When he see that he frown worse than before.

First comes a policeman to testify I cause disturbance, and then comes the old gentleman from next door. He repeat that bit about nothing but the truth so help me God. Then he says I make dreadful noise at night and use abominable language, and dance in obscene fashion. He says when they try to shut the curtains because his wife so terrify of me, I

19

throw stones and break a valuable stain-glass window. He say his wife get serious injury if she'd been hit, and as it is she in terrible nervous condition and the doctor is with her. I think, 'Believe me, if I aim at your wife I hit your wife – that's certain.' 'There was no provocation,' he says. 'None at all.' Then another lady from across the street says this is true. She heard no provocation whatsoever, and she swear that they shut the curtains but I go on insulting them and using filthy language and she saw all this and heard it.

The magistrate is a little gentleman with a quiet voice, but I'm very suspicious of these quiet voices now. He ask me why I don't pay my fine, and I say because I haven't the money. I get the idea they want to find out all about Mr Sims – they listen so very attentive. But they'll find out nothing from me. He ask how long I have the flat and I say I don't remember. I know they want to trip me up like they trip me up about my savings so I won't answer. At last he ask if I have anything to say as I can't be allowed to go on being a nuisance. I think, 'I'm nuisance to you because I have no money that's all.' I want to speak up and tell him how they steal all my savings, so when my landlord asks for month's rent I haven't it to give. I want to tell him the woman next door provoke me since long time and call me bad names but she have a soft sugar voice and nobody hear – that's why I broke her window, but I'm ready to buy another after all. I want to say all I do is sing in that old garden, and I want to say this in decent quiet voice. But I hear myself talking loud and I see my hands wave in the air. Too besides it's no use, they won't believe me, so I don't finish. I stop, and I feel the tears on my face. 'Prove it.' That's all they will say. They whisper, they whisper. They nod, they nod.

Next thing I'm in a car again with a different police-woman, dressed very smart. Not in uniform. I ask her where she's taking me and she says 'Holloway' just that 'Holloway'.

I catch hold of her hand because I'm afraid. But she takes it away. Cold and smooth her hand slide away and her face is china face – smooth like a doll and I think, 'This is the last time I ask anything from anybody. So help me God.'

The car come up to a black castle and little mean streets are all round it. A lorry was blocking up the castle gates. When it get by we pass through and I am in jail. First I stand in a line with others who are waiting to give up handbags and all belongings to a woman behind bars like in a post office. The girl in front bring out a nice compact, look like gold to me, lipstick to match and a wallet full of notes. The woman keep the money, but she give back the powder and lipstick and she half-smile. I have two pounds seven shillings and six-pence in pennies. She take my purse, then she throw me my compact (which is cheap) my comb and my handkerchief like everything in my bag is dirty. So I think, 'Here too, here too.' But I tell myself, 'Girl, what you expect, eh? They all like that. All.'

Some of what happen afterwards I forget, or perhaps better not remember. Seems to me they start by trying to frighten you. But they don't succeed with me for I don't care for nothing now, it's as if my heart hard like a rock and I can't feel.

Then I'm standing at the top of a staircase with a lot of women and girls. As we are going down I notice the railing very low on one side, very easy to jump, and a long way below there's the grey stone passage like it's waiting for you.

As I'm thinking this a uniform woman step up alongside quick and grab my arm. She say, 'Oh no you don't.'

I was just noticing the railing very low that's all – but what's the use of saying so.

Another long line waits for the doctor. It move forward slowly and my legs terribly tired. The girl in front is very young and she cry and cry. 'I'm scared,' she keeps saying. She's lucky in a way – as for me I never will cry again. It all dry up and hard in me now. That, and a lot besides. In the end I tell her to stop, because she doing just what these people want her to do.

She stop crying and start a long story, but while she is

speaking her voice get very far away, and I find I can't see her face clear at all.

Then I'm in a chair, and one of those uniform women is pushing my head down between my knees, but let her push – everything go away from me just the same.

They put me in the hospital because the doctor say I'm sick. I have cell by myself and it's all right except I don't sleep. The things they say you mind I don't mind.

When they clang the door on me I think, 'You shut me in, but you shut all those other dam' devils *out*. They can't reach me now.'

At first it bothers me when they keep on looking at me all through the night. They open a little window in the doorway to do this. But I get used to it and get used to the night chemise they give me. It very thick, and to my mind it not very clean either – but what's that matter to me? Only the food I can't swallow – especially the porridge. The woman ask me sarcastic, 'Hunger striking?' But afterwards I can leave most of it, and she don't say nothing.

One day a nice girl comes around with books and she give me two, but I don't want to read so much. Beside one is about a murder, and the other is about a ghost and I don't think it's at all like those books tell you.

There is nothing I want now. It's no use. If they leave me in peace and quiet that's all I ask. The window is barred but not small, so I can see a little thin tree through the bars, and I like watching it.

After a week they tell me I'm better and I can go out with the others for exercise. We walk round and round one of the yards in that castle – it is fine weather and the sky is a kind of pale blue, but the yard is a terrible sad place. The sunlight fall down and die there. I get tired walking in high heels and I'm glad when that's over.

We can talk, and one day an old woman come up and ask me for dog-ends. I don't understand, and she start muttering at me like she very vexed. Another woman tell me she mean cigarette ends, so I say I don't smoke. But the old woman still look angry, and when we're going in she give me one push and I nearly fall down. I'm glad to get away from these people, and hear the door clang and take my shoes off.

Sometimes I think, 'I'm here because I wanted to sing' and I have to laugh. But there's a small looking glass in my cell and I see myself and I'm like somebody else. Like some strange new person. Mr Sims tell me I too thin, but what he say now to this person in the looking glass? So I don't laugh again.

Usually I don't think at all. Everything and everybody seem small and far away, that is the only trouble.

Twice the doctor come to see me. He don't say much and I don't say anything, because a uniform woman is always there. She look like she thinking, 'Now the lies start.' So I prefer not to speak. Then I'm sure they can't trip me up. Perhaps I there still, or in a worse place. But one day this happen.

We were walking round and round in the yard and I hear a woman singing – the voice come from high up, from one of the small barred windows. At first I don't believe it. Why should anybody sing here? Nobody want to sing in jail, nobody want to do anything. There's no reason, and you have no hope. I think I must be asleep, dreaming, but I'm awake all right and I see all the others are listening too. A nurse is with us that afternoon, not a policewoman. She stop and look up at the window.

It's a smoky kind of voice, and a bit rough sometimes, as if those old dark walls theyselves are complaining, because they see too much misery – too much. But it don't fall down and die in the courtyard; seems to me it could jump the gates of the jail easy and travel far, and nobody could stop it. I don't hear the words – only the music. She sing one verse and she begin another, then she break off sudden. Everybody starts walking again, and nobody says one word. But as we go in I ask the woman in front who was singing. 'That's the Holloway song,' she says. 'Don't you know it yet? She was singing from the punishment cells, and she tell the girls cheerio and never say die.' Then I have to go one way to the hospital block and she goes another so we don't speak again.

When I'm back in my cell I can't just wait for bed. I walk up and down and I think. 'One day I hear that song on trumpets and these walls will fall and rest.' I want to get out so bad I could hammer on the door, for I know now that anything can happen, and I don't want to stay lock up here and miss it.

Then I'm hungry. I eat everything they bring and in the morning I'm still so hungry I eat the porridge. Next time the doctor come he tells me I seem much better. Then I say a little of what really happen in that house. Not much. Very careful.

He look at me hard and kind of surprised. At the door he shake his finger and says, 'Now don't let me see you here again.'

That evening the woman tells me I'm going, but she's so upset about it I don't ask questions. Very early, before it's light she bangs the door open and shouts at me to hurry up. As we're going along the passages I see the girl who gave me the books. She's in a row with others doing exercises. Up Down, Up Down, Up. We pass quite close and I notice she's looking very pale and tired. It's crazy, it's all crazy. This up down business and everything else too. When they give me my money I remember I leave my compact in the cell, so I ask if I can go back for it. You should see that policewoman's face as she shoo me on.

There's no car, there's a van and you can't see through the windows. The third time it stop I get out with one other, a young girl, and it's the same magistrates' court as before.

The two of us wait in a small room, nobody else there, and after a while the girl say, 'What the hell are they doing? I don't want to spend all day here.' She go to the bell and she keep her finger press on it. When I look at her she say, 'Well, what are they *for*?' That girl's face is hard like a board – she could change faces with many and you wouldn't know the difference. But she get results certainly. A policeman come in, all smiling, and we go in the court. The same magistrate, the same frowning man sits below, and when I hear my fine is paid I want to ask who paid it, but he yells at me. 'Silence.'

I think I will never understand the half of what happen, but they tell me I can go, and I understand that. The magistrate ask if I'm leaving the neighbourhood and I say yes, then I'm out in the streets again, and it's the same fine weather, same feeling I'm dreaming.

When I get to the house I see two men talking in the garden. The front door and the door of the flat are both open. I go in, and the bedroom is empty, nothing but the glare streaming inside because they take the Venetian blinds away. As I'm wondering where my suitcase is, and the clothes I leave in the wardrobe, there's a knock and it's the old lady from upstairs carrying my case packed, and my coat is over her arm. She says she sees me come in. 'I kept your things for you.' I start to thank her but she turn her back and walk away. They like that here, and better not expect too much. Too besides, I bet they tell her I'm terrible person.

I go in the kitchen, but when I see they are cutting down the big tree at the back I don't stay to watch.

At the station I'm waiting for the train and a woman asks if I feel well. 'You look so tired,' she says. 'Have you come a long way?' I want to answer, 'I come so far I lose myself on that journey.' But I tell her, 'Yes, I am quite well. But I can't stand the heat.' She says she can't stand it either, and we talk about the weather till the train come in.

I'm not frightened of them any more – after all what else can they do? I know what to say and everything go like a clock works.

I get a room near Victoria where the landlady accept one pound in advance, and next day I find a job in the kitchen of a private hotel close by. But I don't stay there long. I hear of another job going in a big store – altering ladies' dresses and I get that. I lie and tell them I work in very expensive New York shop. I speak bold and smooth faced, and they never check up on me. I make a friend there – Clarice – very light coloured, very smart, she have a lot to do with the customers and she laugh at some of them behind their backs. But I say it's not their fault if the dress don't fit. Special dress for one person only – that's very expensive in London. So it's take in, or let out all the time. Clarice have two rooms not far from the store. She furnish them herself gradual and she gives parties sometimes Saturday nights. It's there I start whistling the Holloway Song. A man comes up to me and says, 'Let's hear that again.' So I whistle it again (I never sing now) and he tells me 'Not bad'. Clarice have an old piano somebody give her to store and he plays the tune, jazzing it up. I say, 'No, not like that,' but everybody else say the way he do it is first class. Well I think no more of this till I get a letter from him telling me he has sold the song and as I was quite a help he encloses five pounds with thanks.

I read the letter and I could cry. For after all, that song was all I had. I don't belong nowhere really, and I haven't money to buy my way to belonging. I don't want to either.

But when that girl sing, she sing to me, and she sing for me. I was there because I was *meant* to be there. It was *meant* I should hear it – this I *know*.

Now I've let them play it wrong, and it will go from me like all the other songs – like everything. Nothing left for me at all.

But then I tell myself all this is foolishness. Even if they played it on trumpets, even if they played it just right, like I wanted – no walls would fall so soon. 'So let them call it jazz,' I think, and let them play it wrong. That won't make no difference to the song I heard.

I buy myself a dusty pink dress with the money.

L. P. HARTLEY

Someone in the Lift

'There's someone coming down in the lift, Mummy!'

'No, my darling, you're wrong, there isn't.'

'But I can see him through the bars – a tall gentleman.'

'You think you can, but it's only a shadow. Now, you'll see, the lift's empty.'

And it always was.

This piece of dialogue, or variations of it, had been repeated at intervals ever since Mr and Mrs Maldon and their son Peter had arrived at the Brompton Court Hotel, where, owing to a domestic crisis, they were going to spend Christmas. New to hotel life, the little boy had never seen a lift before and he was fascinated by it. When either of his parents pressed the button to summon it he would take up his stand some distance away to watch it coming down.

The ground floor had a high ceiling so the lift was visible for some seconds before it touched floor level: and it was then, at its first appearance, that Peter saw the figure. It was always in the same place, facing him in the left-hand corner. He couldn't see it plainly, of course, because of the double grille, the gate of the lift and the gate of the lift-shaft, both of which had to be firmly closed before the lift would work.

He had been told not to use the lift by himself – an unnecessary warning, because he connected the lift with the things that grown-up people did, and unlike most small boys he wasn't over-anxious to share the privileges of his elders: he was content to wonder and admire. The lift appealed to him more as magic than as mechanism.

Acceptance of magic made it possible for him to believe that the lift had an occupant when he first saw it, in spite of the demonstrable fact that when it came to rest, giving its fascinating click of finality, the occupant had disappeared.

'If you don't believe me, ask Daddy,' his mother said.

Peter didn't want to do this, and for two reasons, one of which was easier to explain than the other.

'Daddy would say I was being silly,' he said.

'Oh no, he wouldn't, he never says you're silly.'

This was not quite true. Like all well-regulated modern fathers, Mr Maldon was aware of the danger of offending a son of tender years: the psychological results might be regrettable. But Freud or no Freud, fathers are still fathers, and sometimes when Peter irritated him Mr Maldon would let fly. Although he was fond of him, Peter's private vision of his father was of someone more authoritative and awe-inspiring than a stranger, seeing them together, would have guessed.

The other reason, which Peter didn't divulge, was more fantastic. He hadn't asked his father because, when his father was with him, he couldn't see the figure in the lift.

Mrs Maldon remembered the conversation and told her husband of it. 'The lift's in a dark place,' she said, 'and I dare say he does see something, he's so much nearer to the ground than we are. The bars may cast a shadow and make a sort of pattern that we can't see. I don't know if it's frightening him, but you might have a word with him about it.'

At first Peter was more interested than frightened. Then he began to evolve a theory. If the figure only appeared in his father's absence, didn't it follow that the figure might be, could be, must be, his own father? In what region of his consciousness Peter believed this it would be hard to say; but for imaginative purposes he did believe it and the figure became for him 'Daddy in the lift'. The thought of Daddy in the lift did frighten him, and the neighbourhood of the lift-shaft, in which he felt compelled to hang about, became a place of dread.

Christmas Day was drawing near and the hotel began to deck itself with evergreens. Suspended at the foot of the staircase, in front of the lift, was a bunch of mistletoe, and it was this that gave Mr Maldon his idea.

As they were standing under it, waiting for the lift, he said to Peter:

'Your mother tells me you've seen someone in the lift who isn't there.'

His voice sounded more accusing than he meant it to, and Peter shrank.

'Oh, not now,' he said, truthfully enough. 'Only sometimes.'

'Your mother told me that you always saw it,' his father said, again more sternly than he meant to. 'And do you know who I think it may be?'

Caught by a gust of terror Peter cried, 'Oh, please don't tell me!'

'Why, you silly boy,' said his father reasonably. 'Don't you want to know?'

Ashamed of his cowardice, Peter said he did.

'Why, it's Father Christmas, of course!'

Relief surged through Peter.

'But doesn't Father Christmas come down the chimney?' he asked.

'That was in the old days. He doesn't now. Now he takes the lift!'

Peter thought a moment.

'Will you dress up as Father Christmas this year,' he asked, 'even though it's an hotel?'

'I might.'

'And come down in the lift?'

'I shouldn't wonder.'

After this Peter felt happier about the shadowy passenger behind the bars. Father Christmas couldn't hurt anyone, even if he was (as Peter now believed him to be) his own father. Peter was only six but he could remember two Christmas Eves when his father had dressed up as Santa

29

Claus and given him a delicious thrill. He could hardly wait for this one, when the apparition in the corner would at last become a reality.

Alas, two days before Christmas Day the lift broke down. On every floor it served, and there were five (six counting the basement), the forbidding notice 'Out of Order' dangled from the door-handle. Peter complained as loudly as anyone, though secretly, he couldn't have told why, he was glad that the lift no longer functioned, and he didn't mind climbing the four flights to his room, which opened out of his parents' room but had its own door too. By using the stairs he met the workmen (he never knew on which floor they would be) and from them gleaned the latest news about the lift-crisis. They were working overtime, they told him, and were just as anxious as he to see the last of the job. Sometimes they even told each other to put a jerk into it. Always Peter asked them when they would be finished, and they always answered, 'Christmas Eve at latest.'

Peter didn't doubt this. To him the workmen were infallible, possessed of magic powers capable of suspending the ordinary laws that governed lifts. Look how they left the gates open, and shouted to each other up and down the awesome lift-shaft, paying as little attention to the other hotel visitors as if they didn't exist! Only to Peter did they vouchsafe a word.

But Christmas Eve came, the morning passed, the afternoon passed, and still the lift didn't go. The men were working with set faces and a controlled hurry in their movements; they didn't even return Peter's 'Good night' when he passed them on his way to bed. Bed! He had begged to be allowed to stay up this once for dinner; he knew he wouldn't go to sleep, he said, till Father Christmas came. He lay awake, listening to the urgent voices of the men, wondering if each hammer-stroke would be the last; and then, just as the clamour was subsiding, he dropped off.

Dreaming, he felt adrift in time. Could it be midnight? No, because his parents had after all consented to his going down to dinner. Now was the time. Averting his eyes from the forbidden lift he stole downstairs. There was a clock in the hall, but it had stopped. In the dining-room there was another clock; but dared he go into the dining-room alone, with no one to guide him and everybody looking at him?

He ventured in, and there, at their table, which he couldn't always pick out, he saw his mother. She saw him, too, and came towards him, threading her way between the tables as if they were just bits of furniture, not alien islands under hostile sway.

'Darling,' she said, 'I couldn't find you – nobody could, but here you are!' She led him back and they sat down. 'Daddy will be with us in a minute.' The minutes passed; suddenly there was a crash. It seemed to come from within, from the kitchen perhaps. Smiles lit up the faces of the diners. A man at a near-by table laughed and said, 'Something's on the floor! Somebody'll be for it!' 'What is it?' whispered Peter, too excited to speak out loud. 'Is anyone hurt?' 'Oh, no, darling, somebody's dropped a tray, that's all.'

To Peter it seemed an anti-climax, this paltry accident that had stolen the thunder of his father's entry, for he didn't doubt that his father would come in as Father Christmas. The suspense was unbearable. Can I go into the hall and wait for him?' His mother hesitated and then said yes.

The hall was deserted, even the porter was off duty. Would it be fair, Peter wondered, or would it be cheating and doing himself out of a surprise, if he waited for Father Christmas by the lift? Magic has its rules which mustn't be disobeyed. But he was there now, at his old place in front of the lift; and the lift would come down if he pressed the button.

He knew he mustn't, that it was forbidden, that his father would be angry if he did; yet he reached up and pressed it.

But nothing happened, the lift didn't come, and why? Because some careless person had forgotten to shut the gates – 'monkeying with the lift', his father called it. Perhaps the workmen had forgotten, in their hurry to get home. There was only one thing to do – find out on which floor the gates had been left open, and then shut them.

On their own floor it was, and in his dream it didn't seem strange to Peter that the lift wasn't there, blocking the black hole of the lift-shaft, though he daren't look down it. The gates clicked to. Triumph possessed him, triumph lent him wings; he was back on the ground floor, with his finger on the button. A thrill of power such as he had never known ran through him when the machinery answered to his touch.

But what was this? The lift was coming up from below, not down from above, and there was something wrong with its roof – a jagged hole that let the light through. But the figure was there in its accustomed corner, and this time it hadn't disappeared, it was still there, he could see it through the mazy criss-cross of the bars, a figure in a red robe with white fur edges, and wearing a red cowl on its head: his father, Father Christmas, Daddy in the lift. But why didn't he look at Peter, and why was his white beard streaked with red?

The two grilles folded back when Peter pushed them. Toys were lying at his father's feet, but he couldn't touch them for they too were red, red and wet as the floor of the lift, red as the jag of lightning that tore through his brain. . . .

ELIZABETH BOWEN
Sunday Afternoon

'So here you are!' exclaimed Mrs Vesey to the newcomer who joined the group on the lawn. She reposed for an instant her light, dry fingers on his. 'Henry has come from London,' she added. Acquiescent smiles from the others round her showed that the fact was already known– she was no more than indicating to Henry the role that he was to play. 'What are your experiences? – Please tell us. But nothing dreadful: we are already feeling a little sad.'

'I am sorry to hear that,' said Henry Russel, with the air of one not anxious to speak of his own affairs. Drawing a cane chair into the circle, he looked from face to face with concern. His look travelled on to the screen of lilac, whose dark purple, pink-silver, and white plumes sprayed out in the brilliance of the afternoon. The late May Sunday blazed, but was not warm: something less than a wind, a breath of coldness, fretted the edge of things. Where the lilac barrier ended, across the sun-polished meadows, the Dublin mountains continued to trace their hazy, today almost col-ourless line. The coldness had been admitted by none of the seven or eight people who, in degrees of elderly beauty, sat here full in the sun, at this sheltered edge of the lawn: they continued to master the coldness, or to deny it, as though with each it were some secret *malaise*. An air of fastidious, stylized melancholy, an air of being secluded behind glass, characterized for Henry these old friends in whose shadow he had grown up. To their pleasure at having him back among them was added, he felt, a taboo or warning– he was to tell a little, but not much. He could feel with a shock, as he sat down, how insensibly he had deserted, these last years, the aesthetic of living that he had got from them. As things were, he felt over him their suspended charm. The democratic smell of the Dublin bus, on which he had made the outward journey to join them, had evaporated from his person by the time he was half-way up Mrs Vesey's chestnut avenue. Her house, with its fanlights and tall windows, was a villa in the Italian sense, just near enough to the city to make the country's sweetness particularly acute. Now, the sensations of wartime, that locked his inside being, began as surely to be dispelled – in the influence of this eternalized Sunday afternoon.

'Sad?' he said, 'that is quite wrong.'

'These days, our lives seem unreal,' said Mrs Vesey – with eyes that penetrated his point of view. 'But, worse than that, this afternoon we discover that we all have friends who have died.'

'Lately?' said Henry, tapping his fingers together.

'Yes, in all cases,' said Ronald Cuffe – with just enough dryness to show how much the subject had been beginning to tire him. 'Come, Henry, we look to you for distraction. To us, these days, you are quite a figure. In fact, from all we have heard of London, it is something that you should be alive. Are things there as shocking as they say – or are they more shocking?' he went on, with distaste.

'Henry's not sure,' said someone, 'he looks pontifical.'

Henry, in fact, was just beginning to twiddle this far-off word 'shocking' round in his mind, when a diversion caused some turning of heads. A young girl stepped out of a window and began to come their way across the lawn. She was Maria, Mrs Vesey's niece. A rug hung over her bare arm: she spread out the rug and sat down at her aunt's feet. With folded arms, and her fingers on her thin pointed elbows, she immediately fixed her eyes on Henry Russel. 'Good afternoon,' she said to him, in a mocking but somehow intimate tone.

The girl, like some young difficult pet animal, seemed in a

way to belong to everyone there. Miss Ria Store, the patroness of the arts, who had restlessly been refolding her fur cape, said: 'And where have *you* been, Maria?'

'Indoors.'

Someone said, 'On this beautiful afternoon?'

'Is it?' said Maria, frowning impatiently at the grass.

'Instinct,' said the retired judge, 'now tells Maria it's time for tea.'

'No, this does,' said Maria, nonchalantly showing her wrist with the watch on it. 'It keeps good time, thank you, Sir Isaac.' She returned her eyes to Henry. 'What have you been saying?'

'You interrupted Henry. He was just going to speak.'

'*Is* it so frightening?' Maria said.

'The bombing?' said Henry. 'Yes. But as it does not connect with the rest of life, it is difficult, you know, to know what one feels. One's feelings seem to have no language for anything so preposterous. As for thoughts – '

'At that rate,' said Maria, with a touch of contempt, 'your thoughts would not be interesting.'

'Maria,' said somebody, 'that is no way to persuade Henry to talk.'

'About what is important,' announced Maria, 'it seems that no one can tell one anything. There is really nothing, till one knows it oneself.'

'Henry is probably right,' said Ronald Cuffe, 'in considering that this – this outrage is *not* important. There is no place for it in human experience; it apparently cannot make a place of its own. It will have no literature.'

'Literature!' said Maria. 'One can see, Mr Cuffe, that *you* have always been safe!'

'Maria,' said Mrs Vesey, 'you're rather pert.'

Sir Isaac said, 'What does Maria expect to know?'

Maria pulled off a blade of grass and bit it. Something calculating and passionate appeared in her; she seemed to be crouched up inside herself. She said to Henry sharply: 'But you'll go back, of course?'

'To London? Yes – this is only my holiday. Anyhow, one cannot stay long away.'

Immediately he had spoken Henry realized how subtly this offended his old friends. Their position was, he saw, more difficult than his own, and he could not have said a more cruel thing. Mrs Vesey, with her adept smile that was never entirely heartless, said: 'Then we must hope your time here will be pleasant. Is it so very short?'

'And be careful, Henry,' said Ria Store, 'or you will find Maria stowed away in your baggage. And there would be an embarrassment, at an English port! We can feel her planning to leave us at any time.'

Henry said, rather flatly: 'Why should not Maria travel in the ordinary way?'

'Why should Maria travel at all? There is only one journey now – into danger. We cannot feel that that is necessary for her.'

Sir Isaac added: 'We fear, however, that that is the journey Maria wishes to make.'

Maria, curled on the lawn with the nonchalance of a feline creature, through this kept her eyes cast down. Another cold puff came through the lilac, soundlessly knocking the blooms together. One woman, taken quite unawares, shivered – then changed this into a laugh. There was an aside about love from Miss Store, who spoke with a cold, abstracted knowledge – 'Maria has no experience, none whatever; she hopes to meet heroes – she meets none. So now she hopes to find heroes across the sea. Why, Henry, she might make a hero of you.'

'It is not that,' said Maria, who had heard. Mrs Vesey bent down and touched her shoulder; she sent the girl into the house to see if tea were ready. Presently they all rose and followed – in twos and threes, heads either erect composedly or else deliberately bowed in thought. Henry knew the idea of summer had been relinquished: they would not return to the lawn again. In the dining-room – where the white walls and the glass of the pictures held the reflections of summers – burned the log fire they were so glad to see. With her shoulder against the mantelpiece stood Maria, watching them take their places at the round table. Everything Henry had heard said had fallen off her – in these few minutes all by herself she had started in again on a fresh phase of living that was intact and pure. So much so, that Henry felt the ruthlessness of her disregard for the past, even the past of a few minutes ago. She came forward and put her hands on two chairs – to show she had been keeping a place for him.

Lady Ottery, leaning across the table, said: 'I must ask you – we heard you had lost everything. But that cannot be true?'

Henry said, unwillingly: 'It's true that I lost my flat, and everything in my flat.'

'Henry,' said Mrs Vesey, 'all your beautiful things?'

'Oh dear,' said Lady Ottery, overpowered, 'I thought that could not be possible. I ought not to have asked.'

Ria Store looked at Henry critically. 'You take this too calmly. What has happened to you?'

'It was some time ago. And it happens to many people.'

'But not to everyone,' said Miss Store. 'I should see no reason, for instance, why it should happen to me.'

'One cannot help looking at you,' said Sir Isaac. 'You must forgive our amazement. But there was a time, Henry, when I think we all used to feel that we knew you well. If this is not a painful question, at this juncture, why did you not send your valuables out of town? You could have even shipped them over to us.'

'I was attached to them. I wanted to live with them.'

'And now,' said Miss Store, 'you live with nothing, for ever. Can you really feel that that is life?'

'I do. I may be easily pleased. It was by chance I was out when the place was hit. You may feel – and I honour your point of view – that I should have preferred, at my age, to go into eternity with some pieces of glass and jade and a dozen pictures. But, in fact, I am very glad to remain. To exist.'

'On what level?'

'On any level.'

'Come, Henry,' said Ronald Cuffe, 'that is a cynicism one cannot like in you. You speak of your age: to us, of course, that is nothing. You are at your maturity.'

'Forty-three.'

Maria gave Henry an askance look, as though, after all, he were not a friend. But she then said: 'Why should he wish he was dead?' Her gesture upset some tea on the lace cloth, and she idly rubbed it up with her handkerchief. The tug her rubbing gave to the cloth shook a petal from a Chinese peony in the centre bowl on to a plate of cucumber sandwiches. This little bit of destruction was watched by the older people with fascination, with a kind of appeasement, as though it were a guarantee against something worse.

'Henry is not young and savage, like you are. Henry's life is – or was – an affair of attachments,' said Ria Store. She turned her eyes, under their lids, on Henry. 'I wondered how much of you *has* been blown to blazes.'

'I have no way of knowing,' he said. 'Perhaps you have?'

'Chocolate cake?' said Maria.

'Please.'

For chocolate layer cake, the Vesey cook had been famous since Henry was a boy of seven or eight. The look, then the taste, of the brown segment linked him with Sunday afternoons when he had been brought here by his mother; then, with a phase of his adolescence when he had been unable to eat, only able to look round. Mrs Vesey's beauty, at that time approaching its last lunar quarter, had swum on him when he was about nineteen. In Maria, child of her brother's late marriage, he now saw that beauty, or sort of physical genius, at the start. In Maria, this was without hesitation, without the halting influence that had bound Mrs Vesey up – yes and bound Henry up, from his boyhood, with her – in a circle of quizzical half-smiles. In revenge, he accused the young girl who moved him – who seemed framed, by some sort of anticipation, for the new catastrophic *outward* order of life – of brutality, of being without spirit. At his age, between two generations, he felt cast out. He felt Mrs Vesey might not forgive him for having left her for a world at war.

Mrs Vesey blew out the blue flame under the kettle, and let the silver trapdoor down with a snap. She then gave exactly one of those smiles – at the same time, it was the smile of his mother's friend. Ronald Cuffe picked the petal from the sandwiches and rolled it between his fingers, waiting for her to speak.

'It is cold, *indoors*,' said Mrs Vesey. 'Maria, put another log on the fire – Ria, you say the most unfortunate things. We must remember Henry has had a shock. – Henry, let us talk about something better. You work in an office, then, since the war?'

'In a Ministry – in an office, yes.'

'Very hard? – Maria, that is all you would do if you went to England: work in an office. This is not like a war in history, you know.'

Maria said: 'It is not in history yet .' She licked round her lips for the rest of the chocolate taste, then pushed her chair a little back from the table. She looked secretively at her wrist-watch. Henry wondered what the importance of time could be.

He learned what the importance of time was when, on his way down the avenue to the bus, he found Maria between two chestnut trees. She slanted up to him and put her hand on the inside of his elbow. Faded dark-pink stamen from the flowers above them had moulted down on to her hair. 'You have ten minutes more, really,' she said. 'They sent you off ten minutes before your time. They are frightened someone would miss the bus and come back; then everything would have to begin again. As it is always the same, you would not think it would be so difficult for my aunt.'

'Don't talk like that; it's unfeeling; I don't like it,' said Henry, stiffening his elbow inside Maria's grasp.

'Very well, then: walk to the gate, then back. I shall be able to hear your bus coming. It's true what they said – I'm intending to go away. They will have to make up something without me.'

'Maria, I can't like you. Everything you say is destructive and horrible.'

'Destructive? – I thought you didn't mind.'

'I still want the past.'

'Then how weak you are,' said Maria. 'At tea I admired you. The past – things done over and over again with more trouble than they were ever worth? – However, there's no time to talk about that. Listen, Henry: I must have your address. I suppose you *have* an address now?' She stopped him, just inside the white gate with the green drippings: here he blew stamen off a page of his notebook, wrote on the page and tore it out for her. 'Thank you,' said Maria, 'I might turn up – if I wanted money, or anything. But there will be plenty to do: I can drive a car.'

Henry said: 'I want you to understand that I won't be party to this – *in any way*.'

She shrugged and said: 'You want *them* to understand' – and sent a look back to the house. Whereupon, on his entire being, the suspended charm of the afternoon worked. He protested against the return to the zone of death, and perhaps never ever seeing all this again. The cruciform lilac flowers, in all their purples, and the colourless mountains behind Mrs Vesey's face besought him. The moment he had been dreading, returning desire, flooded him in this tunnel of avenue, with motors swishing along the road outside and Maria standing staring at him. He adored the stoicism of the group he had quitted – with their little fears and their great doubts – the grace of the thing done over again. He thought, with nothing left but our brute courage, we shall be nothing but brutes.

'What is the matter?' Maria said. Henry did not answer: they turned and walked to and fro inside the gates. Shadow played over her dress and hair: feeling the disenchantedness of his look at her she asked again, uneasily, 'What's the matter?'

'You know,' he said, 'when you come away from here, no one will care any more that you are Maria. You will no longer be Maria, as a matter of fact. Those looks, those things that are said to you – they make you, you silly little girl. You are you only inside their spell. You may think action is better – but who will care for you when you only act? You will have an identity number, but no identity. Your whole existence has been in contradistinction. You may think you want an ordinary fate – but there is no ordinary fate. And that extra-ordinariness in the fate of each of us is only recognized by your aunt. I admit that her view of life is too much for me – that is why I was so stiff and touchy today. But where shall we be when nobody has a view of life?'

'You don't expect me to understand you, do you?'

'Even your being a savage, even being scornful – yes, even that you have got from them. – Is that my bus?'

'At the other side of the river: it has still got to cross the bridge. – Henry –' she put her face up. He touched it with kisses thoughtful and cold. 'Goodbye,' he said, 'Miranda.'

'– Maria –'

'Miranda. This is the end of *you*. Perhaps it is just as well.'

'I'll be seeing you –'

'You'll come round my door in London – with your little new number chained to your wrist.'

'The trouble with you is, you're half old.'

Maria ran out through the gates to stop the bus, and Henry got on to it and was quickly carried away.

SEAN O'FAOLAIN

The Woman Who Married Clark Gable

She should have lived in Moscow. If she had been a Russian she would have said: 'O God, life is passing and I have yet to live. All last Easter when the baby clouds were passing over the birch-woods, and the streams were whispering of the coming of summer, and the bells were dancing and singing in the monastery towers, I sat at home and drank vodka and longed for love. I do not know whether life is angry with me because I do not live it, or whether I am angry with life because it will not let me live. Ivan Ivanovitch, for God's sake, meet me tonight by the frog-pond and tell me what is this pain in my heart.' And Ivan would have met her and told her in very simple terms. Instead of that she lived in Dublin (South Circular Road, small red house, red terrace, small garden, near the Old Woman's Hostel – full – and Kilmainham Jail – disused). She nagged her husband virtuously when she should have got drunk with him and poured her virtue down the drains. She went twice a week to the movies, hoovered the house until she had all the pile sucked off the carpets, bought a new knick-knack for the mantelpiece every week, washed the dog, polished the windows, slept after lunch, read *Chit Chat* and *Winifred's Weekly*, went for a walk, and then sat around waiting for her husband to come back from the job.

Every night the conversation was the same.

'Had a hard day, darling?' – from her.

'Not so bad, dearie' – from him.

'What did you have for lunch?'

'A very nice lunch. Pork chop, spinach, chips, rhubarb pie, coffee. Very tasty.'

'I washed Herbie. Look at him. It was an awful job. But he is a pet. Aren't you, Herbie?'

'Nice old 'Erbie. Like your bathie. Soapy-soapy? Not tired, dearie?'

And she would always say she was, very tired, or that she had a stitch in her side, or a pain in her head, and she would put on a miserable face, and he would tell her she ought not to do it, not really, and she would tilt her eyebrows and ask sadly for the evening paper. He would suggest a stroll, or a movie, or have a pipe, or tell her a dirty story, and so to bed, and *da capo* the next day and the next. Before she got into bed she would always say the Rosary, and then she would curl up next to him and wait for him to snore. She liked him; he was an honourable, hardworking, straightforward, generous man; but she did not love him. It must be added that they had no children and she worried about that. It must also be understood that he was a Methodist and went regularly to the tin chapel along the road, and she worried about that too. She was always praying that he might be converted: that was why she said the Rosary every night, though she never told him that. He was English and was rather stubborn about religious matters.

One morning as she kissed him goodbye at the gate of her little garden she drew back hastily and peered at him.

'Darling, you haven't shaved?'

He grinned fatuously, lifted his bowler-hat, said: 'I'm growing a moustache,' and ran. For weeks after that their nightly conversation had an extra five lines:

'I don't like that moustache, darling.'

'It's coming on. Chaps at the works rag me a lot abaht it. But I don't mind. Jealous, I say.'

'But it tickles, darling.'

'Aain't that nice, dearie?'

One night they went to the movies to see *San Francisco*, with Jeanette MacDonald and Clark Gable. This picture dealt with a rake and a good man and a singing heroine, friends in spite of everything, even the singing and the fact that the good man (Spencer Tracy) was a priest. The rake had a squabble with the priest, and although the priest – he was a Boxing Padre – could have knocked him on the canvas for twenty he merely wiped the blood off the corner of his mouth and looked sadly at the rake. In the end there is an earthquake and the earth opens and all sorts of things fall down into holes and the rake kneels down and is converted. They show Mr Gable's boot soles because nobody looking at his face would believe it. Then they all join hands and march down the hill into the camera and the closing, gauzy irides-cent curtains of the cinema, singing the theme-song, 'Sa-a-n Francisco, Open your pearly gates . . .' (etc.), and every-body goes home happy.

She walked home that night in a dreamy silence. She heard none of his remarks about the picture, and when they were back home she kept looking at him in a strange, distant way. She went restlessly in and out of the parlour, threw guilty sidelong glances at him, did not seem to want to go to bed, hardly said a word in answer to his chatter, forgot to pray for his conversion, and lay awake for hours looking out at the tops of the London plane waving faintly against the dull upthrown glow of the city.

She went to the same cinema, alone, the next day; and that night she made him take her to it again; which he was pleased to do because he wanted to know how they got all those things to fall into holes in the ground. All through the picture she held his hand and stole sideward glances at the black line of his Gablesque moustache. That night she put on her pink chiffon nightgown – the one she bought the time she thought she was going to have a baby and only had a miss; and she had worn it again the time she had her gall-stones out; and the time she had the appendix; and the time she went to the nursing home when she tumbled down stairs. She put scent behind her ears and looking at herself in the mirror said,

'Darling, did I ever tell you I had rather a good voice when I was . . . I mean before I married you?' And she swayed

44

and began to hum, 'San Francisco, Open your pearly gates!'

'It sounds like hydraulic pressure,' he ruminated. 'You know, like a lift going down.'

When she lay beside him she looked at his profile and whispered.

'Darling, supposing this was San Francisco. You and me? And the earth begins to shake?'

'Lummy,' he cried. 'Like this?' And he began to bounce up and down on the springs.

She gave a frightened scream.

'Why, dearie, what's wrong?'

'You're so rough,' she said adoringly.

'My poor little upsydaisy, isum frightened?'

She put out the light.

For about two weeks they were happier than at any time since their honeymoon, in that little redbrick house on the South Circular Road. She bought a record of *Open your pearly gates*. She asked him questions about earthquakes and he began to read them up. One Saturday she heard the film was at Bray and, under pretence of a day's outing by the sea, made him take her to it again. This he found a bit boring, but being a kind-hearted chap he humoured her. When it moved on up to Malahide and she wanted to follow it he demurred. To his surprise she crumbled at once and said that if he hit her she wouldn't blame him, and that she probably deserved it. He did no more than tease her when he found a picture of Mr Gable garbed for the boxing-ring pinned up in their parlour the next day. But he did begin to get a bit worried when she bought him a cravat, an old-time three-cornered collar, asked him to take up boxing-lessons, and wanted him to meet her priest and become great friends with him. He drew the line at the priest and the boxing but he did wear the cravat and the collar in which he looked like a horse in demi-harness.

She noticed the worried look on his face the first morning he wore this contraption and decided that he was unhappy because he guessed that she was deceiving him with Mr Gable. She went off to consult her priest.

He heard her problem in complete silence and then said, 'It's a very fine point, I think you'd better give me a week to think it over.' So at the end of the week she went again, this time in a black veil, and he explained to her that the chief end of marriage is, of course, the bearing of children and that what we call Love is, naturally, secondary to this great end. And after all, he said, what *is* Love? Indeed, what are all those curious human manifestations which lead to the great end (which he had already defined)? To a mere celibate these things were all very strange. But then, he added quickly, who are we, anyway, to question the devices of Providence which, indeed, as we may see, are frequently not merely puzzling but baffling? At all events, he hurried on, be that as it might, it appeared to him that, theologically speaking, and always provided that she kept that great end in view, and had no other end in view at any time – he stressed the words *at any time* – there could be no objection to her deciding that she was living with this Mr Mark Cable. Indeed, he added testily, for the matter had caused him a great deal of worry, and caused him to read a great many dull Latin volumes, she could (always provided she kept that great end in view) go on believing that she was living with her grandfather; and he dismissed her abruptly. She left him, a little hurt by the reference to her grandfather, but more content with the propriety of her behaviour than she had ever been since her wedding night.

Her joy was brief. It was on her way home that she purchased the film-magazine which reported, with a large portrait of Mr Clark Gable, that there were rumours flying about New York to the effect that 'our Clark' had lately been seen in gay places in the company of a well-known oil millionairess.

That night she saw at once that her George was giving her worried looks; as well he might since she kept looking at him in a very peculiar fashion.

'Tired, dearie?' he asked.

'A fat lot you care,' she cried tragically.

'But I do care, dearie!'

'You,' she charged with passion, 'care nothing whatsoever for me. What did you have for lunch today?'

'Why,' he mumbled, a bit taken aback by this divergence, 'I 'ad a spot of steak-and-kidney, rhubarb and cuss, black coffee, all very tasty too.'

At this she laughed scornfully.

'Alone?' she challenged.

'Wotcher mean, alone?'

'Were – you – alone?'

'Well, not quite alone. A couple of the chaps as usual.'

'Chaps!'

She uttered what she considered to be a strangled cry, gave a broken sob, ended up with a groan of despair and made a fair shot at hurling herself from the room. He, staring at the dog wagging its tail hopefully, began to examine his conscience; and as any man can always find some little thing somewhere in his conscience, even if it is only a pinched bottom, he played a good deal at finger-under-the-collar before he went up to bed. She did not speak one word to him. Once he asked her if she had a cold, because she was sobbing into her pillow; at which she moaned as if her poor little heart would break, causing him to beg her to tell him if she had a toothache. His patience gave out when she refused to get up and cook his breakfast, for an Englishman will stand much but he will not stand for a breakfast of cold milk and dog-biscuits. He drank neat whisky at lunch and he drank neat whisky (several times) on his way home in the evening, and he tore off his horse-collar and dropped it into the canal, and he had a haircut and shave, and he even had the barber shave off his moustache, and when he squeaked open the garden gate he was full of fight.

She was not. She had bought another film-magazine that afternoon which scornfully denied the story about Mr Clark Gable and the millionairess; said that Mr Gable was very cross about it, in fact. In a high state of nerves she awaited his return and she was trembling when she opened the hall-door. She gave one look at the bald face and collarless neck before her, realized simultaneously that she was being confronted by her husband and had been abandoned by Mr Gable, and the next thing she did was to sink in a faint on the mat and give her poll a terrific wallop off the lino.

It took poor George an hour to bring her around and calm her down, and by that time all the fight had gone out of him. Besides he was too relieved to find that she was her old self again – moaning and groaning at him to his heart's content. When she wanted the evening paper she asked for it (to his great joy) quite snappishly. When, as the night was near ending, he ventured to tell her a dirty story and she laughed loudly and then put on a shocked face and said he ought to be ashamed of himself, he almost winked.

They lived unhappily ever after in complete marital satisfaction.

FRANK SARGESON
Old Man's Story

He was sitting there on the waterfront, and off and on I watched him while he read the newspaper. He looked a frail old man, I don't mean feeble, just frail. Delicate. You see such old men about and you wonder how it is they've lived so long, how it is that some sickness hasn't carried them off long ago. You think perhaps life has always been easy for them, you look at their hands and feel sure about it. Though hands will sometimes deceive you just as much as faces.

It was good to be sitting there on the waterfront. Besides the old man there were ships alongside the wharves to look at, and the sea, and seagulls. The seagulls were making their horrid squabbling noises. It was because of a slice of buttered bread lying close to our seat, the butter gone soft and yellow in the sun. The seagulls wanted it, but didn't dare to come so close to us, and I watched them, wanting to see if they'd have the courage. Then the old man frightened the birds away by saying the word, Terrible! I looked at him and his cheeks had turned red, and I understood it was because of something he'd read in the newspaper.

Have you seen this? he said, and I leaned over to see the column he was pointing to.

Yes, I said. It was about a man, an adult man and a young girl. A Court case.

Terrible! the old man said.

Yes? I said. Maybe you're right. Anyhow, I said, five years in gaol is terrible.

Yes, the old man said, five years in gaol. Terrible!

Oh, I said, I get you. I don't go much on putting people away, I said.

No, the old man said, it's terrible.

But people say, I said, what can you do?

I don't know, the old man said. But I knew of a case once. It didn't get into the newspapers.

Well, the old man told me, and it was quite a story. It had all happened when he was a boy, fourteen years old perhaps, or thereabouts. He'd just finished school and for a time he went and worked on his uncle's farm. It was a nice place, he said, an old place in a part of the country that had been settled very early. The farms round about were all old places, most of them were run by the families that had been the first to settle there. There were old orchards everywhere, and plenty of trees, English trees that had been planted right at the beginning. Some people went in for crops and some ran cows, but besides they'd have poultry and bees, and everybody had an orchard. Life was pretty quiet there, the old man said, there wasn't any hurry and bustle, it was just real old-fashioned country life. Now and then there'd be a picnic in the school grounds, where the trees were very thick and shady, or perhaps they'd hold a dance in the school itself, but that was about all. You couldn't have found a nicer place, the old man said. His uncle's house was an old place just about buried in a tangle of honeysuckle and rambler roses, not the sort of farmhouse it's so easy to find nowadays. The railway ran alongside but it was a branch line, there weren't many trains and they'd run at any old times. Why, the old man said, he could remember one time when the driver stopped the train to get off and buy a watermelon from his uncle. But nobody worried, because people took life differently in those days.

As a boy the old man used to spend his school holidays there, and he'd enjoy himself no end, so when he finished school his people sent him to help his uncle. They thought perhaps he might turn out a farmer. Anyhow it suited him fine. There were just his uncle and his aunt (they'd never had any children), both easy-going, good-natured sorts, and a man they'd had working on the place for years. This man was a little wiry fellow with a mop of curly hair that he never brushed, and a wrinkled face that was always grinning at you. It was a wicked grin, the old man said, one eye'd close up a lot more than the other. Anyhow he was quite a character. He'd turned up one day with a swag on his back, been given a job, and never moved on for years. He was no chicken, in his fifties perhaps; and they used to call him Bandy; though one leg was a lot bandier than the other. He'd had that one broken more times than he could remember was the yarn he told. When he was a boy he'd gone to sea, he said, and several times he'd fallen from aloft. But he told so many yarns about his life in different parts of the world it was hard to say whether they were all true. He was Irish, the old man said, and had the real Irishman's way of telling you far-fetched yarns. Anyhow he milked the cows and was generally useful about the place. He taught the boy to milk and the two of them were in each other's company the most part of each day. Once you got to know him, the old man said, he was a regular hard case to talk to, his aunt would have had a blue-fit if she'd found out. But of course it was only natural for a boy that age to listen to Bandy and never let on. He was curious about life, he had to find things out sooner or later, and thinking it over later on he reckoned he'd learned more from Bandy than he ever had out of his Sunday school books. It was pretty strong stuff, granted, it had a real tang to it, but it was honest stuff all the same. Nor did it ever get him excited so far as he could remember, not in a physical way anyhow. When Bandy'd tell him he'd been with white black brown and yellow and was still clean, he never had any other feeling except a sort of hero-worship for him. It was the same as if Bandy had said he'd had fights with all colours and had always knocked the other fellow out without ever getting a scratch himself. People forget when they grow up, the old man said. Maybe they've learned to play safe by shying away from the strong stuff, but they forget it would never have appealed to them as children in anything like the same way. Children live in a different world, the old man said.

Anyhow, that was the position when the old man was a boy of about fourteen working on his uncle's farm. He was enjoying the life in that old-fashioned neighbourhood, and he was great cobbers with this Bandy, this hard old case; and besides teaching him to milk cows Bandy was every day telling him what was what. Neither his uncle nor his aunt had any idea, he said, they never seemed to worry about his always being with Bandy, and he never told them a thing.

But it turned out things didn't stay like that for very long. One day the boy's aunt went up to town for a holiday, and when she came back she brought home a girl with her. She was quite a young thing, thirteen or fourteen years old perhaps, and small for her age. It seemed she was an orphan and someone had persuaded the old man's aunt to be a good soul and give her a home, to try her out anyhow. Well, her name was Myrtle and she was nothing much to look at. She wore glasses and had curls that hung over her forehead. They made her look a bit silly, the old man said, you felt you'd like to get the scissors and clip them off. She'd annoy you too by always asking, Why? She didn't seem to know much about anything, and you could hardly do a thing without her asking, Why? Still, she seemed to be quite harmless, she helped with the housework and did everything she was told without making any fuss about it. Nobody took much notice of her but she didn't seem to mind.

Later on, though, the boy noticed that a change had come over Bandy. To begin with he'd been like every one else and hardly taken any notice of Myrtle. Then the boy noticed he'd become interested. Up in the cowshed he'd ask, How's Myrtle this morning? Or picking fruit in the orchard he'd say, We'll keep that one for Myrtle. And the curious thing was, the old man said, Myrtle showed signs of being interested the same way. If Bandy was working in the garden anywhere near the house Myrtle would be sure to start banging about on the verandah with a broom. Bandy'd grin at her (that wicked grin, the old man said), and they wouldn't say much, but you could tell there was a sort of situation between them. One day when Myrtle was out on the verandah Bandy suddenly left off digging and picked a bunch of roses (which he wasn't supposed to do) and gave them to the girl. And instead of saying anything she just dropped the broom and ran inside, and Bandy was sort of overcome as well and went away down the garden leaving the boy to dig on his own. It was the kind of thing a boy notices, the old man said, even though he mightn't be able to make head nor tail of it. Another thing was that Bandy wasn't the company he'd been before. He'd be a bit short with the boy for no reason at all, nor would he talk in the old way. If the boy tried to get him to talk on the old subject he wouldn't bite, or else he'd tell him he'd better behave himself or he'd grow up with a dirty mind. He couldn't make it out, the old man said. The idea he'd got of Bandy right from the beginning made it just impossible for him to make it out. And you only had to look at him and look at Myrtle. So far as they were concerned, one and one didn't make two at all.

Then it happened his uncle began to get an idea of the way the wind was blowing. Perhaps he'd been told about the bunch of roses, the boy didn't know. Bandy began to spend his spare time making a garden seat (one of those rustic contraptions, the old man said). It was on the edge of the orchard, but right up against a hedge where you couldn't see it from the house. And one day when it was about finished the boy tried it out by taking a seat. Well, Bandy told him off properly. He hadn't made it for him to sit on, he said. No, he'd made it for Myrtle. But the boy's uncle just happened to be coming up on the other side of the hedge at the time, and he came round and Bandy got told off properly. The boy only heard half of it because his uncle sent him away, but after that nobody could help seeing the difference in Bandy. He went about looking black, the old man said, he'd be always muttering to himself and he'd make a mess of his work, spilling buckets of milk, putting the cows in the wrong paddock and that sort of thing. And by the way Myrtle looked she must have got a talking to as well. She looked scared, the old man said, and often enough she'd look as if she'd been crying. Nor were the pair of them the only ones you could see the difference in. Everybody in the house was affected. The boy couldn't sleep at night for thinking it all over, and he'd hear his uncle and aunt talking in bed in the next room. And he was pretty certain he knew what they were talking about. Why Myrtle wasn't packed off back where she'd come from he couldn't make out, but that didn't happen and for some weeks things just drifted along as they were. He felt very unhappy, the old man said, he was all the time thinking of writing his people to say he was sick of farming and wanted to come back home.

All the same things couldn't last as they were. Myrtle wouldn't eat her meals and Bandy did his work worse and worse. You felt something was going to happen, the old man said, things were absolutely ripe so to speak.

Then one evening the boy saw something. It was one evening when he'd been across to a neighbouring farm for a game of draughts. His aunt didn't like him being out at night on his own, but he'd begged to go, he wanted to get away from what was going on in the house. He couldn't stand it, the old man said. Every night Myrtle'd be sent off to bed immediately she'd done the dishes, and you'd hear Bandy muttering to himself in his room which was a lean-to up against the kitchen wall. Anyhow, coming home this night the boy took a short cut through the orchard, and looking along a row of trees he saw that somebody was sitting on the seat Bandy had made. There was a bit of a moon and he could see something white. He thought of Bandy and Myrtle, of course, and for a time he waited, not knowing whether it would be safe to go closer or not. He thought his heart was beating loud enough to give the show away on its own, and in the dark he felt his cheeks begin to burn. He was thinking of what he might see. But he couldn't help himself, the old man said, he had to go closer. And Bandy and Myrtle were sitting on the seat. Bandy was in his working clothes but Myrtle seemed to be in her nightgown, at any rate the boy could tell she had bare feet. And they were sitting there without saying a word, the old man said, sitting a little apart but holding each other's hands. Every now and then the girl would turn her face to Bandy and he'd lean over to kiss her; or Bandy would turn his face and she'd lean over to kiss him. That was all there was to see, the old man said. Nothing more than that. It amounted to this, that bad old Bandy had got the girl, this young Myrtle, with her silly curls, out on the seat with him, and there was nothing doing except those kisses. And the whole time the boy stood there watching he never heard them say a thing.

It was a tremendous experience for a boy, the old man said, too big for him to be at all clear about until later on in life. All he understood at the time was that he had somehow managed to get life all wrong. Like all boys he thought he'd got to know what was what, but as he stood there in the dark and watched Bandy and Myrtle he understood that he had a lot to learn. He'd been taken in, he thought. It wasn't a pleasant thought, the old man said.

Well, the old man told me the story sitting there on the waterfront. It had all happened a long time ago, and he didn't tell it exactly as I've written it down, but I felt there was something in the story that he wanted to make me see. And I felt it was mainly connected with the part about Bandy and Myrtle sitting on the garden seat, because when he'd told me that part the old man seemed to think his story was finished. He stopped talking and began to fold up his newspaper. But I couldn't leave it at that.

What happened? I said.

Oh, the old man said, my uncle caught the pair of them in

Bandy's room one night, and the girl got packed off back where she'd come from.

I see, I said, and the old man got up to go.

And what about Bandy? I said, and I got up to kick the piece of buttered bread over to the seagulls.

Oh, the old man said, one morning when he was supposed to be milking the cows Bandy hanged himself in the cowshed.

MORLEY CALLAGHAN
A Very Merry Christmas

After midnight on Christmas Eve hundreds of people prayed at the crib of the Infant Jesus which was to the right of the altar under the evergreen-tree branches in St Malachi's church. That night there had been a heavy fall of wet snow, and there was a muddy path up to the crib. Both Sylvanus O'Meara, the old caretaker who had helped to prepare the crib, and Father Gorman, the stout, red-faced, excitable parish priest, had agreed it was the most lifelike tableau of the Child Jesus in a corner of the stable at Bethlehem they had ever had in the church.

But early on Christmas morning Father Gorman came running to see O'Meara, the blood all drained out of his face and his hands pumping up and down at his sides and he shouted, 'A terrible thing has happened. Where is the Infant Jesus? The crib's empty.'

O'Meara, who was a devout, innocent, wondering old man, who prayed a lot and always felt very close to God in the church, was bewildered and he whispered, 'Who could have taken it? Taken it where?'

'Take a look in the crib yourself, man, if you don't believe me,' the priest said, and he grabbed the caretaker by the arm, marched him into the church and over to the crib and showed him that the figure of the Infant Jesus was gone.

'Someone took it, of course. It didn't fly away. But who took it, that's the question?' the priest said. 'When was the last time you saw it?'

'I know it was here last night,' O'Meara said, 'because after the midnight mass when everybody else had gone home I saw Mrs Farrel and her little boy kneeling up here, and when they stood up I wished them a merry Christmas. You don't think she'd touch it, do you?'

'What nonsense, O'Meara. There's not a finer woman in the parish. I'm going over to her house for dinner tonight.'

'I noticed that she wanted to go home, but the little boy wanted to stay there and keep praying by the crib; but after they went home I said a few prayers myself and the Infant Jesus was still there.'

Grabbing O'Meara by the arm the priest whispered excitedly, 'It must be the work of communists or atheists.' There was a sudden rush of blood to his face. 'This isn't the first time they've struck at us,' he said.

'What would communists want with the figure of the Infant Jesus?' O'Meara asked innocently. 'They wouldn't want to have it to be reminded that God was with them. I didn't think they could bear to have Him with them.'

'They'd take it to mock us, of course, and to desecrate the church. O'Meara, you don't seem to know much about the times we live in. Why did they set fire to the church?'

O'Meara said nothing because he was very loyal and he didn't like to remind the priest that the little fire they had in the church a few months ago was caused by a cigarette butt the priest had left in his pocket when he was changing into his vestments, so he was puzzled and silent for a while and then whispered, 'Maybe someone really wanted to take God away, do you think so?'

'Take Him out of the church?'

'Yes. Take Him away.'

'How could you take God out of the church, man? Don't be stupid.'

'But maybe someone thought you could, don't you see?'

'O'Meara, you talk like an old idiot. Don't you realize you play right into the hands of the atheists, saying such things? Do we believe an image is God? Do we worship idols? We do not. No more of that, then. If communists and atheists tried to burn this church once, they'll not stop till they desecrate it. God help us, why is my church marked out for this?' He got terribly excited and rushed away shouting, 'I'm going to phone the police.'

It looked like the beginning of a terrible Christmas Day for the parish. The police came, and were puzzled, and talked to everybody. Newspapermen came. They took pictures of the church and of Father Gorman, who had just preached a sermon that startled the congregation because he grew very eloquent on the subject of vandal outrages to the house of God. Men and women stood outside the church in their best clothes and talked very gravely. Everybody wanted to know what the thief would do with the image of the Infant Jesus. They all were wounded, stirred and wondering. There certainly was going to be something worth talking about at a great many Christmas dinners in the neighbourhood.

But Sylvanus O'Meara went off by himself and was very sad. From time to time he went into the church and looked at the empty crib. He had all kinds of strange thoughts. He told himself that if someone really wanted to hurt God, then just wishing harm to Him really hurt Him, for what other way was there of hurting Him? Last night he had had the feeling that God was all around the crib, and now it felt as if God wasn't there at all. It wasn't just that the image of the Infant Jesus was gone, but someone had done violence to that spot and had driven God away from it. He told himself that things could be done that would make God want to leave a place. It was very hard to know where God was. Of course, He would always be in the church, but where had that part of Him that had seemed to be all around the crib gone?

It wasn't a question he could ask the little groups of astounded parishioners who stood on the sidewalk outside the church, because they felt like wagging their fingers and puffing their cheeks out and talking about what was happening to God in Mexico and Spain.

But when they had all gone home to eat their Christmas dinners, O'Meara, himself, began to feel a little hungry. He went out and stood in front of the church and was feeling thankful that there was so much snow for the children on Christmas Day when he saw that splendid and prominent woman, Mrs Farrel, coming along the street with her little boy. On Mrs Farrel's face there was a grim and desperate expression and she was taking such long fierce strides that the five-year-old boy, whose hand she held so tight, could hardly keep up with her and pull his big red sleigh. Sometimes the little boy tried to lean back and was a dead weight and then she pulled his feet off the ground while he whimpered, 'Oh, gee, oh, gee, let me go.' His red snowsuit was all covered with snow as if he had been rolling on the road.

'Merry Christmas, Mrs Farrel,' O'Meara said. And he called to the boy, 'Not happy on Christmas day? What's the matter, son?'

'Merry Christmas, indeed, Mr O'Meara,' the woman snapped to him. She was not accustomed to paying much attention to the caretaker, a curt nod was all she ever gave him, and now she was far too angry and mortified to bother with him. 'Where's Father Gorman?' she demanded.

'Still at the police station, I think.'

'At the police station! God help us, did you hear that, Jimmie?' she said, and she gave such a sharp tug at the boy's arm that she spun him around in the snow behind her skirts where he cowered, watching O'Meara with a curiously steady pair of fine blue eyes. He wiped away a mat of hair from his forehead as he watched and waited. 'Oh, Lord, this is terrible,' Mrs Farrel said. 'What will I do?'

'What's the matter, Mrs Farrel?'

'I didn't do anything,' the child said. 'I was coming back here. Honest I was, mister.'

'Mr O'Meara,' the woman began, as if coming down from a great height to the level of an unimportant and simpleminded old man, 'maybe you could do something for us. Look on the sleigh.'

O'Meara saw that an old coat was wrapped around something on the sleigh, and stooping to lift it, he saw the figure of the Infant Jesus there. He was so delighted he only looked up at Mrs Farrel and shook his head in wonder and said, 'It's back and nobody harmed it at all.'

'I'm ashamed, I'm terribly ashamed, Mr O'Meara. You don't know how mortified I am,' she said, 'but the child really didn't know what he was doing. It's a disgrace to us, I know. It's my fault that I haven't trained him better, though God knows I've tried to drum respect for the church into him.' She gave such a jerk at the child's hand he slid on his knee in the snow keeping his eyes on O'Meara.

Still unbelieving, O'Meara asked, 'You mean he really took it from the church?'

'He did, he really did.'

'Fancy that. Why, child, that was a terrible thing to do,' O'Meara said, 'Whatever got into you?' Completely mystified he turned to Mrs Farrel, but he was so relieved to have the figure of the Infant Jesus back without there having been any great scandal that he couldn't help putting his hand gently on the child's head.

'It's all right, and you don't need to say anything,' the child said, pulling away angrily from his mother, and yet he never took his eyes off O'Meara, as if he felt there was some bond between them. Then he looked down at his mitts, fumbled with them and looked up steadily and said, 'It's all right, isn't it, mister?'

'It was early this morning, right after he got up, almost the first thing he must have done on Christmas Day,' Mrs Farrel said. 'He must have walked right in and picked it up and taken it out to the street.'

'But what got into him?'

'He makes no sense about it. He says he had to do it.'

'And so I did, 'cause it was a promise,' the child said. 'I promised last night, I promised God that if He would make Mother bring me a big red sleigh for Christmas I would give Him the first ride on it.'

'Don't think I've taught the child foolish things,' Mrs Farrel said. 'I'm sure he meant no harm. He didn't understand at all what he was doing.'

'Yes, I did,' the child said stubbornly.

'Shut up, child,' she said, shaking him.

O'Meara knelt down till his eyes were on a level with the child's and they looked at each other till they felt close together and he said, 'But why did you want to do that for God?'

' 'Cause it's a swell sleigh, and I thought God would like it.'

Mrs Farrel, fussing and red-faced, said, 'Don't you worry. I'll see he's punished by having the sleigh taken away from him.'

But O'Meara, who had picked up the figure of the Infant Jesus, was staring down at the red sleigh; and suddenly he had a feeling of great joy, of the illumination of strange good tidings, a feeling that this might be the most marvellous Christmas Day in the whole history of the city, for God must surely have been with the child, with him on a joyous, carefree holiday sleigh ride, as he ran along those streets and pulled the sleigh. And O'Meara turned to Mrs Farrel, his face bright with joy, and said, commandingly, with a look in his eyes that awed her, 'Don't you dare say a word to him, and don't you dare touch that sleigh, do you hear? I think God did like it.'

RHYS DAVIES

Gents Only

While he was busy burying a woman one June afternoon, Lewis the Hearse's wife left him for ever, going by the three o'clock train and joining her paramour at Stickell junction, where they were seen by Matt Morgan waiting for their connection. She left a letter for her husband, a plate of tart for his tea, and that sense of awful desolation a gone person can leave in a house.

What was in that letter no one ever knew, not even Lewis' sister Bloddie, who – for the news was up all the hillsides of Crwtch the same evening – came flying down from her farm up where the old BC tomb had been found. But from that afternoon Lewis was a changed man. Not that he had been a specially bright bit of spring sunshine before, though he was quite a decent-looking man in his way. His manner betokened a sombre nature which was not entirely due to his calling. Because of his reasonable prices and his craftsmanship in coffins, all the people of Crwtch respected him.

'A servant you'll have to take,' Bloddie declared shrilly, and her bosom heaved like the Bay of Biscay because he wouldn't show her the letter. 'Forever running down here I can't be. . . . The house she left clean. I will say.' She looked at the uneaten tart – for Lewis' wife was Crwtch's best tart maker – jealously. 'If that tart you don't want I can take it.'

Lewis lifted his brooding head at last. 'Take it!' he barked, so fierce that she jumped back. 'And your own carcass too.'

But what Crwtch never expected was the decision he came to the very next day. He tore down from outside his house the wooden tablet announcing his name and profession and

63

in its place screwed a new one just painted in the work shed behind the house.

This announced: *J. J. Lewis, Gent's Undertaker*. Seeing him screw it up, Daniels Long Time, captain of the amateur Fire Brigade and so called because people said his engine was always a long time coming when needed, stopped and asked: 'What is it meaning, Lewis?'

Shaking his screwdriver, Lewis barked: 'My last woman I buried yesterday. From now on, men's funerals only.' And he went in, slamming the door.

No one could believe it. For days it was the talk at every hearth, in every shop and pub in Crwtch. Everybody waited for the next woman to go. A man died and Lewis buried him as usual, very reasonable and the coffin up to standard. Except for this funeral Lewis had not appeared out of doors, not even to go to chapel. His sister Bloddie said he cleaned and cooked for himself, ordering things by his apprentice, Shenkin. At this funeral everybody looked at him inquisitively but could collect nothing but a bleak decision in the uprightness of his body walking behind his lovely crystal hearse.

Then Polly Red Rose went of old age. Licensee of the best pub in Crwtch (now carried on by her son), Polly was respected by both sexes and all creeds. Surely Lewis, who had often enjoyed a glass of the Red Rose beer, would not say no to burying her? The son knocked at Lewis' door. But before he could take off his black bowler and step inside, Lewis said clearly, not angry, but firm as a rock:

'No use coming in. See the plate outside? Gents only, or boys, and no exceptions, sorry to say. Good day.'

Now, there was not another undertaker within fifteen miles of Crwtch, the one in Stickell, a stranger. And not only would he charge extra for travelling his contrivance thirty miles in all, but it was known that his carriages were shabby, being more used in a town the size of Stickell. Everybody knew how Lewis' coffins (to say nothing of his moderate charges) were not only good value but would surely last longer than anybody else's. And so, when the women of Crwtch began to boil against this reflection on their sex and solicited their men to do something about it, even the men more or less began to agree.

'If I was a man,' Mrs Hopcyns the Boot declared to her husband, right in front of a woman customer buying boots, 'horse-whip him I would.'

'Sore he is,' Hopcyns the Boot said mildly. 'Give him a bit of time to get over the Mrs leaving him like that. Come round he will in a year or two.'

'Anybody would think,' said the customer, kicking off a boot and flushed from bending, 'that men don't mind about it. Forced to bury Polly Red Rose he ought to have been.'

'How?' enquired Hopcyns. 'No law there is about it. Same as I am not bound to sell you a pair of boots!'

'Catching it is, is it!' simmered the customer. In Crwtch there was only one of all trades, except farming, so there was no competition for customers.

The first outcome of all the agitation, however, was that the Big Men of Horeb chapel went in deputation to Lewis. They wore their formal Sunday black, watch-chains, and umbrellas, and in array they looked impressive. Lewis received them readily enough in his parlour, where were the samples of wood, metals, and glass wreaths. But he did not sit down like them, and, before they could speak, he launched like a judge having the last word:

'Lord of himself a man is. Private his soul. Between me and my destiny it is what I have decided in the matter of my funerals. But this I will say: Not only to vex the women of Crwtch is my intention; vex the women of the whole world I would. Yet small of mind is that. This is my true reason – women will see there is a man at last who will not sit down under their carryings-on and shamelessness. A good example I have begun, in a time gone loose and no respect for the vows of the marriage day. No more now. I have decided.'

The Big Men looked at each other, and it was plain there was no stout movement to contradict Lewis or attempt coaxing. At last one said, however: 'But Lewis, Lewis, come now. Surely similar all are in death, and in a hearse there are no trousers or petticoats, properly speaking. The same shroud of Heaven covers all.'

Another, who had a crinkled little old face like an old apple in the loft, added: 'Yes, persons only in the cemetery and not men and women. No carryings-on *there*; the only place safe from such it is. Every door marked "Private", and no back door either. Agree with you I would, Lewis, if the cemetery was a place of this and that; only right it would be for you to say no to taking women there. But surely it is not?'

'Obliged I am for the visit,' said Lewis, far away. 'Just now I am starching white collars.' Indeed, starch was whitening his fingers, and he had the air of one with many household tasks to do.

No doubt at all a door was shut fast in his soul. For him no more the peaches and the blossoms of women in the world. The Big Men filed out in the sunshine and adjourned to the vestry of Horeb to consider the manner of their report to their wives. . . . But Crwtch's protest did not stop there. The following week those ten of the business-men who call themselves the Chamber of Trade, meeting once a month in The Red Rose, sought conference with Lewis.

Though, as before, resolutely calm, Lewis made sharp interruption of their mild wheedling: 'Look now, this you must do. Put a big advertisement in the newspaper – "Chance for Undertaker in Well-off Small Town. Present Undertaker Gents Only. Apply to Crwtch Chamber of Trade". See?'

Reproachful, one of the members protested in sorrow: 'A stranger in *your* business is not welcome, Lewis, and well you do know it. Surprised at you I am.' And he added significantly: 'Ointment for bruises there are always, and many in pretty boxes.'

Lewis knew what the member meant. Under the special circumstances he would not become a social outcast if he took a fancy to someone and brought her under his roof, though in Crwtch this was the most abhorrent sin of all. But he said cynically:

'Ointments cost money, and down by half is my business. And will be for ever.'

After the failure of the Chamber of Trade, the Society of Merched y Te itself made attempts. This society of teetotal women formed to spread the ideal of temperance was – no one knew why – of powerful influence in Crwtch and nobody willingly incurred its displeasure. The mother of one of its members having died, the daughter made great groan of the awful cost of the funeral by the undertaker at Stickell, with the coffin looking like one from a factory. The Merched, twenty strong, assembled one August afternoon and marched in procession to Lewis' house. But, apprised of their intention by his spy, Shenkin the apprentice, Lewis had not only locked and barred his door but had nailed a notice on it: *'J. J. Lewis. In Business to Men Only. No Others Admitted. By Order, J. J. Lewis.'*

It is plain that women of affairs, particularly when in concourse, would not be daunted by such a notice. They knocked, they rapped and banged, called through the letter-box and rattled it with fancy umbrellas, tactless as any reforming society can be. There was no reply. Presently the noise was such – it was a hot day and tempers were rising – that a crowd of about two hundred collected, and from his cottage PC Evans the Spike telephoned the Sergeant in Stickell, putting on his helmet first. The Sergeant said that no man is obliged to open the door of his house to the public and that the crowd must be dispersed if it was creating a nuisance. Perspiring, Evans the Spike stepped out, went back for his baton, and then, after plunging into the crowd and enquiring the meaning of this uproar, gave the Sergeant's decision and posted himself in Lewis' doorway.

'Truth of the matter is,' called one of the Merched indignantly, 'supporting the sly old fish the men are. . . . . A letter will be written!' she finished with great ominousness.

But it was Bloddie who moved in the affair with better craft. She became incensed that her brother persisted in deliberately throwing away good business. Some years younger than he was, she hoped to benefit one day from the tidy little fortune he could be making.

It was during a visit to her friend's farm over the hill one afternoon that she saw light – in the person of her friend's orphan niece who had just come from the mining valleys to work at the farm. About twenty, Lottie's lovely head shone fresh as a buttercup, and all her presence breathed strong of an obedient nature waiting to devote itself entire to a person. Though dainty-looking she had no nerves and was strong as an ox. Better still, there was a smile behind the naughty blue of her eye, and even better still, she had deficiencies – she did not like hard work, and her lazy mind seemed vacant and only waiting for the one thing to come along and keep her comfortable.

Bloddie conferred with her old friend, who had taken Lottie to live with her because there was no one else to take her. 'Aye,' agreed the aunt at once, 'sweeten him up she could, no doubt. Welcome you are to her, Bloddie.'

'Look how he used to be,' Bloddie remembered, fired, 'as a young man! No 'ooman in Crwtch was safe from him. . . . A man with extremes in his nature he is, evident,' she added, putting her finger on his character accurately.

But how to get Lottie into Lewis' notice was the problem. Bloddie lay in bed of nights brooding. She was the only woman – for a sister is not a woman – who was allowed into her brother's house, and even she was treated with short shrift though he accepted the bit of green stuff or bacon she brought down from the farm. Then one morning she rose and said clearly to herself: 'A new shock often kills an old one.'

Thereafter she took to calling on Lewis frequently, always with presents for his meals, and even daring to follow him into the work shed that abutted on the back lane and talking to him while he made a coffin. Subtly she got to know this and that from his short grunts. One day, splashing the varnish down on a beautiful cut coffin – for Crwtch men still remained faithful to him and his moderate charges – he growled: 'No good you keep coming here, Bloddie. Shenkin the apprentice can do my business for the house. Tomorrow, going by the first train to Stickell he is to buy wallpaper and a chicken in the market.'

'Wallpapering the parlour are you?' she said idly. 'Coffin for Josh Jones that is? Nice wood.'

'Going to him it is the day after tomorrow,' Lewis grunted, and drew the final brush with great delicacy along the lid.

'Would you bury *me*, Johnnie?' she ventured, very sisterly.

'No,' he said.

But later he gave her a cup of tea (the first since his wife had run away, never to be heard of again), and she took it as a good omen of relenting and melting. She dared to stay until quite late that night and went out to the work shed again to fetch the bag of shopping she had left there. 'There,' she said, turning the key of the back kitchen door for him, 'all locked up and everything done for you! Surely a woman in the house is a price above rubies?' She had even washed up and polished the grate.

'You be off now,' he growled, reading a trade paper. 'Your views don't carry weight with me.'

The next morning, a mild October morning very sweet in the nose, Bloddie let herself and the girl Lottie into Lewis' back-lane door as dawn was breaking. She had left the door unlocked the night before. Lottie was giggling and very ready for the prank, being bored with the lonely farm. They crept into the work shed and Bloddie lit a candle. The lid of Josh Jones' coffin lay ajar on the beautiful varnished casket resting on the trestles.

'There!' said Bloddie. 'And if you do your piece proper a man with money you might marry. Starved he is.'

She moved the lid and helped Lottie into the coffin. She arranged the bright, cool yellow hair and the clean-ironed pink muslin dress that showed legs plain, and in the narrow frame the shapely girl looked like Heaven come to earth. Even Bloddie herself, lifting the candle, exclaimed in wonder: 'Beautiful enough to eat you look, a wedding cake! . . . Now what are you going to say?'

Lottie, her long lashes beating her cheeks, repeated in a pleading voice: 'An orphan I am and looking for someone to take care of me. Cruel everybody has been to me. Last night I ran away from the gipsies and came in by here. Die I want to, for the world I cannot stand no more.' And she smiled a tearful and pleading smile – for the simplest girl can make a good actress when needed – and lifted her arms like swan necks. 'My father's face you got, only younger. Kiss me and let me rest by here.'

'Champion!' said Bloddie admiringly. 'Now take patience, for a long time he might be. A big piece of work you might do for Crwtch, and earn a fortune for yourself too.' She arranged the lid over the coffin as before, leaving a slit of space open, and put out the candle.

'Cosy it is,' Lottie sighed. 'There's nice the wood smells!'

But when Bloddie had gone and an hour passed without Lewis arriving, Lottie, of indolent nature and having been up early, fell fast asleep. The work shed was dark. It had only a small cob-webbed window in the shade of a tree, where a rising wind began to mutter and creak in growing noise.

Bloddie did not go back to the farm as she intended. She went to call on a friend in Mary Ann Street who cut dresses for her, and what with a cup of tea and one thing and another, time passed. Her friend made broth and afterwards they went to visit Mrs Leyshon, who was confined of a son. In the afternoon Bloddie looked at a clock.

'Jawch, I must go now,' she said, suddenly feeling excited. She bought a currant loaf in the baker's and then made quick for her brother's house. 'There's pale you are looking!' her friend said in parting. 'Not well you are feeling?' But Bloddie did not know if she felt well or not.

Lewis, in his shirt-sleeves, answered the door to her timid knock. He stood aside with nothing special in the grudging cast of his face.

'Well,' she said, expectant. 'Things well with you today? Down to do a bit of shopping I am.' In the living room she laid the currant loaf on the table. There was no sign of Lottie anywhere. 'A loaf of currant bread for you, Johnnie.'

There was conversation on several small matters, Lewis grunting as usual, and she tidying the hearth, her eyes restless and her ears cocked to the ceiling. 'Oh, Johnnie,' she burst at last out of her dry throat, 'faint I am for a cup of tea.'

'Get yourself one,' he said, surly. 'I got work in the shed. That Shenkin haven't come back from Stickell yet.' And he went out to the back.

She drank the tea quick for strength. And her queer excitement could be held no more. She went out to the back, down the slice of weedy garden, and peered into the open door of the dusky shed. A dribbling lit candle was stuck on a chest of tools, with Lewis sitting beside it polishing a brass name plate. On the trestle Josh Jones' coffin lay with the lid closed tight over it. Bloddie, stooping, twisted into the shed. Her knees were bending.

'Oh, Johnnie . . .' she began, quavering, in a small going voice.

In the candle-light his shiny little eyes looked up, occupied. 'What now?' he grunted, and went back to his polishing. 'You go and have your tea.'

Breathing hard, she crept across to the coffin. Her hand came out stealthily and made to lift the lid. It would not move. The six big ornamental screws were brassy in the candle-light. 'Johnnie,' she whispered, bending and feeling her head go round, 'what you screwed down the lid for?'

'Ready to go to Josh Jones tomorrow, of course. Lids don't jump about in my hearse.'

She gave the coffin a violent push. But it did not budge. Sure enough it was full as an egg. Beating the lid with her hands, she shrieked: 'You looked inside before screwing it down? . . . Oh, Johnnie!' she wailed.

'What's the matter with you, woman!' he barked. 'Look inside for what? The coffin's been screwed down since first thing this morning. You've been drinking!'

'Lottie is in there!' she screamed. 'Niece of Ceridwen.'

'I don't know any Lottie,' he shouted, irritable. 'That's enough now. I won't have you coming here in the drink.'

Babbling, and her fat little fists without real strength, she began turning the screws. He called out to her to leave his coffin alone, but, still polishing the brass plate, he did not rise from his bench. Six screws she had to loosen. She flung off the lid.

The coffin was empty except for Lewis' big black ledger and many bricks. She spun round with a snarl.

'Oh, wicked old fox that you are, oh –' And this and that.

He rose tremendous, the shining plate in an arm, like Moses. 'Out of my house with you, out now and till Doomsday!'

Sobbing in rage and fright, she ran up the garden, he at her heels. But she called up the criticism of hell on him, and he on her. In the living-room her eye caught the currant loaf. She snatched it up and took it with her through the front door, which slammed behind her for the last time.

Up at the farm she found Lottie in bed not only with a cold but with fright. Fed and comforted, however, the girl dried her tears. 'I went to sleep,' she related, 'and I was woke up by candle grease dropping hot on my face. Red his whiskers were by the candle! I said what you said, but he shouted at me: "A good mind I got to lock you up in this coffin till I call the policeman for a burglar! You be off back to the gipsies. Supply free nights' lodging for trollops I don't. . . ." And he wouldn't help me out of the coffin and wouldn't touch me at all. I lost my head and said where I was from, too. . . .'

Afterwards the aunt tried to console her friend. 'Let the old rascal go, Bloddie. A man he is no more. Cut off the old dolt is.'

'Pew!' breathed Bloddie, stertorous, 'but I thought poor Lottie had been coffined right enough.'

'Never mind,' said Ceridwen; 'not so frivolous and empty-headed it might make her.'

It was the last attempt to make Lewis Gents Only (as he came to be called) relent from his hard vow. He remained faithful to it until he retired from business and went to live in Swansea. All women continued to be buried by the Stickell undertaker, but the man who bought Lewis' business and stock in hand of course changed this. It must be said that though mention of Lewis always made Crwtch women bridle, when he left he went in dignity and with the good wishes and respect of most men. He had that upright look of a man who knows his own mind and abides by its decisions, and in his face independence mingled solemnly with the natural pride of a craftsman. His history is still discussed in the parlour bar of The Red Rose; and it is often the starting point of a deep debate — was he justified or not in refusing to undertake women?

GRAHAM GREENE
The Blue Film

'Other people enjoy themselves,' Mrs Carter said.

'Well,' her husband replied, 'we've seen . . .'

'The reclining Buddha, the emerald Buddha, the floating markets,' Mrs Carter said. 'We have dinner and then go home to bed.'

'Last night we went to Chez Eve. . . .'

'If you weren't with *me*,' Mrs Carter said, 'you'd find . . . you know what I mean, Spots.'

It was true, Carter thought, eyeing his wife over the coffee-cups: her slave bangles chinked in time with her coffee-spoon: she had reached an age when the satisfied woman is at her most beautiful, but the lines of discontent had formed. When he looked at her neck he was reminded of how difficult it was to unstring a turkey. Is it my fault, he wondered, or hers – or was it the fault of her birth, some glandular deficiency, some inherited characteristic? It was sad how when one was young, one so often mistook the signs of frigidity for a kind of distinction.

'You promised we'd smoke opium,' Mrs Carter said.

'Not here, darling. In Saigon. Here it's "not done" to smoke.'

'How conventional you are.'

'There'd be only the dirtiest of coolie places. You'd be conspicuous. They'd stare at you.' He played his winning card. 'There'd be cockroaches.'

'I should be taken to plenty of Spots if I wasn't with a husband.'

He tried hopefully, 'The Japanese strip-teasers . . .' but

she had heard all about them. 'Ugly women in bras,' she said. His irritation rose. He thought of the money he had spent to take his wife with him and to ease his conscience – he had been away too often without her, but there is no company more cheerless than that of a woman who is not desired. He tried to drink his coffee calmly: he wanted to bite the edge of the cup.

'You've spilt your coffee,' Mrs Carter said.

'I'm sorry.' He got up abruptly and said, 'All right. I'll fix something. Stay here.' He leant across the table. 'You'd better not be shocked,' he said. 'You've asked for it.'

'I don't think I'm usually the one who is shocked,' Mrs Carter said with a thin smile.

Carter left the hotel and walked up towards the New Road. A boy hung at his side and said, 'Young girl?'

'I've got a woman of my own,' Carter said gloomily.

'Boy?'

'No thanks.'

'French films?'

Carter paused. 'How much?'

They stood and haggled awhile at the corner of the drab street. What with the taxi, the guide, the films, it was going to cost the best part of eight pounds, but it was worth it, Carter thought, if it closed her mouth for ever from demanding 'Spots'. He went back to fetch Mrs Carter.

They drove a long way and came to a halt by a bridge over a canal, a dingy lane overcast with indeterminate smells. The guide said, 'Follow me.'

Mrs Carter put a hand on Carter's arm. 'Is it safe?' she asked.

'How would I know?' he replied, stiffening under her hand.

They walked about fifty unlighted yards and halted by a bamboo fence. The guide knocked several times. When they were admitted it was to a tiny earth-floored yard and a wooden hut. Something – presumably human – was humped in the dark under a mosquito-net. The owner showed them into a tiny stuffy room with two chairs and a portrait of the King. The screen was about the size of a folio volume.

The first film was peculiarly unattractive and showed the rejuvenation of an elderly man at the hands of two blonde masseuses. From the style of the women's hairdressing the film must have been made in the late twenties. Carter and his wife sat in mutual embarrassment as the film whirled and clicked to a stop.

'Not a very good one,' Carter said, as though he were a connoisseur.

'So that's what they call a blue film,' Mrs Carter said. 'Ugly and not exciting.'

A second film started.

There was very little story in this. A young man – one couldn't see his face because of the period soft hat – picked up a girl in the street (her cloche hat extinguished her like a meat-cover) and accompanied her to her room. The actors were young: there was some charm and excitement in the picture. Carter thought, when the girl took off her hat, I know that face, and a memory which had been buried for more than a quarter of a century moved. A doll over a telephone, a pin-up girl of the period over the double bed. The girl undressed, folding her clothes very neatly: she leant over to adjust the bed, exposing herself to the camera's eye and to the young man: he kept his head turned from the camera. Afterwards, she helped him in turn to take off his clothes. It was only then he remembered – that particular playfulness confirmed by the birthmark on the man's shoulder.

Mrs Carter shifted on her chair. 'I wonder how they find the actors,' she said hoarsely.

'A prostitute,' he said. 'It's a bit raw, isn't it? Wouldn't you like to leave?' he urged her, waiting for the man to turn his head. The girl knelt on the bed and held the youth around the waist – she couldn't have been more than twenty. No, he made a calculation, twenty-one.

'We'll stay,' Mrs Carter said, 'we've paid.' She laid a dry hot hand on his knee.

'I'm sure we could find a better place than this.'

'No.'

The young man lay on his back and the girl for a moment left him. Briefly, as though by accident, he looked at the camera. Mrs Carter's hand shook on his knee. 'Good God,' she said, 'it's you.'

'It *was* me,' Carter said, 'thirty years ago.' The girl was climbing back on to the bed.

'It's revolting,' Mrs Carter said.

'I don't remember it as revolting,' Carter replied.

'I suppose you went and gloated, both of you.'

'No, I never saw it.'

'Why did you do it? I can't look at you. It's shameful.'

'I asked you to come away.'

'Did they pay you?'

'They paid her. Fifty pounds. She needed the money badly.'

'And you had your fun for nothing?'

'Yes.'

'I'd never have married you if I'd known. Never.'

'That was a long time afterwards.'

'You still haven't said why. Haven't you any excuse?' She stopped. He knew she was watching, leaning forward, caught up herself in the heat of that climax more than a quarter of a century old.

Carter said, 'It was the only way I could help her. She'd never acted in one before. She wanted a friend.'

'A friend,' Mrs Carter said.

'I loved her.'

'You couldn't love a tart.'

'Oh yes, you can. Make no mistake about that.'

'You queued for her, I suppose. '

'You put it too crudely,' Carter said.

'What happened to her?'

'She disappeared. They always disappear.'

The girl leant over the young man's body and put out the light. It was the end of the film. 'I have new ones coming next week,' the Siamese said, bowing deeply. They followed their guide back down the dark lane to the taxi.

In the taxi Mrs Carter said, 'What was her name?'

'I don't remember.' A lie was easiest.

As they turned into the New Road she broke her bitter silence again. 'How could you have brought yourself . . . ? It's so degrading. Suppose someone you knew – in business – recognized you.'

'People don't talk about seeing things like that. Anyway, I wasn't in business in those days.'

'Did it never worry you?'

'I don't believe I have thought of it once in thirty years.'

'How long did you know her?'

'Twelve months perhaps.'

'She must look pretty awful by now if she's alive. After all she was common even then.'

'I thought she looked lovely,' Carter said.

They went upstairs in silence. He went straight to the bathroom and locked the door. The mosquitoes gathered around the lamp and the great jar of water. As he undressed he caught glimpses of himself in the small mirror: thirty years had not been kind: he felt his thickness and his middle age. He thought: I hope to God she's dead. Please, God, he said, let her be dead. When I go back in there, the insults will start again.

But when he returned Mrs Carter was standing by the mirror. She had partly undressed. Her thin bare legs reminded him of a heron waiting for fish. She came and put her arms round him: a slave bangle joggled against his shoulder. She said, 'I'd forgotten how nice you looked.'

'I'm sorry. One changes.'

'I didn't mean that. I like you as you are.'

She was dry and hot and implacable in her desire. 'Go on,' she said, 'go on,' and then she screamed like an angry and hurt bird. Afterwards she said, 'It's years since that happened,' and continued to talk for what seemed a long half hour excitedly at his side. Carter lay in the dark silent, with a feeling of loneliness and guilt. It seemed to him that he had betrayed that night the only woman he loved.

SAMUEL BECKETT

Still

Bright at last close of a dark day the sun shines out at last and
goes down. Sitting quite still at valley window normally turn
head now and see it the sun low in the southwest sinking.
Even get up certain moods and go stand by western window
quite still watching it sink and then the afterglow. Always
quite still some reason some time past this hour at open
window facing south in small upright wicker chair with
armrests. Eyes stare out unseeing till first movement some
time past close though unseeing still while still light. Quite
still again then all quite quiet apparently till eyes open again
while still light though less. Normally turn head now ninety
degrees to watch sun which if already gone then fading
afterglow. Even get up certain moods and go stand by western window till quite dark and even some evenings some
reason long after. Eyes then open again while still light and
close again in what if not quite a single movement almost.
Quite still again then at open window facing south over the
valley in this wicker chair though actually close inspection
not still at all but trembling all over. Close inspection namely
detail by detail all over to add up finally to this whole not still
at all but trembling all over. But casually in this failing light
impression dead still even the hands clearly trembling and
the breast faint rise and fall. Legs side by side broken right
angles at the knees as in that old statue some old god
twanged at sunrise and again at sunset. Trunk likewise dead
plumb right up to top of skull seen from behind including
nape clear of chairback. Arms likewise broken right angles at
the elbows forearms along armrests just right length fore-

arms and rests for hands clenched lightly to rest on ends. So quite still again then all quite quiet apparently eyes closed which to anticipate when they open again if they do in time then dark or some degree of starlight or moonlight or both. Normally watch night fall however long from this narrow chair or standing by western window quite still either case. Quite still namely staring at some one thing alone such as tree or bush a detail alone if near if far the whole if far enough till it goes. Or by eastern window certain moods staring at some point on the hillside such as that beech in whose shade once quite still till it goes. Chair some reason always same place same position facing south as though clamped down whereas in reality no lighter no more movable imaginable. Or anywhere any ope staring out at nothing just failing light quite still till quite dark though of course no such thing just less light still when less did not seem possible. Quite still then all this time eyes open when discovered then closed then opened and closed again no other movement any kind though of course not still at all when suddenly or so it looks this movement impossible to follow let alone describe. The right hand slowly opening leaves the armrest taking with it the whole forearm complete with elbow and slowly rises opening further as it goes and turning a little deasil till midway to the head it hesitates and hangs half open trembling in mid air. Hangs there as if half inclined to return that is sink back slowly closing as it goes and turning the other way till as and where it began clenched lightly on end of rest. Here because of what comes now not midway to the head but almost there before it hesitates and hangs there trembling as if half inclined etc. Half no but on the verge when in its turn the head moves from its place forward and down among the ready fingers where no sooner received and held it weighs on down till elbow meeting armrest brings this last movement to an end and all still once more. Here back a little way to that suspense before head to rescue as if hand's need the greater and on down in what if not quite a single movement almost till elbow against rest. All quite still again then head in hand namely thumb on outer edge of right socket index ditto left and middle on left cheekbone plus as the hours pass lesser contacts each more or less now more now less with the faint stirrings of the various parts as night wears on. As if even in the dark eyes closed not enough and perhaps even more than ever necessary against that no such thing the further shelter of the hand. Leave it so all quite still or try listening to the sounds all quite still head in hand listening for a sound.

R. K. NARAYAN
An Astrologer's Day

Punctually at midday he opened his bag and spread out his professional equipment, which consisted of a dozen cowrie shells, a square piece of cloth with obscure mystic charts on it, a notebook, and a bundle of palmyra writing. His forehead was resplendent with sacred ash and vermilion, and his eyes sparkled with a sharp abnormal gleam which was really an outcome of a continual searching look for customers, but which his simple clients took to be a prophetic light and felt comforted. The power of his eyes was considerably enhanced by their position – placed as they were between the painted forehead and the dark whiskers which streamed down his cheeks: even a half-wit's eyes would sparkle in such a setting. To crown the effect he wound a saffron-coloured turban around his head. This colour scheme never failed. People were attracted to him as bees are attracted to cosmos or dahlia stalks. He sat under the boughs of a spreading tamarind tree which flanked a path running through the Town Hall Park. It was a remarkable place in many ways: a surging crowd was always moving up and down this narrow road morning till night. A variety of trades and occupations was represented all along its way: medicine sellers, sellers of stolen hardware and junk, magicians, and, above all, an auctioneer of cheap cloth, who created enough din all day to attract the whole town. Next to him in vociferousness came a vendor of fried groundnut, who gave his ware a fancy name each day, calling it 'Bombay Ice-Cream' one day, and on the next 'Delhi Almond,' and on the third 'Raja's Delicacy,' and so on and so forth, and people flocked to him. A considerable portion of this crowd dallied before the astrologer too. The astrologer transacted his business by the light of a flare which crackled and smoked up above the groundnut heap nearby. Half the enchantment of the place was due to the fact that it did not have the benefit of municipal lighting. The place was lit up by shop lights. One or two had hissing gaslights, some had naked flares stuck on poles, some were lit up by old cycle lamps, and one or two, like the astrologer's, managed without lights of their own. It was a bewildering criss-cross of light rays and moving shadows. This suited the astrologer very well, for the simple reason that he had not in the least intended to be an astrologer when he began life; and he knew no more of what was going to happen to others than he knew what was going to happen to himself next minute. He was as much a stranger to the stars as were his innocent customers. Yet he said things which pleased and astonished everyone: that was more a matter of study, practice, and shrewd guesswork. All the same, it was as much an honest man's labour as any other, and he deserved the wages he carried home at the end of a day.

He had left his village without any previous thought or plan. If he had continued there he would have carried on the work of his forefathers – namely, tilling the land, living, marrying, and ripening in his cornfield and ancestral home. But that was not to be. He had to leave home without telling anyone, and he could not rest till he left it behind a couple of hundred miles. To a villager it is a great deal, as if an ocean flowed between.

He had a working analysis of mankind's troubles: marriage, money, and the tangles of human ties. Long practice had sharpened his perception. Within five minutes he understood what was wrong. He charged three pies per question, never opened his mouth till the other had spoken for at least ten minutes, which provided him enough stuff for a dozen answers and advices. When he told the person before him, gazing at his palm, 'In many ways you are not getting the fullest results for your efforts,' nine out of ten were disposed to agree with him. Or he questioned: 'Is there any woman in your family, maybe even a distant relative, who is not well disposed towards you?' Or he gave an analysis of character: 'Most of your troubles are due to your nature. How can you be otherwise with Saturn where he is? You have an impetuous nature and a rough exterior.' This endeared him to their hearts immediately, for even the mildest of us loves to think that he has a forbidding exterior.

The nuts vendor blew out his flare and rose to go home. This was a signal for the astrologer to bundle up too, since it left him in darkness except for a little shaft of green light which strayed in from somewhere and touched the ground before him. He picked up his cowrie shells and paraphernalia and was putting them back into his bag when the green shaft of light was blotted out; he looked up and saw a man standing before him. He sensed a possible client and said: 'You look so careworn. It will do you good to sit down for a while and chat with me.' The other grumbled some reply vaguely. The astrologer pressed his invitation; whereupon the other thrust his palm under his nose, saying: 'You call yourself an astrologer?' The astrologer felt challenged and said, tilting the other's palm towards the green shaft of light: 'Yours is a nature . . .' 'Oh, stop that,' the other said. 'Tell me something worth while. . . .'

Our friend felt piqued. 'I charge only three pies per question, and what you get ought to be good enough for your money. . . .' At this the other withdrew his arm, took out an anna, and flung it out to him, saying: 'I have some questions to ask. If I prove you are bluffing, you must return that anna to me with interest.'

'If you find my answers satisfactory, will you give me five rupees?'

'No.'

'Or will you give me eight annas?'

'All right, provided you give me twice as much if you are wrong,' said the stranger. This pact was accepted after a little further argument. The astrologer sent up a prayer to heaven as the other lit a cheroot. The astrologer caught a glimpse of his face by the matchlight. There was a pause as cars hooted on the road, *jutka* drivers swore at their horses, and the babble of the crowd agitated the semi-darkness of the park. The other sat down, sucking his cheroot, puffing out, sat there ruthlessly. The astrologer felt very uncomfortable. 'Here, take your anna back. I am not used to such challenges. It is late for me today. . . .' He made preparations to bundle up. The other held his wrist and said: 'You can't get out of it now. You dragged me in while I was passing.' The astrologer shivered in his grip; and his voice shook and became faint. 'Leave me today. I will speak to you tomorrow.' The other thrust his palm in his face and said: 'Challenge is challenge. Go on.' The astrologer proceeded with his throat drying up: 'There is a woman . . .'

'Stop,' said the other. 'I don't want all that. Shall I succeed in my present search or not? Answer this and go. Otherwise I will not let you go till you disgorge all your coins.' The astrologer muttered a few incantations and replied: 'All right. I will speak. But you will give me a rupee if what I say is convincing? Otherwise I will not open my mouth, and you may do what you like.' After a good deal of haggling the other agreed. The astrologer said: 'You were left for dead. Am I right?'

'Ah, tell me more.'

'A knife has passed through you once?' said the astrologer.

'Good fellow!' He bared his chest to show the scar. 'What else?'

'And then you were pushed into a well nearby in the field. You were left for dead.'

'I should have been dead if some passer-by had not chanced to peep into the well,' exclaimed the other, overwhelmed by enthusiasm. 'When shall I get at him?' he asked, clenching his fist.

'In the next world,' answered the astrologer. 'He died four months ago in a far-off town. You will never see any more of him.' The other groaned on hearing it. The astrologer proceeded:

'Guru Nayak – '

'You know my name!' the other said, taken aback.

'As I know all other things. Guru Nayak, listen carefully to what I have to say. Your village is two days' journey due north of this town. Take the next train and be gone. I see once again great danger to your life if you go from home.' He took out a pinch of sacred ash and held it to him. 'Rub it on your forehead and go home. Never travel southward again, and you will live to be a hundred.'

'Why should I leave home again?' the other said reflectively. 'I was only going away now and then to look for him and to choke out his life if I met him.' He shook his head regretfully. 'He has escaped my hands. I hope at least he died as he deserved.' 'Yes,' said the astrologer. 'He was crushed under a lorry.' The other looked gratified to hear it.

The place was deserted by the time the astrologer picked up his articles and put them into his bag. The green shaft was also gone, leaving the place in darkness and silence. The stranger had gone off into the night, after giving the astrologer a handful of coins.

It was nearly midnight when the astrologer reached home. His wife was waiting for him at the door and demanded an explanation. He flung the coins at her and said: 'Count them. One man gave all that.'

'Twelve and a half annas,' she said, counting. She was overjoyed. 'I can buy some jaggery and coconut tomorrow. The child has been asking for sweets for so many days now. I will prepare some nice stuff for her.'

'The swine has cheated me! He promised me a rupee,' said the astrologer. She looked up at him. 'You look worried. What is wrong?'

'Nothing.'

After dinner, sitting on the *pyol*, he told her: 'Do you know a great load is gone from me today? I thought I had the blood of a man on my hands all these years. That was the reason why I ran away from home, settled here, and married you. He is alive.'

She gasped. 'You tried to kill!'

'Yes, in our village, when I was a silly youngster. We drank, gambled, and quarrelled badly one day – why think of it now? Time to sleep,' he said, yawning, and stretched himself on the *pyol*.

WILLIAM SANSOM

Difficulty with a Bouquet

Seal, walking through his garden, said suddenly to himself:
'I would like to pick some flowers and take them to Miss D.'

The afternoon was light and warm. Tall chestnuts fanned
themselves in a pleasant breeze. Among the hollyhocks
there was a good humming as the bees tumbled from flower
to flower. Seal wore an open shirt. He felt fresh and fine,
with the air swimming coolly under his shirt and around his
ribs. The summer's afternoon was free. Nothing pressed
him. It was a time when some simple, disinterested impulse
might well be hoped to flourish.

Seal felt a great joy in the flowers around him and from
this a brilliant longing to give. He wished to give quite
inside himself, uncritically, without thinking for a moment:
'Here am I, Seal, wishing something.' Seal merely wanted to
give some of his flowers to a fellow being. It had happened
that Miss D was the first person to come to mind. He was in
no way attached to Miss D. He knew her slightly, as a plain,
elderly girl of about twenty who had come to live in the flats
opposite his garden. If Seal had ever thought about Miss D at
all, it was because he disliked the way she walked. She
walked stiffly, sailing with her long body while her little legs
raced to catch up with it. But he was not thinking of this
now. Just by chance he had glimpsed the block of flats as he
had stooped to pick a flower. The flats had presented the
image of Miss D to his mind.

Seal chose common, ordinary flowers. As the stems broke
he whistled between his teeth. He had chosen these ordinary flowers because they were the nearest to hand: in the

second place, because they were fresh and full of life. They were neither rare nor costly. They were pleasant, fresh, unassuming flowers.

With the flowers in his hand, Seal walked contentedly from his garden and set foot on the asphalt pavement that led to the block of flats across the way. But as his foot touched the asphalt, as the sly glare of an old man fixed his eye for the moment of its passing, as the traffic asserted itself, certain misgivings began to freeze his impromptu joy. 'Good heavens,' he suddenly thought, 'what am I doing?' He stepped outside himself and saw Seal carrying a bunch of cheap flowers to Miss D in the flats across the way.

'These are cheap flowers,' he thought. 'This is a sudden gift. I shall smile as I hand them to her. We shall both know that there is no ulterior reason for the gift and thus the whole action will smack of goodness – of goodness and simple brotherhood. And somehow . . . for that reason this gesture of mine will appear to be the most calculated pose of all. Such a simple gesture is improbable. The improbable is to be suspected. My gift will certainly be regarded as an affection.

'Oh, if only I had some reason – aggrandisement, financial gain, seduction – any of the accepted motives that would return my flowers to social favour. But no – I have none of these in me. I only wish to give and to receive nothing in return.'

As he walked on, Seal could see himself bowing and smiling. He saw himself smile too broadly as he apologized by exaggeration for his good action. His neck flinched with disgust as he saw himself assume the old bravados. He could see the mocking smile of recognition on the face of Miss D.

Seal dropped the flowers into the gutter and walked slowly back to his garden.

From her window high up in the concrete flats, Miss D watched Seal drop the flowers. How fresh they looked! How they would have livened her barren room! 'Wouldn't it have been nice,' thought Miss D, 'if that Mr Seal had been bringing *me* that pretty bouquet of flowers! Wouldn't it have been nice if he had picked them in his own garden and – well, just brought them along, quite casually, and made me a present of the delightful afternoon.' Miss D dreamed on for a few minutes.

Then she frowned, rose, straightened her suspender belt, hurried into the kitchen. 'Thank God he didn't,' she sighed to herself. 'I should have been most embarrassed. It's not as if he wanted me. It would have been just too maudlin for words.'

PATRICK WHITE
Willy-Wagtails by Moonlight

The Wheelers drove up to the Mackenzies' punctually at
six-thirty. It was the hour for which they had been asked.
My God, thought Jum Wheeler. It had been raining a little,
and the tyres sounded blander on the wet gravel.

In front of the Mackenzies', which was what is known as a
Lovely Old Home – colonial style – amongst some carefully
natural-looking gums, there stood a taxi.

'Never knew Arch and Nora ask us with anyone else,'
Eileen Wheeler said.

'Maybe they didn't. Even now. Maybe it's someone they
couldn't get rid of.'

'Or an urgent prescription from the chemist's.'

Eileen Wheeler yawned. She must remember to show
sympathy, because Nora Mackenzie was going through a
particularly difficult one.

Anyway, they were there, and the door stood open on the
lights inside. Even the lives of the people you know, even
the lives of Nora and Arch look interesting for a split second,
when you drive up and glimpse them through a lit
doorway.

'It's that Miss Cullen,' Eileen said.

For there was Miss Cullen, doing something with a brief-
case in the hall.

'Ugly bitch,' Jum said.

'Plain is the word,' corrected Eileen.

'Arch couldn't do without her. Practically runs the business.'

Certainly that Miss Cullen looked most methodical,

shuffling the immaculate papers, and slipping them into a new pigskin brief-case in Arch and Nora's hall.

'Got a figure,' Eileen conceded.

'But not a chin.'

'Oh, hello, Miss Cullen. It's stopped raining.'

It was too bright stepping suddenly into the hall. The Wheelers brightly blinked. They looked newly made.

'Keeping well, Miss Cullen, I hope?'

'I have nothing to complain about, Mr Wheeler,' Miss Cullen replied.

She snapped the catch. Small, rather pointed breasts under the rain-coat. But, definitely, no chin.

Eileen Wheeler was fixing her hair in the reproduction Sheraton mirror.

She had been to the hairdresser's recently, and the do was still set too tight.

'Well, good-bye now,' Miss Cullen said.

When she smiled there was a hint of gold, but discreet, no more than a bridge. Then she would draw her lips together, and lick them ever so slightly, as if she had been sucking a not unpleasantly acid sweetie.

Miss Cullen went out the door, closing it firmly but quietly behind her.

'That was Miss Cullen,' said Nora Mackenzie coming down. 'She's Arch's secretary.'

'He couldn't do without her,' she added, as though they did not know.

Nora was like that. Eileen wondered how she and Nora had tagged along together, ever since Goulburn, all those years.

'God, she's plain!' Jum said.

Nora did not exactly frown, but pleated her forehead the way she did when other people's virtues were assailed. Such attacks seemed to affect her personally, causing her almost physical pain.

'But Mildred is so kind,' she insisted.

Nora Mackenzie made a point of calling her husband's

employees by first names, trying to make them part of a family which she alone, perhaps, would have liked to exist.

'She brought me some giblet soup, all the way from Balgowlah, that time I had virus 'flu.'

'Was it good, darling?' Eileen asked.

She was going through the routine, rubbing Nora's cheek with her own. Nora was pale. She must remember to be kind.

Nora did not answer, but led the way into the lounge-room.

Nora said:

'I don't think I'll turn on the lights for the present. They hurt my eyes, and it's so restful sitting in the dusk.'

Nora *was* pale. She had, in fact, just taken a couple of Disprin.

'Out of sorts, dear?' Eileen asked.

Nora did not answer, but offered some dry martinis.

Very watery, Jum knew from experience, but drink of a kind.

'Arch will be down presently,' Nora said. 'He had to attend to some business, some letters Miss Cullen brought. Then he went in to have a shower.'

Nora's hands were trembling as she offered the dry martinis, but Eileen remembered they always had.

The Wheelers sat down. It was all so familiar, they did not have to be asked, which was fortunate, as Nora Mackenzie always experienced difficulty in settling guests into chairs. Now she sat down herself, far more diffidently than her friends. The cushions were standing on their points.

Eileen sighed. Old friendships and the first scent of gin always made her nostalgic.

'It's stopped raining,' she said, and sighed.

'Arch well?' Jum asked.

As if he cared. She had let the ice get into the cocktail, turning it almost to pure water.

'He has his trouble,' Nora said. 'You know, his back.'

Daring them to have forgotten.

Nora loved Arch. It made Eileen feel ashamed.

So fortunate for them to have discovered each other. Nora Leadbetter and Arch Mackenzie. Two such bores. And with bird-watching in common. Though Eileen Wheeler had never believed Nora did not make herself learn to like watching birds.

At Goulburn, in the early days, Nora would come out to Glen Davie sometimes to be with Eileen at week-ends. Mr Leadbetter had been manager at the Wales for a while. He always saw that his daughter had the cleanest notes. Nora was shy, but better than nothing, and the two girls would sit about on the veranda those summer evenings, buffing their nails, and listening to the sheep cough in the home paddock. Eileen gave Nora lessons in making-up. Nora had protested, but was pleased.

'Mother well, darling?' Eileen asked, sipping that sad, watery gin.

'Not exactly *well*,' Nora replied, painfully.

Because she had been to Orange, to visit her widowed mother, who suffered from Parkinson's disease.

'You know what I mean, dear,' said Eileen.

Jum was dropping his ash on the carpet. It might be better when poor bloody Arch came down.

'I have an idea that woman, that Mrs Galloway, is unkind to her,' Nora said.

'Get another,' Eileen advised. 'It isn't like after the War.'

'One can never be sure,' Nora debated. 'One would hate to hurt the woman's feelings.'

Seated in the dusk Nora Mackenzie was of a moth colour. Her face looked as though she had been rubbing it with chalk. Might have, too, in spite of those lessons in make-up. She sat and twisted her hands together.

How very red Nora's hands had been, at Goulburn, at the convent, to which the two girls had gone. Not that they belonged to *those*. It was only convenient. Nora's hands had been red and trembly after practising a tarantella, early, in the frost. So very early all of that. Eileen had learnt about life shortly after puberty. She had tried to tell Nora one or two things, but Nora did not want to hear. Oh, no, no, *please*, Eileen, Nora cried. As though a boy had been twisting her arm. She had those long, entreating, sensitive hands.

And there they were still. Twisting together, making their excuses. For what they had never done.

Arch came in then. He turned on the lights, which made Nora wince, even those lights which barely existed in all the neutrality of Nora's room. Nora did not comment, but smiled, because it was Arch who had committed the crime.

Arch said:

'You two toping hard as usual.'

He poured himself the rest of the cocktail.

Eileen laughed her laugh which people found amusing at parties.

Jum said, and bent his leg, if it hadn't been for Arch and the shower, they wouldn't have had the one too many.

'A little alcohol releases the vitality,' Nora remarked ever so gently.

She always grew anxious at the point where jokes became personal.

Arch composed his mouth under the handle-bars moustache, and Jum knew what they were in for.

'Miss Cullen came out with one or two letters,' Arch was taking pains to explain. 'Something she thought should go off tonight. I take a shower most evenings. Summer, at least.'

'Such humidity,' Nora helped.

Arch looked down into his glass. He might have been composing further remarks, but did not come out with them.

That silly, bloody English-air-force-officer's moustache. It was the only thing Arch had ever dared. War had given him the courage to pinch a detail which did not belong to him.

'That Miss Cullen, useful girl,' Jum suggested.

'Runs the office.'

'Forty, if a day,' Eileen said, whose figure was beginning to slacken off.

Arch said he would not know, and Jum made a joke about Miss Cullen's *cul-de-sac*.

The little pleats had appeared again in Nora Mackenzie's chalky brow. 'Well,' she cried, jumping up, quite girlish, 'I do hope the dinner will be a success.'

And laughed.

Nora was half-way through her second course with that woman at the Chanticleer. Eileen suspected there would be avocadoes stuffed with prawns, chicken *Mornay*, and *crêpes Suzette*.

Eileen was right.

Arch seemed to gain in authority sitting at the head of his table.

'I'd like you to taste this wine,' he said. 'It's very light.'

'Oh, yes?' said Jum.

The wine was corked , but nobody remarked. The second bottle, later on, was somewhat better. The Mackenzies were spreading themselves tonight.

Arch flipped his napkin once or twice, emphasizing a point. He smoothed the handle-bars moustache, which should have concealed a harelip, only there wasn't one. Jum dated from before the moustache, long, long, very long.

Arch said:

'There was a story Armitage told me at lunch. There was a man who bought a mower. Who suffered from indigestion. Now, how, exactly, did it . . . go?'

Jum had begun to make those little pellets out of bread. It always fascinated him how grubby the little pellets turned out. And himself not by any means dirty.

Arch failed to remember the point of the story Armitage had told.

It was difficult to understand how Arch had made a success of his business. Perhaps it was that Miss Cullen, breasts and all, under the rain-coat. For a long time Arch had messed around. Travelled in something. Separator parts. Got the agency for some sort of phoney machine for supplying *ozone* to public buildings. The Mackenzies lived at Burwood then. Arch continued to mess around. The War was quite a godsend. Arch was the real adje type. Did a conscientious job. Careful with his allowances, too.

Then, suddenly, after the War, Arch Mackenzie had launched out, started the import-export business. Funny the way a man will suddenly hit on the idea to which his particular brand of stupidity can respond.

The Mackenzies had moved to the North Shore, to the house which still occasionally embarrassed Nora. She felt as though she ought to apologize for success. But there was the bird-watching. Most week-ends they went off to the bush, to the Mountains or somewhere. She felt happier in humbler circumstances. In time she got used to the tape recorder which they took along. She made herself look upon it as a necessity rather than ostentation.

Eileen was dying for a cigarette.

'May I smoke, Arch?'

'We're amongst friends, aren't we?'

Eileen did not answer that. And Arch fetched the ash-tray they kept handy for those who needed it.

Nora in the kitchen dropped the beans. Everybody heard, but Arch asked Jum for a few tips on investments, as he always did when Nora happened to be out of the room. Nora had some idea that the Stock Exchange was immoral.

Then Nora brought the dish of little, pale tinned peas.

'Ah! *Pet – ty pwah!*' said Jum.

He formed his full, and rather greasy lips into a funnel through which the little rounded syllables poured most impressively.

Nora forgot her embarrassment. She envied Jum his courage in foreign languages. Although there were her lessons in Italian, she would never have dared utter in public.

'Can you bear *crêpes Suzette*?' Nora had to apologize.

'Lovely, darling.' Eileen smiled.

She would have swallowed a tiger. But was, *au fond*, at her gloomiest.

What was the betting Nora would drop the *crêpes Suzette*?

It was those long, trembly hands, on which the turquoise ring looked too small and innocent. The Mackenzies were still in the semi-precious bracket in the days when they became engaged.

'How's the old bird-watching?'

Jum had to force himself, but after all he had drunk their wine.

Arch Mackenzie sat deeper in his chair, almost completely at his ease.

'Got some new tapes,' he said. 'We'll play them later. Went up to Kurrajong on Sunday, and got the bell-birds. I'll play you the lyre-bird, too. That was Mount Wilson.'

'Didn't we hear the lyre-bird last time?' Eileen asked.

Arch said:

'Yes.'

Deliberately.

'But wouldn't you like to hear it again? It's something of a collector's piece.'

Nora said they'd be more comfortable drinking their coffee in the lounge.

Then Arch fetched the tape recorder. He set it up on the Queen Anne walnut piecrust. It certainly was an impressive machine.

'I'll play you the lyre-bird.'

'The *pièce de résistance*? Don't you think we should keep it?'

'He can never wait for the lyre-bird.'

Nora had grown almost complacent. She sat holding her coffee, smiling faintly through the steam. The children she had never had with Arch were about to enter.

'Delicious coffee,' Eileen said.

She had finished her filter-tips. She had never felt drearier.

The tape machine had begun to snuffle. There was quite an unusual amount of crackle. Perhaps it was the bush. Yes, that was it. The bush!

'Well, it's really quite remarkable how you people have the patience,' Eileen Wheeler had to say.

'Ssh!'

Arch Mackenzie was frowning. He had sat forward in the period chair.

'This is where it comes in.'

His face was tragic in the shaded light.

'Get it?' he whispered.

His hand was helping. Or commanding.

'Quite remarkable,' Eileen repeated.

Jum was shocked to realize he had only two days left in which to take up the ICI rights for old Thingummy.

Nora sat looking at her empty cup. But lovingly.

Nora could have been beautiful, Eileen saw. And suddenly felt old, she who had stripped once or twice at amusing parties. Nora Mackenzie did not know about that.

Somewhere in the depths of the bush Nora was calling that it had just turned four o'clock, but she had forgotten to pack the thermos.

The machine snuffled.

Arch Mackenzie was listening. He was biting his moustache.

'There's another passage soon.' He frowned.

'Darling,' Nora whispered, 'after the lyre-bird you might slip into the kitchen and change the bulb. It went while I was making the coffee.'

Arch Mackenzie's frown deepened. Even Nora was letting him down.

But she did not see. She was so in love.

It might have been funny if it was not also pathetic. People were horribly pathetic, Eileen Wheeler decided, who had her intellectual moments. She was also feeling sick. It was Nora's *crêpes Suzette*, lying like blankets.

'You'll realize there are one or two rough passages,' Arch said, coming forward when the tape had ended. 'I might cut it.'

'It could do with a little trimming,' Eileen agreed. 'But perhaps it's more natural without.'

'Am I a what's-this, a masochist,' she asked.

'Don't forget the kitchen bulb,' Nora prompted.

Very gently. Very dreamy.

Her hair had strayed, in full dowdiness, down along her white cheek.

'I'll give you the bell-birds for while I'm gone.'

Jum's throat had begun to rattle. He sat up in time, though, and saved his cup in the same movement.

'I remember the bell-birds,' he said.

'Not these ones, you don't. These are new. These are the very latest. The best bell-birds.'

Arch had started the tape, and stalked out of the room, as if to let the bell-birds themselves prove his point.

'It is one of our loveliest recordings,' Nora promised.

They all listened or appeared to.

When Nora said:

'Oh, dear' – getting up – 'I do believe' – panting almost – 'the bell-bird tape' – trembling – 'is damaged.'

Certainly the crackle was more intense.

'Arch will be so terribly upset.'

She had switched off the horrifying machine. With surprising skill for one so helpless. For a moment it seemed to Eileen Wheeler that Nora Mackenzie was going to hide the offending tape somewhere in her bosom. But she thought better of it, and put it aside on one of those little superfluous tables.

'Perhaps it's the machine that's broken,' suggested Jum.

'Oh, no,' said Nora, 'it's the tape. I know. We'll have to give you something else.'

'I can't understand,' – Eileen grinned – 'how you ever got around, Nora, to being mechanical.'

'If you're determined,' Nora said.

Her head was lowered in concentration.

'If you want a thing enough.'

She was fixing a fresh tape.

'And we do love our birds. Our Sundays together in the bush.'

The machine had begun its snuffling and shuffling again. Nora Mackenzie raised her head, as if launched on an invocation.

Two or three notes of bird-song fell surprisingly pure and clear, out of the crackle, into the beige and string-coloured room.

'This is one,' Nora said, 'I don't think I've ever heard before.'

She smiled, however, and listened to identify.

'Willy-Wagtails,' Nora said.

Willy-Wagtails were suited to tape. The song tumbled and exulted.

'It must be something,' Nora said, 'that Arch made while I was with Mother. There were a couple of Sundays when he did a little field-work on his own.'

Nora might have given way to a gentle melancholy for all she had foregone if circumstances had not heightened the pitch. There was Arch standing in the doorway. Blood streaming.

'Blasted bulb collapsed in my hand!'

'Oh, darling! Oh *dear*!' Nora cried.

The Wheelers were both fascinated. There was the blood dripping on the beige wall-to-wall.

How the willy-wagtails chortled.

Nora Mackenzie literally staggered at her husband, to take upon herself, if possible, the whole ghastly business.

'Come along, Arch,' she moaned. 'We'll fix. In just a minute,' Nora panted.

And simply by closing the door, she succeeded in blotting the situation, all but the drops of blood that were left behind on the carpet.

'Poor old Arch! Bleeding like a pig!' Jum Wheeler said, and laughed.

Eileen added:

'We shall suffer the willy-wags alone.'

Perhaps it was better like that. You could relax. Eileen began to pull. Her step-ins had eaten into her.

The willy-wagtails were at it again.

'Am I going crackers?' asked Jum. 'Listening to those bloody birds!'

When somebody laughed. Out of the tape. The Wheelers sat. Still.

Three-quarters of the bottle! Snuffle crackle. *Arch Mackenzie, you're a fair trimmer!* Again that rather brassy laughter.

'Well, I'll be blowed!' said Jum Wheeler.

'Bet it's that Miss Cullen,' Eileen said.

The Wheeler spirits soared as surely as plummets dragged the notes of the wagtail down.

But it's far too rocky, and far too late. Besides, it's willy-wagtails we're after. How Miss Cullen laughed. *Willy-wagtails by moonlight!* Arch was less intelligible, as if he had listened to too many birds, and caught the habit. Snuffle crackle went the machine . . . *the buttons are not made to undo* . . . Miss Cullen informed. *Oh stop it. Arch!* ARCH! *You're* TEARING *me!*

So that the merciless machine took possession of the room. There in the crackle of twigs, the stench of ants, the two Wheelers sat. There was that long, thin Harry Edwards, Eileen remembered, with bony wrists, had got her down behind the barn. She had hated it at first. All mirth had been exorcized from Miss Cullen's recorded laughter. Grinding out. Grinding out. So much of life was recorded by now. Returning late from a country dance, the Wheelers had fallen down amongst the sticks and stones, and made what is called love, and risen in the grey hours, to find themselves numb and bulging.

If only the tape, if you knew the trick with the wretched switch.

Jum Wheeler decided not to look at his wife. Little guilty, pockets were turning themselves out in his mind. That woman at the Locomotive Hotel. Pockets and pockets of putrefying trash. Down along the creek, amongst the tussocks and the sheep pellets, the sun burning his boy's skin, he played his overture to sex. Alone.

This sort of thing's all very well, Miss Cullen decided. *It's time we turned practical. Are you sure we can find our way back to the car?*

Always trundling. Crackling. But there were the blessed wagtails again.

'Wonder if they forgot the machine?'

'Oh, God! Hasn't the tape bobbed up in Pymble?'

A single willy-wagtail sprinkled its grace-notes through the stuffy room.

'Everything's all right,' Nora announced. 'He's calmer now. I persuaded him to take a drop of brandy.'

'That should fix him,' Jum said.

But Nora was listening to the lone wagtail. She was standing in the bush. Listening. The notes of bird-song falling like mountain water, when they were not chiselled in moonlight.

'There is nothing purer,' Nora said, 'than the song of the wagtail. Excepting Schubert,' she added, 'some of Schubert.'

She was so shyly glad it had occurred to her.

But the Wheelers just sat.

And again Nora Mackenzie was standing alone amongst the inexorable moonlit gums. She thought perhaps she had always felt alone, even with Arch, while grateful even for her loneliness.

'Ah, there you are!' Nora said.

It was Arch. He stood holding out his bandaged wound. Rather rigid. He could have been up for court martial.

'I've missed the willy-wagtails,' Nora said, raising her face to him, exposing her distress, like a girl. 'Some day you'll have to play it to me. When you've the time. And we can concentrate.'

The Wheelers might not have existed.

As for the tape it had discovered silence.

Arch mumbled they'd all better have something to drink.

Jum agreed it was a good idea.

'Positively brilliant,' Eileen said.

MARY LAVIN
Sarah

Sarah had a bit of a bad name. That was the worst her neighbours would say of her, although there was a certain fortuity about her choice of fathers for the three strapping sons she'd borne – all three outside wedlock.

Sarah was a great worker, strong and tireless, and a lot of women in the village got her in to scrub for them. Nobody was ever known to be unkind to her. And not one of her children was born in the County Home. It was the most upright matron in the village who slapped life into every one of them.

'She's unfortunate, that's all,' this matron used to say. 'How could she know any better – living with two rough brothers? And don't forget she had no father herself!'

If Sarah had been one to lie in bed on a Sunday and miss Mass, her neighbours might have felt differently about her, there being greater understanding in their hearts for sins against God than for sins against his Holy Church. But Sarah found it easy to keep the Commandments of the church. She never missed Mass. She observed abstinence on all days abstinence was required. She frequently did the Stations of the Cross as well. And on Lady Day when an annual pilgrimage took place to a holy well in the neighbouring village Sarah was an example to all – with her shoes off walking over the sharp flinty stones, doing penance like a nun. If on that occasion some outsider showed disapproval of her, Sarah's neighbours were quicker than Sarah herself to take offence. All the same, charity was tempered with prudence, and women with grown sons, and women not long married, took care not to hire her.

So when Oliver Kedrigan's wife, a newcomer to the locality, spoke of getting Sarah in to keep house for her while she was going up to Dublin for a few days, two of the older women in the district felt it their duty to step across to Kedrigan's and offer a word of advice.

'I know she has a bit of a bad name,' Kathleen conceded, 'but she's a great worker. I hear it's said she can bake bread that's nearly as good as my own.'

'That may be!' said one of the women, 'but if I was you, I'd think twice before I'd leave her to mind your house while you're away!'

'Who else is there I can get?' Kathleen said stubbornly.

'Why do you want anyone? You'll only be gone for three days, isn't that all?'

'Three days is a long time to leave a house in the care of a man.'

'I'd rather let the roof fall in on him than draw Sarah Murray about my place!' said the woman. 'She has a queer way of looking at a man. I wouldn't like to have her give my man one of those looks.' Kathleen got their meaning at last.

'I can trust Oliver,' she said coldly.

'It's not right to trust any man too far,' the women said, shaking their heads.

'Oliver isn't that sort,' Kathleen said, and her pale papery face smiled back contempt for the other women.

Stung by that smile, the women stood up and prepared to take their leave.

'I suppose you know your own business,' said the first one who had raised the subject, 'but I wouldn't trust the greatest saint ever walked with Sarah Murray.'

'I'd trust Oliver with any woman in the world,' Kathleen said.

'Well he's your man, not ours,' said the two women, speaking together as they went out the door. Kathleen looked after them resentfully. She may not have been too happy herself about hiring Sarah but as she closed the door on the women she made up her mind for once and for all to do so, goaded on by pride in her legitimate power over her man. She'd let everyone see she could trust him.

As the two women went down the road they talked for a while about the Kedrigans but gradually they began to talk about other things, until they came to the lane leading up to the cottage where Sarah Murray lived with her brothers and the houseful of children. Looking up at the cottage their thoughts went back to the Kedrigans again and they came to a stand. 'What ever took possession of Oliver Kedrigan to marry that bleached out bloodless thing?' one of them said.

'I don't know,' said the other one. 'But I wonder why she's going up to Dublin?'

'Why do you think!' said the first woman, contemptuous of her companion's ignorance. 'Not that she looks to me like a woman would ever have a child, no matter how many doctors she might go to – in Dublin or elsewhere.'

Sarah went over to Mrs Kedrigan's the morning Mrs Kedrigan was going away and she made her a nice cup of tea. Then she carried the suitcase down to the road and helped Kathleen on to the bus because it was a busy time for Oliver. He had forty lambing ewes and there was a predatory vixen in a nearby wood that was causing him alarm. He had had to go out at the break of day to put up a new fence.

But the bus was barely out of sight, when Oliver's cart rattled back into the yard. He'd forgotten to take the wire-cutters with him. He drew up outside the kitchen door and called to Sarah to hand him out the clippers, so he wouldn't have to get down off the cart. But when he looked down at her, he gave a laugh. 'Did you rub sheep-raddle into your cheeks?' he asked, and he laughed again – a loud happy laugh that could give no offence. And Sarah took none. But her cheeks went redder, and she angrily swiped a bare arm across her face as if to stem the flux of the healthy blood in her face. Oliver laughed for the third time. 'Stand back or you'll frighten the horse and he'll bolt,' he said, as he jerked the reins and the cart rattled off out of the yard again.

Sarah stared after him, keeping her eyes on him until the cart was like a toy cart in the distance, with a toy horse under it, and Oliver himself a toy farmer made out of painted wood.

When Kathleen came home the following Friday her house was cleaner than it had ever been. The boards were scrubbed white as rope, the windows glinted and there was bread cooling on the sill. Kathleen paid Sarah and Sarah went home. Her brothers were glad to have her back to clean the house and make the beds and bake. She gave them her money. The children were glad to see her too because while she was away their uncles made them work all day footing turf and running after sheep like collie dogs.

Sarah worked hard as she had always done, for a few months. Then one night as she was handing round potato-cakes to her brothers and the children who were sitting around the kitchen table with their knives and forks at the ready in their hands, the elder brother Pat gave a sharp look at her. He poked Joseph, the younger brother, in the ribs with the handle of his knife. 'For God's sake,' he said, 'will you look at her!'

Sarah ignored Pat's remark, except for a toss of her head. She sat down and ate her own supper greedily, swilling it down with several cups of boiling tea. When she'd finished she got up and went out into the wagon-blue night. Her brothers stared after her. 'Holy God,' Pat said, 'something will have to be done about her this time.'

'Ah what's the use of talking like that?' Joseph said, twitching his shoulders uneasily. 'If the country is full of blackguards, what can we do about it?'

Pat put down his knife and fork and thumped the table with his closed fist.

'I thought the talking-to she got from the priest the last time would knock sense into her. The priest said a Home was the only place for the like of her. I told him we'd have no part in putting her away – God Almighty what would we do without her? There must be a woman in the house! – but we can't stand for much more of this.'

Joseph was still pondering over the plight they'd be in without her. 'Her brats need her too,' he said, 'leastways until they can be sent out to service themselves.' He looked up. 'That won't be long now though; they're shaping into fine strong boys.'

But Pat stood up. 'All the same something will have to be done. When the priest hears about this he'll be at me again. And this time I'll have to give him a better answer than the other times.'

Joseph shrugged his shoulders. 'Ah tell him you can get no rights of her. And isn't it the truth?' He gave an easy-going chuckle. 'Tell him to tackle the job himself!'

Pat gave a sort of a laugh too but it was less easy. 'Do you remember what he said the last time? He said if she didn't tell the name of the father, he'd make the new born infant open its mouth and name him.'

'How well he didn't do it! Talk is easy!' Joseph said.

'He didn't do it,' said Pat, 'because Sarah took care not to let him catch sight of the child till the whole thing was put to the back of his mind by something else – the Confirmation – or the rewiring of the chapel.'

'Well, can't she do the same with this one?' Joseph said. He stood up. 'There's one good thing about the whole business, and that is that Mrs Kedrigan didn't notice anything wrong with her, or she'd never have given her an hour's work!'

Pat twitched with annoyance. 'How could Mrs Kedrigan notice anything? Isn't it six months at least since she was working in Kedrigan's?'

'It is I suppose,' Joseph said.

The two brothers moved about the kitchen for a few minutes in silence. The day with its solidarity of work and eating was over and they were about to go their separate ways when Joseph spoke.

'Pat?'

'What?'

'Oh nothing,' said Joseph. 'Nothing at all.'

'Ah quit your hinting! What are you trying to say? Speak out man.'

'I was only wondering,' said Joseph. 'Have you any idea at all who could be the father of this one?'

'Holy God,' Pat cried in fury. 'Why would you think I'd know the father of this one any more than the others? But if you think I'm going to stay here all evening gossiping like a woman, you're making a big mistake. I'm going out. I'm going over to the quarry field to see that heifer is all right that was sick this morning.'

'Ah the heifer'll be all right,' Joseph said. But feeling his older brother's eyes were on him he shrugged his shoulders. 'You can give me a shout if she's in a bad way and you want me.' Then when he'd let Pat get as far as the door he spoke again. 'I won't say anything to her, I suppose, when she comes in?' he asked.

Pat swung around. 'And what would you say, I'd like to know? Won't it be beyond saying anyway in a few weeks when everyone in the countryside will see for themselves what's going on?'

'That's right,' said Joseph.

Sarah went out every night, as she had always done, when dusk began to crouch over the fields. And her brothers kept silent tongues in their heads about the child she was carrying. She worked even better than before and she sang at her work. She carried the child deep in her body and she boldly faced an abashed congregation at Mass on Sundays, walking down the centre aisle and taking her usual place under the fourth station of the cross.

Meantime Mrs Kedrigan too was expecting her long-delayed child, but she didn't go to Mass: the priest came to her. She was looking bad. By day she crept from chair to chair around the kitchen, and only went out at night for a bit of a walk up and down their own lane. She was self-conscious about her condition and her nerves were frayed. Oliver used to have to sit up half the night with her and hold her moist hands in his until she fell asleep, but all the same she woke often and was frightened and peevish and, in bursts of hysteria, she called him a cruel brute. One evening she was taking a drop of tea by the fire. Oliver had gone down to the Post Office to see if there was a letter from the Maternity Hospital in Dublin, where she had engaged a bed for the following month. When he came back Oliver had a letter in his hand. Before he gave it to her, he told her what was in it. It was an anonymous letter and it named him as the father of the child Sarah Murray was going to bring into the world in a few weeks. He told Kathleen it was an unjust accusation.

'For God's sake, say something, Katty,' he said. 'You don't believe the bloody letter, do you?' Kathleen didn't answer. 'You don't believe it, sure you don't.' He went over to the window and laid his burning face against the cold pane of glass. 'What will I do, Katty?'

'You'll do nothing,' Kathleen said, speaking for the first time. 'Nothing. Aren't you innocent? Take no notice of that letter.'

She stooped and with a wide and grotesque swoop she plucked up the letter. Then she got to her feet and put the letter under a plate on the dresser and began to get the tea ready with slow, tedious journeyings back and forth across the silent kitchen. Oliver stood looking out at the fields until the tea was ready and once or twice he looked at his wife with curiosity. At last he turned away from the window and went over to the dresser. 'I'll tear up the letter,' he said.

'You'll do nothing of the kind,' Kathleen said, and with a lurch she reached the dresser before him. 'Here's where that letter belongs.'

There was a sound of crackling and a paper-ball went into the heart of the flames. Oliver watched it burn, and although he thought it odd that he didn't see the writing on it, he still believed that it was Sarah's letter that coiled into a black spiral in the grate.

The next evening Sarah was sitting by the fire as Kathleen Kedrigan had been sitting by hers. She too was drinking a cup of tea, and she didn't look up when her brothers came into the kitchen. No one spoke, but after a minute or two Sarah went to get up to prepare the supper. Her brother Pat pushed her down again on the chair. The cup shattered against the range and the tea slopped over the floor.

'Is this letter yours? Did you write it?' he shouted at her, holding out a letter addressed to Oliver Kedrigan – a letter that had gone through the post, and been delivered and opened. 'Do you hear me talking to you? Did you write this letter?'

'What business is it of yours?' Sarah said sullenly, and again she tried to get to her feet.

'Sit down, I tell you,' Pat shouted, and he pressed her back. 'Answer my question. Did you write this letter?'

Sarah stared dully at the letter in her brother's hand. The firelight flickered in her yellow eyes. 'Give it to me,' she snarled, and she snatched it from him. 'What business is it of yours, you thief?'

'Did you hear that, Pat? She called you a thief!' the younger brother shouted.

'Shut up, you,' Pat said. He turned back to his sister. 'Answer me. Is it true what it says in this letter?'

'How do I know what it says! And what if it is true? It's no business of yours.'

'I'll show you whose business it is!' Pat said. For a minute he stood as if not knowing what to do. Then he ran into the room off the kitchen where Sarah slept with the three children. He came out with an armful of clothes, a red dress, a coat, and a few bits of underwear. Sarah watched him. There was no one holding her down now but she didn't attempt to rise. Again her brother stood for a moment in the middle of the floor irresolute. Then he heard the outer door rattle in a gust of wind, and he ran towards it and dragging it open he threw out the armful of clothing, and ran back into the room. This time he came out with a jumper and a red cap, an alarm clock and a few other odds and ends. He threw them out the door, too.

'Do you know it's raining, Pat?' the younger brother asked cautiously.

'What do I care if it's raining?' Pat said. He went into the other room a third time. He was a while in there rummaging and when he came out he had a picture-frame, a prayer book, a pair of high-heeled shoes, a box of powder and a little green velvet box stuck all over with pearly shells.

Sarah sprang to her feet. 'My green box. Oh! Give me my box!' She tried to snatch it from him.

But Joseph suddenly put out a foot and tripped her.

When Sarah got to her feet Pat was standing at the door throwing her things out one by one, but he kept the green box till last and when he threw it out he fired it with all his strength as far as it would go as if trying to reach the dunghill at the other end of the yard. At first Sarah made as if to run out to get the things back. Then she stopped and started to pull on her coat, but her brother caught her by the hair, at the same time pulling the coat off her. Then, by the hair he dragged her across the kitchen and pushed her out into the rain, where she slipped and fell again on the wet slab stone of the doorway. Quickly then he shut out the sight from his eyes by banging the door closed.

'That ought to teach her,' he said. 'Carrying on with a married man! No one is going to say I put up with that kind of thing. I didn't mind the other times when it was probably old Molloy or his like that would have been prepared to pay for his mistakes if the need arose, but I wasn't going to stand for a thing like this.'

'You're sure it was Kedrigan?'

'Ah! didn't you see the letter yourself! Wasn't it Sarah's writing? And didn't Mrs Kedrigan herself give it to me this morning?'

113

'Sarah denied it, Pat,' Joseph said. His spurt of courage had given out and his hands were shaking as he went to the window and pulled back a corner of the bleached and neatly-sewn square of a flour bag that served as a curtain.

'She did! And so did he, I suppose? Well, she can deny it somewhere else now.'

'Where do you suppose she'll go?'

'She can go where she bloody well likes. And shut your mouth, you. Keep away from that window! Can't you sit down? Sit down, I tell you.'

All this took place at nine o'clock on a Tuesday night. The next morning at seven o'clock, Oliver Kedrigan went to a fair in a neighbouring town where he bought a new ram. He had had his breakfast in the town and he wanted to get on with his work, but he went to the door of the kitchen to see his wife was all right and called in to her from the yard. 'Katty! Hand me the tin of raddle. It's on top of the dresser.'

Kathleen Kedrigan came to the door and she had the tin of raddle in her hand.

'You won't be troubled with any more letters,' she said.

Oliver laughed self-consciously. 'That's a good thing, anyhow,' he said. 'Hurry, give me the raddle.'

His wife held the tin in her hand, but she didn't move. She leaned against the jamb of the door. 'I see you didn't hear the news?'

'What news?'

'Sarah Murray got what was coming to her last night. Her brothers turned her out of the house, and threw out all her things after her.'

Oliver's face darkened.

'That was a cruel class of thing for brothers to do. Where did she go?'

'She went where she and her likes belong; into a ditch on the side of the road!'

Oliver said nothing. His wife watched him closely and she

clenched her hands. 'You can spare your sympathy. She won't need it.'

Oliver looked up.

'Where did she go?'

'Nowhere,' Kathleen said slowly.

Oliver tried to think clearly. It had been a bad night, wet and windy. 'She wasn't out all night in the rain?' he asked, a fierce light coming into his eyes.

'She was,' Kathleen said, and she stared at him. 'At least that's where they found her in the morning, dead as a rat. And the child dead beside her!'

Her pale eyes held his, and he stared uncomprehendingly into them. Then he looked down at her hand that held the tin of red sheep-raddle.

'Give me the raddle!' he said, but before she had time to hand it to him he yelled at her again. 'Give me the raddle. Give it to me. What are you waiting for? Give me the God-damn' stuff.'

ELIZABETH TAYLOR

The Fly-paper

On Wednesdays, after school, Sylvia took the bus to the outskirts of the nearest town for her music lesson. Because of her docile manner, she did not complain of the misery she suffered in Miss Harrison's darkened parlour, sitting at the old-fashioned upright piano with its brass candlesticks and loose, yellowed keys. In the highest register there was not the faintest tinkle of a note, only the hollow sound of the key being banged down. Although that distant octave was out of her range, Sylvia sometimes pressed down one of its notes, listening mutely to Miss Harrison's exasperated railings about her – Sylvia's – lack of aptitude, or even concentration. The room was darkened in winter by a large fir-tree pressing against – in windy weather tapping against – the window, and in summer even more so by holland blinds, half-drawn to preserve the threadbare carpet. To add to all the other miseries, Sylvia had to peer short-sightedly at the music-book, her glance going up and down between it and the keyboard, losing her place, looking hunted, her lips pursed.

It was now the season of the drawn blinds, and she waited in the lane at the bus-stop, feeling hot in her winter coat, which her grandmother insisted on her wearing, just as she insisted on the music lessons. The lane buzzed in the heat of the late afternoon – with bees in the clover, and flies going crazy over some cow-pats on the road.

Since her mother's death, Sylvia had grown glum and sullen. She was a plain child, plump, mature for her eleven years. Her greasy hair was fastened back by a pink plastic slide; her tweed coat, of which, last winter, she had been

116

rather proud, had cuffs and collar of mock ocelot. She carried, beside her music case, a shabby handbag, once her mother's.

The bus seemed to tremble and jingle as it came slowly down the road. She climbed on, and sat down on the long seat inside the door, where a little air might reach her.

On the other long seat opposite her, was a very tall man; quite old, she supposed, for his hair was carefully arranged over his bald skull. He stared at her. She puffed with the heat and then, to avoid his glance, she slewed round a little to look over her shoulder at the dusty hedges – the leaves all in late summer darkness. She was sure that he was wondering why she wore a winter's coat on such a day, and she unbuttoned it and flapped it a little to air her armpits. The weather had a threat of change in it, her grandmother had said, and her cotton dress was too short. It had already been let down and had a false hem, which she now tried to draw down over her thighs.

'Yes, it is very warm,' the man opposite her suddenly said, as if agreeing with someone else's remark.

She turned in surprise, and her face reddened, but she said nothing.

After a while, she began to wonder if it would be worth getting off at the fare-stage before the end of her journey and walk the rest of the way. Then she could spend the money on a lolly. She had to waste half-an-hour before her lesson, and must wander about somewhere to pass the time. It would be better to be wandering about with a lolly to suck. Her grandmother did not allow her to eat sweets – bathing the teeth in acid, she said it was.

'I believe I have seen you before,' the man opposite said. 'Either wending your way to or from a music-lesson, I imagine.' He looked knowingly at her music-case.

'To,' she said sullenly.

'A budding Myra Hess,' he went on. 'I take it that you play the piano, as you seem to have no instrument secreted about your person.'

She did not know what he meant, and stared out the window, frowning, feeling so hot and anguished.

'And what is your name?' he asked. 'We shall have to keep it in mind for the future when you are famous.'

'Sylvia Wilkinson,' she said under her breath.

'Not bad. Not bad, Sylvia. No doubt one day I shall boast that I met the great Sylvia Wilkinson on a bus one summer's afternoon. Name-dropping, you know. A harmless foible of the humble.'

He was very neat and natty, but his reedy voice had a nervous tremour. All this time, he had held an unlighted cigarette in his hand, and gestured with it, but made no attempt to find matches.

'I expect at school you sing the beautiful song, "Who is Sylvia?" Do you?'

She shook her head, without looking at him and, to her horror, he began to sing, quaveringly, 'Who is Sylvia? What is she-he?'

A woman sitting a little further down the bus, turned and looked at him sharply.

He's mad, Sylvia decided. She was embarrassed, but not nervous, not nervous at all, here in the bus with other people, in spite of all her grandmother had said about not getting into conversations with strangers.

He went on singing, wagging his cigarette in time.

The woman turned again and gave him a longer stare. She was homely-looking, Sylvia decided – in spite of fair hair going very dark at the roots. She had a comfortable, protective manner, as if she were keeping an eye on the situation for Sylvia's sake.

Suddenly, he broke off his singing and returned her stare. 'I take it, Madam,' he said, 'that you do not appreciate my singing.'

'I should think it's hardly the place,' she said shortly. 'That's all,' and turned her head away.

'Hardly the place!' he said, in a low voice, as if to himself, and with feigned amazement. 'On a fair summer's afternoon, while we bowl merrily along the lanes. Hardly the place – to express one's joy of living! I am sorry,' he said to Sylvia, in a louder voice. 'I had not realized we were going to a funeral.'

Thankfully, she saw that they were coming nearer to the outskirts of the town. It was not a large town, and its outskirts were quiet.

'I hope you don't mind me chatting to you,' the man said to Sylvia. 'I am fond of children. I am known as being *good* with them. Well known for that. I treat them on my own level, as one should.'

Sylvia stared – almost glared – out of the window, twisted round in her seat, her head aching with the stillness of her eyes.

It was flat country, intersected by canals. On the skyline, were the clustered chimneys of a brick-works. The only movement out there was the faintest shimmering of heat.

She was filled by misery; for there seemed nothing in her life now but acquiescence to hated things, and her grandmother's old ways setting her apart from other children. Nothing she did was what she wanted to do – school-going, church-going, now this terrible music lesson ahead of her. Since her mother's death, her life had taken a sharp turn for the worse, and she could not see how it would ever be any better. She had no faith in freeing herself from it, even when she was grown-up.

A wasp zigzagged across her and settled on the front of her coat. She was obliged to turn. She sat rigid, her head held back, her chin tucked in, afraid to make a movement.

'Allow me!' The awful man opposite had reached across the bus, and flapped a crumpled handkerchief at her. The wasp began to fuss furiously, darting about her face.

'We'll soon settle you, you little pest,' the man said, making matters worse.

The bus-conductor came between them. He stood carefully still for a moment, and then decisively clapped his hands together, and the wasp fell dead to the ground.

'Thank you,' Sylvia said to him, but not to the other.

They were passing bungalows now, newly-built, and with unmade gardens. Looking directly ahead of her, Sylvia got up, and went to the platform of the bus, standing there in a slight breeze, ready for the stopping-place.

Beyond the bus-shelter, she knew that there was a little general shop. She would comfort herself with a bright red lolly on a stick. She crossed the road and stood looking in the window, at jars of boiled sweets, and packets of detergents and breakfast cereals. There was a notice about ice-creams, but she had not enough money.

She turned to go into the empty, silent shop when the now familiar and dreaded voice came from beside her. 'Would you care to partake of an ice, this hot afternoon?'

He stood between her and the shop, and the embarrassment she had suffered on the bus gave way to terror.

'An ice?' he repeated, holding his head on one side, looking at her imploringly.

She thought that if she said 'yes', she could at least get inside the shop. Someone must be there to serve, someone whose protection she might depend upon. Those words of warning from her grandmother came into her head, cautionary tales, dark with unpleasant hints.

Before she could move, or reply, she felt a hand lightly but firmly touch her shoulder. It was the glaring woman from the bus, she was relieved to see.

'Haven't you ever been told not to talk to strangers?' she asked Sylvia, quite sharply, but with calm common sense in her brusqueness. 'You'd better be careful,' she said to the man menacingly. 'Now come along, child, and let this be a lesson to you. Which way were you going?'

Sylvia nodded ahead.

'Well, best foot forward, and keep going. And *you*, my man, can kindly step in a different direction, or I'll find a policeman.'

At this last word, Sylvia turned to go, feeling flustered, but important.

'You should *never*,' the woman began, going along beside her. 'There's some funny people about these days. Doesn't your mother warn you?'

'She's dead.'

'Oh, well, I'm sorry about that. My God, it's warm.' She pulled her dress away from her bosom, fanning it. She had a shopping-basket full of comforting, homely groceries, and Sylvia looked into it, as she walked beside her.

'Wednesday's always my day,' the woman said. 'Early-closing here, so I take the bus up to Horseley. I have a relative who has the little general store there. It makes a change, but not in this heat.'

She rambled on about her uninteresting affairs. Once, Sylvia glanced back, and could see the man still standing there, gazing after them.

'I shouldn't turn round,' the woman said. 'Which road did you say?'

Sylvia hadn't, but now did so.

'Well, you can come my way. That would be better, and there's nothing much in it. Along by the gravel-pits. I'll have a quick look round before we turn the corner.'

When she did so, she said that she thought they were being followed, at a distance. 'Oh, it's disgraceful,' she said. 'And with all the things you read in the papers. You can't be too careful, and you'll have to remember that in the future. I'm not sure I ought not to inform the police.'

Along this road, there were disused gravel-pits, and chic-ory and convolvulus. Rusty sorrel and rustier tin-cans gave the place a derelict air. On the other side, there were allotments, and ramshackle tool-sheds among dark nettles.

'It runs into Hamilton Road,' the woman explained.

'But I don't have to be there for another half-hour,' Sylvia said nervously. She could imagine Miss Harrison's face if she turned up on the doorstep all that much too soon, in the middle of a lesson with the bright-looking girl she had often met leaving.

'I'm going to give you a nice cup of tea, and make sure you're all right. Don't you worry.'

Thankfully, she turned in at the gate of a little red brick house at the edge of the waste land. It was ugly, but very neat, and surrounded by hollyhocks. The beautifully shining windows were draped with frilly, looped-up curtains, with plastic flowers arranged between them.

Sylvia followed the woman down a side path to the back door, trying to push her worries from her mind. She was all right this time, but what of all the future Wednesdays, she wondered – with their perilous journeys to be made alone.

She stood in the kitchen and looked about her. It was clean and cool there. A budgerigar hopped in a cage. Rather listlessly, but not knowing what else to do, she went to it and ran her finger-nail along the wires.

'There's my baby boy, my little Joey,' the woman said in a sing-song, automatic way, as she held the kettle under the tap. 'You'll feel better when you've had a cup of tea,' she added, now supposedly addressing Sylvia.

'It's very kind of you.'

'Any woman would do the same. There's a packet of Oval Marie in my basket, if you'd like to open it and put them on this plate.'

Sylvia was glad to do something. She arranged the biscuits carefully on the rose-patterned plate. 'It's very nice here,' she said. Her grandmother's house was so dark and cluttered; Miss Harrison's even more so. Both smelt stuffy, of thick curtains and old furniture. She did not go into many houses, for she was so seldom invited anywhere. She was a dull girl, whom nobody liked very much, and she knew it.

'I must have everything sweet and fresh,' the woman said complacently.

The kettle began to sing.

I've still got to get home, Sylvia thought in a panic. She stared up at a fly-paper hanging in the window – the only disconcerting thing in the room. Some of the flies were still half alive, and striving hopelessly to free themselves. But they were caught forever.

She heard footsteps on the path, and listened in surprise; but the woman did not seem to hear, or lift her head. She was spooning tea from the caddy into the teapot.

'Just in time, Herbert,' she called out.

Sylvia turned round as the door opened. With astonished horror, she saw the man from the bus step confidently into the kitchen.

'Well done, Mabel!' he said, closing the door behind him. 'Don't forget one for the pot!' He smiled, smoothing his hands together, surveying the room.

Sylvia spun round questioningly to the woman, who was now bringing the teapot to the table, and she noticed for the first time that there were three cups and saucers laid there.

'Well, sit down, do,' the woman said, a little impatiently. 'It's all ready.'

FRED URQUHART

But German Girls Walk Different

Ever since I was a kid I've been crazy about horses. I've always wanted one of my own. But there was fat chance of that, living in a tenement in Glasgow – even if the old man had had the money to buy me one. And anyway, even if the old lady hadn't cut up rough, what would the neighbours have said if I'd kept it tethered in the back-green?

When I joined the Army I fancied myself in the Guards riding one of these great shiny chargers. But the Guards were mechanized by then, and anyway I wasn't big enough to be a Guardsman. So I just had to go into the bleeding infantry. And all I want now is to get demobbed and get back to Civvy Street as quick as I can with Marta. There'll be ructions with the old lady about that, I guess. I don't know how kindly she'll take to a German daughter-in-law. But maybe things'll be all right. The old lady's not a bad old spud if you take her in the right way.

It's funny what three months in your life do. Three months ago there I was right in the middle of Germany, and the only things that worried me were the non-fratting and the fact that I couldn't get to ride one of the many beautiful German horses I saw. But all that was changed by Blister Hill in one night.

Blister's a Canadian who's attached to our unit. He's a great boy for *winning* things. Everything he sees that he wants he just goes and grabs, and if people complain – well, it's just too bad. Blister's 'won' it and nothing can be done.

At first Blister had several brushes with our C.O. about

this. Our C.O. is a bit like a schoolmaster; that's why we christened him 'The Beak'. It started one day when a bloke came into our R.H.Q. and handed me a sheaf of papers and said: 'That's for the C.O.'

I must have looked puzzled. I was wondering what this bloke who's a truck-driver was doing with papers for the C.O. For the fellow said: 'You'll laugh when you read these. I had to laugh myself. I had my truck parked by the side of the road last night, and the old geezer himself came along and raised no end of a stink. "Don't you know it's illegal to park an army vehicle by the roadside, my man?" he says. "Write out one hundred times *It is a punishable offence to park an army vehicle by the side of a road*, and bring it to my office in the morning." '

'I sat up half the night doing them,' the bloke said. 'Don't laugh, will you?'

But it was no laughing matter. As that guy on the radio says: 'It makes you think!' Anyway, it made some of our blokes think, and it helped a lot when some of them who didn't know what their politics were put in their votes at the election.

Blister, of course, is the sort of guy who knows how to vote without letting anything or anybody influence him. 'Private enterprise all the time for me,' he says. 'My own, and my friends.'

Blister took a sort of shine to me. You know how it is. He said I was such a little guy I needed protecting. 'Got to keep you from getting tied up with any of these husky German fräuleins,' he said. 'If one of them gets her talons on you, you'll be mincemeat in no time.'

And so Blister and me have palled around ever since he joined our crowd. I've learned a lot from him about winning things. I used to think I was pretty hot in the old days in Glasgow, but I knew nothing until I fell in with Blister. My old lady used to say: 'The quickness of the hand deceives the left foot!' But even that couldn't describe Blister. He leaves me dizzy. I've often said to him it's not right to win things off people the way he does. 'Even though they are Jerries!' I've said.

But although he's left me dizzy often, he's never left me as dizzy as that night he brought me the horse.

I'd told him sometimes how I'd always wished I could have a horse and how I'd have liked to be a jockey. And I'd told him about wanting to go in the Guards and not being big enough. But I never thought it had sunk in. Two-three times he said: 'Aw, but we'll get you a horse, Chuck! We can easy win a horse. Leave that to your Uncle Blis!' But I never cottoned on to it much. I just thought he was talking big in his own Canadian way.

And then one night he came into our billet grinning all over. 'Get your boots on, brother!' he said. 'Get on your boots and bring your saddle! We're gonna ride the range to-night! Yippee!'

'Ach, I'm no' goin' oot the night,' I said. 'I'm ower tired, and I cannie be fashed.'

'Come on!' he cried. 'There ain't gonna be no empty saddles in the old corral to-night! Get booted and spurred. We're gonna roam the range together!'

'I dinnie want to go oot,' I said.

But he took hold of me and put my boots on, then he picked me up and carried me out. And all the time he kept singing a lot of cowboy songs. He caused such a commotion that the rest of the chaps in the billet came along to see what was up.

And like me they nearly passed out when they saw the horse. It was a black German cavalry horse: a super bit of work.

'Well, what do you think of Old Faithful, chum?' Blister said, unhitching it from a post and leading it up to me. 'Will he suit your nibs?'

'Where'd ye get him?' I said.

Blister shrugged and patted the horse's neck. 'I won him,' he said.

'But ye cannie win a horse,' I said. 'No' a horse o' this size, anyway!'

'I was walking in the country,' Blister said. 'And as I walked along I passed a field where this horse was grazing. Now, horses are very inquisitive animals. As soon as this horse saw me, it galloped up and nodded to me over the fence. So I nodded back and said: "How do, old fella!" Well, I walked along, and the horse walked along beside me. Then we came to a gate. So I leaned on the gate, and as I was leaning I thought about you, kid, and how you'd always wanted a horse, and I said to myself: "Blister, it ain't good for that kid to go on wanting a horse that bad. It's bad for his psychology, Blister," I says. "Frustration and all that." And I was so busy thinking all this I didn't notice what my hand was doing, but it must have been playing with the latch of the gate, for when I started to walk away I discovered that the horse had nosed open the gate and was following me. The Pied Piper!'

'He's a nice horse,' he said.

'He's a nice horse sure enough,' I said. 'But – oh, it's an awful big But! What are we goin' to do with him? We cannie hide a horse like we could hide a blanket or a chicken or a keg o' rum.'

'Ye'll have to take him back, Blister,' I said.

'Can't, buddy,' he said. 'I couldn't find his field now even if you paid me!'

'He's yours now,' he said. 'You won him. C'mon, get on his back.' And before I knew where I was he'd lifted me on the horse.

For the next two or three minutes I hadn't time to think of anything but keeping myself from sliding off the horse's back. Blister, of course, had forgotten to win a saddle – though he'd gotten a bridle all right. And all the time I kept thinking about the Beak and about him making inquiries, and about where we were to hide the horse. You see, you can hardly hide a horse under your bed. Not a horse of this size, anyway.

I said this to Blister after I'd galloped two-three times up and down the lane beside our billet. I was all for taking the horse back, and so were the other chaps. But Blister was stubborn. There's a bit of the mule about Blister; maybe that's why the horse took to him. 'We'll put him in the old Frau's washing-house at the foot of the garden,' he said. 'For to-night, anyway. We'll decide what to do about him to-morrow.'

The other chaps were up in arms about this. Frau Gottlieb wasn't a bad old kipper, but she could be a holy terror when roused; and they all thought a great muckle horse amongst her washing would be just the thing to make her rush straight to the Beak. And so we had a great discussion. Some of the fellows, like me, were all for turning the horse loose and letting it find its own way back to its field. But Blister said, 'It's goin' into the old Frau's wash-house.'

I argued and argued with him while we were doing this, telling him we'd have the Beak down on us like a load of bricks. 'It's all very well winning a rug or a bottle of whisky,' I said. 'But a great muckle horse is a different matter. How do ye expect me to take it hame to Glesca? I couldnie very well hide it in ma kitbag, could I? Just you picture me walkin' doon the gang-plank off the leave-boat with that horse on ma back!'

I never slept that night for worrying. And the next morning we had a round-table discussion about it while we were shaving in the wash-house. One of the lads had aye to be standing at the door, keeking to see that Frau Gottlieb wasn't coming. But luckily she never appeared.

Blister was still stubborn. 'I won't take him back,' he said. 'He followed me here. He likes me, don't you, old boy?' And he nodded to the horse and winked, and the bloody horse neighed back at him. 'I tell you what,' Blister said. 'We'll leave the decision until after breakfast. I'll lock the wash-house door and put the key in my pocket, so the old Frau won't be able to find out. Maybe the Lord will be on our side and solve the problem for us.'

But the Lord must have slept late that morning, for after breakfast we were called on parade, and there was the C.O.

with an old Jerry farmer and a young girl who spoke some English. My knees were knocking together, but I couldn't keep my eyes offen this dame. She was the classiest bit of work I'd seen since I came to Germany. All the time the Beak was talking I watched her. I was so busy watching that I scarcely heard the Beak say that if the horse wasn't returned he'd make every man-jack in the unit write out a thousand times *Thou Shalt Not Steal*. And as I watched her I suddenly thought of a wonderful scheme. I saw it all in a flash. Me and Blister would take the horse back to their farm and we'd say we'd found it wandering on the road, and then the old guy and his daughter would fall on our necks and hail us as conquering heroes and whatnot, and then – domino! – the girl would fall for me.

But I'd reckoned again without Blister, for when I looked for him after parade he was nowhere to be seen. And when I went to the wash-house the door was open and the horse gone.

Blister came back about an hour later and said: 'Well, I've done it. I couldn't bear the thought of writing that thing out a thousand times. Hope you're satisfied, buddy.'

I could have killed him. I told him what I'd been planning, and then I said: 'But now ye've ruined it, you – you big cheese!'

Blister said nothing, and he kept out of my way all that day. I looked for him after supper, for I wanted to know where this girl's farm was; I thought maybe he and I could walk along there and maybe we'd see the girl and then, maybe, with Blister to give me courage, I'd be able to speak to her. But Blister was nowhere to be seen, and he didn't appear until just before lights out. He stood inside the door and beckoned me. 'Come here, you,' he said, jerking his thumb outside. 'This what you want?'

The horse was tethered to the wash-house door.

Well, to cut a long story short, there was the same pantomime the next morning with the old Jerry farmer and his daughter at our Beak, looking again for their horse. But after it me and Blister got busy. We nipped over to the wash-house and took the horse to the farm. 'We found him wandering on the road,' Blister said. 'You should lock him up more carefully, mister. Lots of them soldiers aren't to be trusted.'

The old farmer almost fell on our necks. He couldn't do enough to entertain us, and speaking for myself I was perfectly willing to stay in his comfortable farm-kitchen as long as it was Marta who was pouring out the wine and handling round cakes.

I was still dizzy as we walked back to our billet. But Blister was kinda moody. He said nothing all the way except to tell me to stop acting like a kid when I gave two-three hop-skips and a jump. 'This love business!' he said.

I didn't answer, but just after that when we passed a couple of Yankee soldiers and I heard one of them say: 'But German girls walk different,' I nudged him and said: 'D'ye hear that, chum? Doesn't that prove things to you?'

'I heard,' he said. And then he sighed and said: 'He was an awful nice horse.'

All the same, it looks now the way things are panning out that maybe I'll get the horse as well as Marta, for the old farmer said to me only yesterday that he would give us the horse as a wedding-present. But I'm not so sure about that. It will maybe be hard enough going with the old lady if I take home Marta without having the horse thrown in.

ANGUS WILSON
A Visit in Bad Taste

'He looks very much older' said Margaret. 'It's aged him dreadfully and made him servile.'

'I should imagine that prison does tend to kill one's independence' said her husband drily.

'Oh yes that's all very well, Malcolm, you can afford to be rational, to explain away, to account for. But he's my brother and no amount of reasons can make it any better to have him sitting there fingering his tie when he talks, loosening his collar with his finger, deferring every opinion to you, calling old Colonel Gordon sir, jumping up with every move I make. It's like a rather pathetic minor public schoolboy of nineteen applying for a job, and he's sixty, Malcolm, remember that – sixty.'

'I think you know' said Malcolm Tarrant, as he replaced his glass of port on the little table by his side 'that public school has always meant a lot more to Arthur than we can quite understand. The only time that I visited him in Tamcaster I was struck by the importance that they all attached to it. As a bank manager there and a worthy citizen of the town it was in some kind of way a passport to power, not just the place you'd been at school at. And now, I imagine, it's assumed an importance out of all perspective, a kind of lifebuoy to a drowning sailor. We're inclined to imagine prison as peopled with public schoolboys, each with a toothbrush moustache and an assumed military rank, "ex-public schoolboy gaoled", but they only make so much of it because it's so unusual. God knows what sort of awful snobbery the presence of a "public schoolman" arouses among the old lags, or the warders too for

131

that matter – people speak so often of the horrors of War but they never mention the most awful of them – the mind of the non-commissioned officer. Depend upon it, whatever snobbery there was, Arthur got full benefit from it.'

Margaret's deep, black eyes showed no sign of her distress, only her long upper lip stiffened and the tapir's nose that would have done credit to an Edward Lear drawing showed more white. The firelight shone upon her rich silver brocade evening dress as she rustled and shimmered across the room to place a log on the great open fire. She put the tiny liqueur glass of light emerald – how Malcolm always laughed at her feminine taste for crême de menthe! – upon the mantelpiece between the Chelsea group of Silenus and a country girl and the plain grey bowl filled with coppery and red-gold chrysanthemums.

'If you mean that Arthur is vulgar' she cried 'always has been, yes, yes. At least, not always' and her thin lips, so faintly rouged, relaxed into tenderness 'not when we were children. But increasingly so. My dear, how could I think otherwise, married to that terrible little woman. – 'How do you keep the servants from thieving, Margaret?'' – ''Give that class an inch and they'll take an ell'' – dreadful, vulgar little Fascist-minded creature.'

'Dear Margaret' said Malcolm, and he smiled the special smile of admiring condescension that he kept for his wife's political opinions. 'Remember that in Myra's eyes you were a terrible Red.'

'It isn't a question of politics, Malcolm' said his wife and she frowned – to her husband she was once again the serious-minded, simple student he had found so irresistible at Cambridge nearly forty years ago. 'It's a question of taste. No, it was a terrible marriage and a terrible life. It was the one excuse I could make for him at the time. To have lived for so many years against such a background was excuse enough for any crime, yes, even that one. I felt it all through the trial as I sat and watched Myra being the injured wife, with that ghastly family round her.'

'That's where we differ' said Malcolm and for a moment his handsome, high-cheekboned face with its Roman nose showed all his Convenanting ancestry 'I could never excuse his actions. I tried to rid myself of prejudice against them, to see him as a sick man rather than as a criminal' it was not for nothing one felt that the progressive weeklies were so neatly piled on the table beside him 'but when he refused psychiatric treatment the whole thing became impossible.'

Margaret smiled at her husband maternally as she speared a crystallized orange from its wooden box with the little two pronged fork. 'It must be wonderful to have everything all cut and dried like you, darling' she said 'only people don't fit into pigeon holes according to the demands of reason. Arthur would never go to a psychoanalyst, you old goose; in the first place he thinks it isn't respectable, and then deep down, of course, he would be frightened of it, he would think it was witchcraft.'

'No doubt you're right. No doubt Arthur does still live in the Middle Ages' he moved his cigar dexterously so that the long grey ash fell into the ashtray rather than on to his suit, he narrowed his eyes 'I still find his actions disgusting, inexcusable.'

'Offences against children' said Margaret and she spoke the phrase in inverted commas, contemptuously 'I suppose there is no woman whose blood does not get heated when she reads that in the newspaper. But somehow it all seemed so different when I saw it at the trial. Arthur seemed so shrunken and small, so curiously remote for the principal actor, as though he'd done it all inadvertently. He probably had, too,' she added fiercely, striking the arm of her chair with her hand 'in order to forget that dreadful, bright woman – that awful, chromium-plated, cocktail-cabinet, old-oak-lounge home. And then those ghastly people – the parents – there are some kinds of working class people I just cannot take – servile and defiant, obstinate and shifty. I believe every word Arthur said when he told of their menaces, their sudden visits, their demands for money. Oh!

they'd had their pound of flesh all right' she said bitterly 'in unhappiness and fear. Even the children, Malcolm, it sounds so moving in the abstract, poor little creatures not comprehending, their whole lives distorted by a single incident. When Rupert and Jane were little, I used to think that if anyone harmed them I would put his eyes out with hot irons. But these children weren't like that – that cretinous boy with the sudden look of cunning in his eyes and that awful, painted, oversexed girl.'

'It's a pity you ever went to the trial' said Malcolm, but Margaret could not agree. 'I had to suffer it all' she cried 'it was the only way. But that Dostoyevskeyan mood is over. I don't want any more of it, I want it to be finished.' She fitted a cigarette into one of the little cardboard holders that stood in a glass jar on her work-table, then suddenly she turned on her husband fiercely 'Why has he come here? Why? Why?' she cried.

'I imagine because he's lonely' said Malcolm.

'Of course he is. What can be expected? But he'll be just as lonely here. We aren't his sort of people, Malcolm. Oh! Not just because of what's happened, we never have been. This isn't his kind of house.' She thought with pleasure of all they had built up there – the taste, the tolerance, the ease of living, the lack of dogmatism. Her eyes lighted on the Chelsea and the Meissen figures, the John drawings, the Spanish metal-work, the little pale yellow spinet – eclectic but good. Her ears heard once more Ralph Tarrant telling them of his ideas for Hamlet, Mrs Doyle speaking of her life with the great man, Professor Crewe describing his theory of obsolete ideas, Dr Modjka his terrible meeting with Hitler. Arthur had no place there.

'You want me to ask him to go' said Malcolm slowly. Margaret bent over the fire, crouching on a stool in the hearth, holding out her hands to the warmth. 'Yes' she said in a low voice 'I do.' 'Before he's found his feet?' Malcolm was puzzled. 'He knows I think that he must move eventually, but for the moment . . .' 'The moment!' broke in Margaret savagely. 'If he stays now he stays for ever, I'm as certain of that as that I stand. Don't ask me *how* I know, but I do.' 'Ah! well. It won't be a very pleasant talk' said her husband 'but perhaps it will be for the best.'

Only the frou-frou of Margaret's skirt broke the silence as she moved about the room, rearranging the sprigs of winter jasmine, drawing the heavy striped satin curtains across to cover a crack of light. Suddenly she sat down again on the stool and began to unwrap some sewing from a little silk bundle.

'I think the last chapter of Walter's book very pretentious' she said in a voice harder and clearer than normal. 'He's at his worst when he's doing the great Panjandrum.'

'Poor Walter' said Malcolm 'You can't go on playing Peter Pan *and* speak with the voice of authority . . .'

They had not long been talking, when Arthur came in. His suit looked over-pressed, his tie was too 'club', his hair had too much brilliantine for a man of his age. All his actions were carried out overconsciously, with military precision; as he sat down he jerked up his trousers to preserve the crease, he removed a white handkerchief from his shirtcuff, wiped his little toothbrush moustache and cleared his throat – 'Sorry to have been so long' he said 'Nature's call, you know'. Malcolm smiled wryly and Margaret winced.

'You don't take sugar, do you Arthur?' she said as she handed him his coffee.

'Will you have a glass of port, old man?' asked Malcolm, adapting his phraseology to his brother-in-law.

'Oh! thanks very much' said Arthur in quick, nervous tones, fingering his collar. Then feeling that such diffidence was unsuitable, he added 'Port, eh? Very fruity, very tasty.'

There was a long pause, then Margaret and Malcolm spoke at once.

'I've just been saying that Walter Howard's new book . . .' she began.

'Did you have an opportunity to look at the trees we've planted?' said Malcolm. Then, as Margaret blushing, turned her head away, he continued 'We ought really to have more trees down, if this fuel shortage is going to materialize. I'll get on to Bowers about it.'

'Oh not this week, darling' said Margaret 'Mrs Bowers is away with her mother who's ill and young Peter's got flu. Poor Bowers is terribly overworked.'

'Next week then' said Malcolm 'I must say I've never known such a set for illness.'

'Give them an inch and they'll take an ell' said Arthur.

The reiteration of her sister-in-law's phrase enraged Margaret. 'What nonsense you do talk, Arthur' she cried. 'I should have thought the last few months would have taught you some sense.' She blushed scarlet as she realized what she had said, then more gently she added 'You don't know the Bowers. Why Mrs Bowers is the best friend I have round here.'

Arthur felt the old order was on its mettle, he was not prepared to be placated. 'I'm afraid my respect for your precious British workmen has not been increased where I come from' he said defiantly.

'I doubt if you saw the British workman at his best in prison' said Malcolm carefully, and as his brother-in-law was about to continue the argument, he added 'No, Arthur, let's leave it at that – Margaret and I have our own ideas on these things and we're too old to change them now.'

Arthur's defiance vanished. He fingered the knot of his tie and mumbled something about 'respecting them for it'. There was a silence for some minutes, then Malcolm said abruptly 'Where do you plan to go from here?' Arthur was understood to say that he hadn't thought about it.

'I think you should' said Malcolm 'Why don't you go abroad?'

'The Colonies?' questioned Arthur with a little laugh.

'I know it's conventional, but why not? You can always count on me if you need any money.'

Arthur did not speak for a moment. Then 'You *want* me to go from here?' he asked. Margaret was determined to fight her own battle, so 'Yes, Arthur' she replied 'You must. It won't do here, we don't fit in together.'

'I doubt if *I* fit in anywhere' Arthur's voice was bitter.

Malcolm would have dispelled the mood with a 'nonsense, old man', but Margaret again took up the task. 'No, Malcolm, perhaps he's right' suddenly her voice became far away, with a dramatic note. 'When Malcolm was at the Ministry in London during the raids and Rupert was flying over Germany, I had to realize that they might both be killed and then, of course *I* wouldn't have fitted in. I took my precautions. I always carried something that would finish me off quickly if I needed it. Remember, Arthur, if anything should happen I shall always understand and respect you.'

Malcolm looked away, embarrassed. These moments of self-dramatization of Margaret's made him feel that he had married beneath him.

Arthur sat, thinking – the colonies or suicide, neither seemed to be what he was needing.

'Well' he said finally 'I'm very tired, I'll be toddling off to bed, I think. A real long night'll do me good.'

Margaret got up and stroked his hair.

'Ee,' he said 'it's a moocky do, lass, as Nurse used to say.'

This direct appeal to sentiment repelled her 'You'll find whisky and a syphon in your room' she said formally.

'Yes, have a good nightcap' said Malcolm to the erect over-military back of his brother-in-law.

'Thank God that's over' he sighed a few minutes later. 'Poor old Arthur. I expect he'll find happiness sometime, somewhere.'

'No, Malcolm' said Margaret fiercely 'it's been an unpleasant business, but if it's not to turn sour on us, we've got to face it. Arthur will *never* be happy, he's rotten, dead. But we aren't, and if we're going to live, we can't afford to let his rottenness infect us.'

Malcolm stared at his wife with admiration – to face reality, that was obviously the way to meet these things, not to try to escape. He thought for a few minutes of what she had said – of Arthur's rottenness – socially and personally – and of all that they stood for – individually alive, socially progressive. But for all the realism of her view, it somehow did not satisfy him. He remained vaguely uneasy the whole evening.

ROALD DAHL
The Hitch-hiker

I had a new car. It was an exciting toy, a big B.M.W. 3·3 Li, which means 3·3 litre, long wheelbase, fuel injection. It had a top speed of 129 m.p.h. and terrific acceleration. The body was pale blue. The seats inside were darker blue and they were made of leather, genuine soft leather of the finest quality. The windows were electrically operated and so was the sun-roof. The radio aerial popped up when I switched on the radio, and disappeared when I switched it off. The powerful engine growled and grunted impatiently at slow speeds, but at sixty miles an hour the growling stopped and the motor began to purr with pleasure.

I was driving up to London by myself. It was a lovely June day. They were haymaking in the fields and there were butter-cups along both sides of the road. I was whispering along at seventy miles an hour, leaning back comfortably in my seat, with no more than a couple of fingers resting lightly on the wheel to keep her steady. Ahead of me I saw a man thumbing a lift. I touched the footbrake and brought the car to a stop beside him. I always stopped for hitch-hikers. I knew just how it used to feel to be standing on the side of a country road watching the cars go by. I hated the drivers for pretending they didn't see me, especially the ones in big cars with three empty seats. The large expensive cars seldom stopped. It was always the smaller ones that offered you a lift, or the old rusty ones, or the ones that were already crammed full of children and the driver would say, 'I think we can squeeze in one more.'

The hitch-hiker poked his head through the open window and said, 'Going to London, guv'nor?'

'Yes,' I said. 'Jump in.'

He got in and I drove on.

He was a small ratty-faced man with grey teeth. His eyes were dark and quick and clever, like a rat's eyes, and his ears were slightly pointed at the top. He had a cloth cap on his head and he was wearing a greyish-coloured jacket with enormous pockets. The grey jacket, together with the quick eyes and the pointed ears, made him look more than anything like some sort of a huge human rat.

'What part of London are you headed for?' I asked him.

'I'm goin' right through London and out the other side,' he said. 'I'm goin' to Epsom, for the races. It's Derby Day today.'

'So it is,' I said. 'I wish I were going with you. I love betting on horses.'

'I never bet on horses,' he said. 'I don't even watch 'em run. That's a stupid silly business.'

'Then why do you go?' I asked.

He didn't seem to like that question. His little ratty face went absolutely blank and he sat there staring straight ahead at the road, saying nothing.

'I expect you help to work the betting machines or something like that,' I said.

'That's even sillier,' he answered. 'There's no fun working them lousy machines and selling tickets to mugs. Any fool could do that.'

There was a long silence. I decided not to question him any more. I remembered how irritated I used to get in my hitch-hiking days when drivers kept asking *me* questions. Where are you going? Why are you going there? What's your job? Are you married? Do you have a girl-friend? What's her name? How old are you? And so on and so forth. I used to hate it.

'I'm sorry,' I said. 'It's none of my business what you do. The trouble is, I'm a writer, and most writers are terribly nosey parkers.'

'You write books?' he asked.

'Yes.'

'Writin' books is okay,' he said. 'It's what I call a skilled trade. I'm in a skilled trade too. The folks I despise is them that spend all their lives doin' crummy old routine jobs with no skill in 'em at all. You see what I mean?'

'Yes.'

'The secret of life,' he said, 'is to become very very good at somethin' that's very very 'ard to do.'

'Like you,' I said.

'Exactly. You and me both.'

'What makes you think that *I'm* any good at my job?' I asked. 'There's an awful lot of bad writers around.'

'You wouldn't be drivin' about in a car like this if you weren't no good at it,' he answered. 'It must've cost a tidy packet, this little job.'

'It wasn't cheap.'

'What can she do flat out?' he asked.

'One hundred and twenty-nine miles an hour,' I told him.

'I'll bet she won't do it.'

'I'll bet she will.'

'All car makers is liars,' he said. 'You can buy any car you like and it'll never do what the makers say it will in the ads.'

'This one will.'

'Open 'er up then and prove it,' he said. 'Go on, guv'nor, open 'er right up and let's see what she'll do.'

There is a roundabout at Chalfont St Peter and immediately beyond it there's a long straight section of dual carriageway. We came out of the roundabout on to the carriageway and I pressed my foot down on the accelerator. The big car leaped forward as though she'd been stung. In ten seconds or so, we were doing ninety.

'Lovely!' he cried. 'Beautiful! Keep goin'!'

I had the accelerator jammed right down against the floor and I held it there.

'One hundred!' he shouted . . . 'A hundred and five! . . . A hundred and ten! . . . A hundred and fifteen! Go on! Don't slack off!'

I was in the outside lane and we flashed past several cars as though they were standing still – a green Mini, a big cream-coloured Citroën, a white Land-Rover, a huge truck with a container on the back, an orange-coloured Volkswagen Mini-bus . . .

'A hundred and twenty!' my passenger shouted, jumping up and down. 'Go on! Go on! Get 'er up to one-two-nine!'

At that moment, I heard the scream of a police siren. It was so loud it seemed to be right inside the car, and then a policeman on a motor-cycle loomed up alongside us on the inside lane and went past us and raised a hand for us to stop.

'Oh, my sainted aunt!' I said. 'That's torn it!'

The policeman must have been doing about a hundred and thirty when he passed us, and he took plenty of time slowing down. Finally, he pulled into the side of the road and I pulled in behind him. 'I didn't know police motor-cycles could go as fast as that,' I said rather lamely.

'That one can,' my passenger said. 'It's the same make as yours. It's a B.M.W. R90S. Fastest bike on the road. That's what they're usin' nowadays.'

The policeman got off his motor-cycle and leaned the machine sideways on to its prop stand. Then he took off his gloves and placed them carefully on the seat. He was in no hurry now. He had us where he wanted us and he knew it.

'This is real trouble,' I said. 'I don't like it one bit.'

'Don't talk to 'im any more than is necessary, you understand,' my companion said. 'Just sit tight and keep mum.'

Like an executioner approaching his victim, the policeman came strolling slowly towards us. He was a big meaty man with a belly, and his blue breeches were skintight around his enormous thighs. His goggles were pulled up on to the helmet, showing a smouldering red face with wide cheeks.

We sat there like guilty schoolboys, waiting for him to arrive.

'Watch out for this man,' my passenger whispered. ' 'Ee looks mean as the devil.'

The policeman came round to my open window and

placed one meaty hand on the sill. 'What's the hurry?' he said.

'No hurry, officer,' I answered.

'Perhaps there's a woman in the back having a baby and you're rushing her to hospital? Is that it?'

'No, officer.'

'Or perhaps your house is on fire and you're dashing home to rescue the family from upstairs?' His voice was dangerously soft and mocking.

'My house isn't on fire, officer.'

'In that case,' he said, 'you've got yourself into a nasty mess, haven't you? Do you know what the speed limit is in this country?'

'Seventy,' I said.

'And do you mind telling me exactly what speed you were doing just now?'

I shrugged and didn't say anything.

When he spoke next, he raised his voice so loud that I jumped. *'One hundred and twenty miles per hour!'* he barked. 'That's *fifty* miles an hour over the limit!'

He turned his head and spat out a big gob of spit. It landed on the wing of my car and started sliding down over my beautiful blue paint. Then he turned back again and stared hard at my passenger. 'And who are you?' he asked sharply.

'He's a hitch-hiker,' I said. 'I'm giving him a lift.'

'I didn't ask you,' he said. 'I asked him.'

' 'Ave I done somethin' wrong?' my passenger asked. His voice was as soft and oily as haircream.

'That's more than likely,' the policeman answered. 'Anyway, you're a witness. I'll deal with you in a minute. Driving-licence,' he snapped, holding out his hand.

I gave him my driving-licence.

He unbuttoned the left-hand breast-pocket of his tunic and brought out the dreaded book of tickets. Carefully, he copied the name and address from my licence. Then he gave it back to me. He strolled round to the front of the car and read the number from the number-plate and wrote that down as well. He filled in the date, the time and the details of my offence. Then he tore out the top copy of the ticket. But before handing it to me, he checked that all the information had come through clearly on his own carbon copy. Finally, he replaced the book in his tunic pocket and fastened the button.

'Now you,' he said to my passenger, and he walked around to the other side of the car. From the other breast-pocket he produced a small black notebook. 'Name?' he snapped.

'Michael Fish,' my passenger said.

'Address?'

'Fourteen, Windsor Lane, Luton.'

'Show me something to prove this is your real name and address,' the policeman said.

My passenger fished in his pockets and came out with a driving-licence of his own. The policeman checked the name and address and handed it back to him. 'What's your job?' he asked sharply.

'I'm an 'od carrier.'

'A *what*?'

'An 'od carrier.'

'Spell it.'

'H-O-D C-A- . . .'

'That'll do. And what's a hod carrier, may I ask?'

'An 'od carrier, officer, is a person 'oo carries the cement up the ladder to the bricklayer. And the 'od is what 'ee carries it in. It's got a long 'andle, and on the top you've got two bits of wood set at an angle . . .'

'All right, all right. Who's your employer?'

'Don't 'ave one. I'm unemployed.'

The policeman wrote all this down in the black notebook. Then he returned the book to its pocket and did up the button.

'When I get back to the station I'm going to do a little checking up on you,' he said to my passenger.

'Me? What've I done wrong?' the rat-faced man asked.

'I don't like your face, that's all,' the policeman said. 'And we just might have a picture of it somewhere in our files.' He strolled round the car and returned to my window.

'I suppose you know you're in serious trouble,' he said to me.

'Yes, officer.'

'You won't be driving this fancy car of yours again for a very long time, not after *we've* finished with you. You won't be driving *any* car again come to that for several years. And a good thing, too. I hope they lock you up for a spell into the bargain.'

'You mean prison?' I asked, alarmed.

'Absolutely,' he said, smacking his lips. 'In the clink. Behind the bars. Along with all the other criminals who break the law. *And* a hefty fine into the bargain. Nobody will be more pleased about that than me. I'll see you in court, both of you. You'll be getting a summons to appear.'

He turned away and walked over to his motor-cycle. He flipped the prop stand back into position with his foot and swung his leg over the saddle. Then he kicked the starter and roared off up the road out of sight.

'Phew!' I gasped. 'That's done it.'

'We was caught,' my passenger said. 'We was caught good and proper.'

'I was caught, you mean.'

'That's right,' he said. 'What you goin' to do now, guv'nor?'

'I'm going straight up to London to talk to my solicitor,' I said. I started the car and drove on.

'You mustn't believe what 'ee said to you about goin' to prison,' my passenger said. 'They don't put nobody in the clink just for speedin'.'

'Are you sure of that?' I asked.

'I'm positive,' he answered. 'They can take your licence away and they can give you a whoppin' big fine, but that'll be the end of it.'

I felt tremendously relieved.

'By the way,' I said, 'Why did you lie to him?'

'Who, me?' he said. 'What makes you think I lied?'

'You told him you were an unemployed hod carrier. But you told *me* you were in a highly skilled trade.'

'So I am,' he said. 'But it don't pay to tell everythin' to a copper.'

'So what *do* you do?' I asked him.

'Ah,' he said slyly. 'That'd be tellin', wouldn't it?'

'Is it something you're ashamed of?'

'Ashamed?' he cried. 'Me, ashamed of my job? I'm about as proud of it as anybody could be in the entire world!'

'Then why won't you tell me?'

'You writers really is nosey parkers, aren't you?' he said. 'And you ain't goin' to be 'appy, I don't think, until you've found out exactly what the answer is?'

'I don't really care one way or the other,' I told him, lying.

He gave me a crafty little ratty look out of the sides of his eyes. 'I think you do care,' he said. 'I can see it on your face that you think I'm in some kind of a very peculiar trade and you're just achin' to know what it is.'

I didn't like the way he read my thoughts. I kept quiet and stared at the road ahead.

'You'd be right, too,' he went on. 'I *am* in a very peculiar trade. I'm in the queerest peculiar trade of 'em all.'

I waited for him to go on.

'That's why I 'as to be extra careful 'oo I'm talkin' to, you see. 'Ow am I to know, for instance, you're not another copper in plain clothes?'

'Do I look like a copper?'

'No,' he said. 'You don't. And you ain't. Any fool could tell that.'

He took from his pocket a tin of tobacco and a packet of cigarette papers and started to roll a cigarette. I was watching him out of the corner of one eye, and the speed with which he performed this rather difficult operation was incredible. The cigarette was rolled and ready in about five seconds. He ran his tongue along the edge of the paper, stuck it down and popped the cigarette between his lips. Then, as if from nowhere, a lighter appeared in his hand. The lighter flamed. The cigarette was lit. The lighter disappeared. It was altogether a remarkable performance.

'I've never seen anyone roll a cigarette as fast as that,' I said.

'Ah,' he said, taking a deep suck of smoke. 'So you noticed.'

'Of course I noticed. It was quite fantastic.'

He sat back and smiled. It pleased him very much that I had noticed how quickly he could roll a cigarette. 'You want to know what makes me able to do it?' he asked.

'Go on then.'

'It's because I've got fantastic fingers. These fingers of mine,' he said, holding up both hands high in front of him, 'are quicker and cleverer than the fingers of the best piano player in the world!'

'Are you a piano player?'

'Don't be daft,' he said. 'Do I look like a piano player?'

I glanced at his fingers. They were so beautifully shaped, so slim and long and elegant, they didn't seem to belong to the rest of him at all. They looked more like the fingers of a brain surgeon or a watchmaker.

'My job,' he went on, 'is a hundred times more difficult than playin' the piano. Any twerp can learn to do that. There's titchy little kids learnin' to play the piano in almost any 'ouse you go into these days. That's right, ain't it?'

'More or less,' I said.

'Of course it's right. But there's not one person in ten million can learn to do what I do. Not one in ten million! 'Ow about that?'

'Amazing,' I said.

'You're darn right it's amazin',' he said.

'I think I know what you do,' I said. 'You do conjuring tricks. You're a conjurer.'

'Me?' he snorted. 'A conjurer? Can you picture me goin'

round crummy kids' parties makin' rabbits come out of top 'ats?'

'Then you're a card player. You get people into card games and deal yourself marvellous hands.'

'Me! A rotten card-sharper!' he cried. 'That's a miserable racket if ever there was one.'

'All right. I give up.'

I was taking the car along slowly now, at no more than forty miles an hour, to make quite sure I wasn't stopped again. We had come on to the main London–Oxford road and were running down the hill towards Denham.

Suddenly, my passenger was holding up a black leather belt in his hand. 'Ever seen this before?' he asked. The belt had a brass buckle of unusual design.

'Hey!' I said. 'That's mine, isn't it? It *is* mine! Where did you get it?'

He grinned and waved the belt gently from side to side. 'Where d'you think I got it?' he said. 'Off the top of your trousers, of course.'

I reached down and felt for my belt. It was gone.

'You mean you took it off me while we've been driving along?' I asked, flabbergasted.

He nodded, watching me all the time with those little black ratty eyes.

'That's impossible,' I said. 'You'd have had to undo the buckle and slide the whole thing out through the loops all the way round. I'd have seen you doing it. And even if I hadn't seen you, I'd have felt it.'

'Ah, but you didn't, did you?' he said, triumphant. He dropped the belt on his lap, and now all at once there was a brown shoelace dangling from his fingers. 'And what about this, then?' he exclaimed, waving the shoelace.

'What about it?' I said.

'Anyone around 'ere missin' a shoelace?' he asked, grinning.

I glanced down at my shoes. The lace of one of them was missing. 'Good grief!' I said. 'How did you do that? I never saw you bending down.'

'You never saw nothin',' he said proudly. 'You never even saw me move an inch. And you know why?'

'Yes,' I said. 'Because you've got fantastic fingers.'

'Exactly right!' he cried. 'You catch on pretty quick, don't you?' He sat back and sucked away at his home-made cigarette, blowing the smoke out in a thin stream against the windshield. He knew he had impressed me greatly with those two tricks, and this made him very happy. 'I don't want to be late,' he said. 'What time is it?'

'There's a clock in front of you,' I told him.

'I don't trust car clocks,' he said. 'What does your watch say?'

I hitched up my sleeve to look at the watch on my wrist. It wasn't there. I looked at the man. He looked back at me, grinning.

'You've taken that, too,' I said.

He held out his hand and there was my watch lying in his palm. 'Nice bit of stuff, this,' he said. 'Superior quality. Eighteen-carat gold. Easy to flog, too. It's never any trouble gettin' rid of quality goods.'

'I'd like it back, if you don't mind,' I said rather huffily.

He placed the watch carefully on the leather tray in front of him. 'I wouldn't nick anything from you, guv'nor,' he said. 'You're my pal. You're giving me a lift.'

'I'm glad to hear it,' I said.

'All I'm doin' is answerin' your questions,' he went on. 'You asked me what I did for a livin' and I'm showin' you.'

'What else have you got of mine?'

He smiled again, and now he started to take from the pocket of his jacket one thing after another that belonged to me – my driving-licence, a key-ring with four keys on it, some pound notes, a few coins, a letter from my publishers, my diary, a stubby old pencil, a cigarette-lighter, and last of all, a beautiful old sapphire ring with pearls around it belonging to my wife. I was taking the ring up to the jeweller in London because one of the pearls was missing.

'Now *there's* another lovely piece of goods,' he said, turning the ring over in his fingers. 'That's eighteenth century, if I'm not mistaken, from the reign of King George the Third.'

'You're right,' I said, impressed. 'You're absolutely right.'

He put the ring on the leather tray with the other items.

'So you're a pickpocket,' I said.

'I don't like that word,' he answered. 'It's a coarse and vulgar word. Pickpockets is coarse and vulgar people who only do easy little amateur jobs. They lift money from blind old ladies.'

'What do you call yourself, then?'

'Me? I'm a fingersmith. I'm a professional fingersmith.' He spoke the words solemnly and proudly, as though he were telling me he was the President of the Royal College of Surgeons or the Archbishop of Canterbury.

'I've never heard that word before,' I said. 'Did you invent it?'

'Of course I didn't invent it,' he replied. 'It's the name given to them who's risen to the very top of the profession. You've 'eard of a goldsmith and a silversmith, for instance. They're experts with gold and silver. I'm an expert with my fingers, so I'm a fingersmith.'

'It must be an interesting job.'

'It's a marvellous job,' he answered. 'It's lovely.'

'And that's why you go to the races?'

'Race meetings is easy meat,' he said. 'You just stand around after the race, watchin' for the lucky ones to queue up and draw their money. And when you see someone collectin' a big bundle of notes, you simply follows after 'im and 'elps yourself. But don't get me wrong, guv'nor. I never takes nothin' from a loser. Nor from poor people neither. I only go after them as can afford it, the winners and the rich.'

'That's very thoughtful of you,' I said. 'How often do you get caught?'

'Caught?' he cried, disgusted. '*Me* get caught! It's only pickpockets get caught. Fingersmiths never. Listen, I could take the false teeth out of your mouth if I wanted to and you wouldn't even catch me!'

'I don't have false teeth,' I said.

'I know you don't,' he answered. 'Otherwise I'd 'ave 'ad 'em out long ago!'

I believed him. Those long slim fingers of his seemed able to do anything.

We drove on for a while without talking.

'That policeman's going to check up on you pretty thoroughly,' I said. 'Doesn't that worry you a bit?'

'Nobody's checkin' up on me,' he said.

'Of course they are. He's got your name and address written down most carefully in his black book.'

The man gave me another of his sly, ratty little smiles. 'Ah,' he said. 'So 'ee 'as. But I'll bet 'ee ain't got it all written down in 'is memory as well. I've never known a copper yet with a decent memory as well. Some of 'em can't even remember their own names.'

'What's memory got to do with it?' I asked. 'It's written down in his book, isn't it?'

'Yes, guv'nor, it is. But the trouble is, 'ee's lost the book. 'Ee's lost both books, the one with my name in it *and* the one with yours.'

In the long delicate fingers of his right hand, the man was holding up in triumph the two books he had taken from the policeman's pockets. 'Easiest job I ever done,' he announced proudly.

I nearly swerved the car into a milk-truck, I was so excited.

'That copper's got nothin' on either of us now,' he said.

'You're a genius!' I cried.

' 'Ee's got no names, no addresses, no car number, no nothin',' he said.

'You're brilliant!'

'I think you'd better pull in off this main road as soon as possible,' he said. 'Then we'd better build a little bonfire and burn these books.'

'You're a fantastic fellow,' I exclaimed.

'Thank you, guv'nor,' he said. 'It's always nice to be appreciated.'

MURIEL SPARK

The Ormolu Clock

The Hotel Stroh stood side by side with the Guesthouse Lublonitsch, separated by a narrow path that led up the mountain, on the Austrian side, to the Yugoslavian border. Perhaps the old place had once been a great hunting tavern. These days, though, the Hotel Stroh was plainly a disappointment to its few drooping tenants. They huddled together like birds in a storm; their flesh sagged over the unscrubbed tables on the dark back veranda, which looked over Herr Stroh's untended fields. Usually, Herr Stroh sat somewhat apart, in a mist of cognac, his lower chin resting on his red neck, and his shirt open for air. Those visitors who had come not for the climbing but simply for the view sat and admired the mountain and were sloppily waited upon until the weekly bus should come and carry them away. If they had cars, they rarely stayed long – they departed, as a rule, within two hours of arrival, like a comic act. This much was entertainingly visible from the other side of the path, at the Guesthouse Lublonitsch.

I was waiting for friends to come and pick me up on their way to Venice. Frau Lublonitsch welcomed all her guests in person. When I arrived I was hardly aware of the honour, she seemed so merely a local woman – undefined and dumpy as she emerged from the kitchen wiping her hands on her brown apron, with her grey hair drawn back tight, her sleeves rolled up, her dingy dress, black stockings, and boots. It was only gradually that her importance was permitted to dawn upon strangers.

There was a Herr Lublonitsch, but he was of no account,

152

even though he got all the martial courtesies. He sat punily with his drinking friends at one of the tables in front of the inn, greeting the guests as they passed in and out and receiving as much attention as he wanted from the waitresses. When he was sick Frau Lublonitsch took his meals with her own hands to a room upstairs set aside for his sickness. But she was undoubtedly the boss.

She worked the hired girls fourteen hours a day, and they did the work cheerfully. She was never heard to complain or to give an order; it was enough that she was there. Once, when a girl dropped a tray with five mugs of soup, Frau Lublonitsch went and fetched a cloth and submissively mopped up the mess herself, like any old peasant who had suffered worse than that in her time. The maids called her Frau Chef. 'Frau Chef prepares special food when her husband's stomach is bad,' one of them told me.

Appended to the guesthouse was a butcher's shop, and this was also a Lublonitsch possession. A grocer's shop had been placed beside it, and on an adjacent plot of ground – all Lublonitsch property – a draper's shop was nearing completion. Two of her sons worked in the butcher's establishment; a third had been placed in charge of the grocer's; and the youngest son, now ready to take his place, was destined for the draper's.

In the garden, strangely standing on a path between the flowers for decorating the guests' tables and the vegetables for eating, facing the prolific orchard and overhung by the chestnut trees that provided a roof for outdoor diners, grew one useless thing – a small, well-tended palm tree. It gave an air to the place. Small as it was, this alien plant stood as high as the distant mountain peaks when seen from the perspective of the great back porch where we dined. It quietly dominated the view.

Ordinarily, I got up at seven, but one morning I woke at half past five and came down from my room on the second floor to the yard, to find someone to make me some coffee.

Standing in the sunlight, with her back to me, was Frau Lublonitsch. She was regarding her wide kitchen garden, her fields beyond it, her outbuildings and her pigsties where two aged women were already at work. One of the sons emerged from an outbuilding carrying several strings of long sausages. Another led a bullock with a bag tied over its head to a tree and chained it there to await the slaughterers. Frau Lublonitsch did not move but continued to survey her property, her pigs, her pig-women, her chestnut trees, her bean-stalks, her sausages, her sons, her tall gladioli, and – as if she had eyes in the back of her head – she seemed aware, too, of the good thriving guesthouse behind her, and the butcher's shop, the draper's shop, and the grocer's.

Just as she turned to attack the day's work, I saw that she glanced at the sorry Hotel Stroh across the path. I saw her mouth turn down at the corners with the amusement of one who has a certain foreknowledge; I saw a landowner's recognition in her little black eyes.

You could tell, even before the local people told you, that Frau Lublonitsch had built up the whole thing from nothing by her own wits and industry. But she worked pitiably hard. She did all the cooking. She supervised the household, and, without moving hurriedly, she sped into the running of the establishment like the maniac drivers from Vienna who tore along the highroad in front of her place. She scoured the huge pans herself, wielding her podgy arm round and round; clearly, she trusted none of the girls to do the job properly. She was not above sweeping the floor, feeding the pigs, and serving in the butcher's shop, where she would patiently hold one after another great sausage under her customer's nose for him to smell its quality. She did not sit down, except to take her dinner in the kitchen, from her rising at dawn to her retiring at one in the morning.

Why does she do it, what for? Her sons are grown up, she's got her guesthouse, her servants, her shops, her pigs, fields, cattle—

At the café across the river, where I went in the late

afternoon, they said, 'Frau Lublonitsch has got far more than that. She owns all the strip of land up to the mountain. She's got three farms. She may even expand across the river and down this way to the town.'

'Why does she work so hard? She dresses like a peasant,' they said. 'She scours the pots.' Frau Lublonitsch was their favourite subject.

She did not go to church, she was above church. I had hoped to see her there, wearing different clothes and perhaps sitting with the chemist, the dentist, and their wives in the second-front row behind the count and his family; or perhaps she might have taken some less noticeable place among the congregation. But Frau Lublonitsch was a church unto herself, and even resembled in shape the onion-shaped spires of the churches around her.

I climbed the lower slopes of the mountains while the experts in their boots did the thing earnestly up on the sheer crags above the clouds. When it rained, they came back and reported, 'Tito is sending the bad weather.' The maids were bored with the joke, but they obliged with smiles every time, and served them up along with the interminable veal.

The higher mountain reaches were beyond me except by bus. I was anxious, however, to scale the peaks of Frau Lublonitsch's nature.

One morning, when everything was glittering madly after a nervous stormy night, I came down early to look for coffee. I had heard voices in the yard some moments before, but by the time I appeared they had gone indoors. I followed the voices to the dark stone kitchen and peered in the doorway. Beyond the chattering girls, I caught sight of a further doorway, which usually remained closed. Now it was open.

Within it was a bedroom reaching far back into the house. It was imperially magnificent. It was done in red and gold. I saw a canopied bed, built high, splendidly covered with a scarlet quilt. The pillows were piled up at the head – about four of them, very white. The bed head was deep dark wood, touched with gilt. A golden fringe hung from the canopy. In some ways this bed reminded me of the glowing bed by which van Eyck ennobled the portrait of Jan Arnolfini and his wife. All the rest of the Lublonitsch establishment was scrubbed and polished local wood, but this was a very poetic bed.

The floor of the bedroom was covered with a carpet of red which was probably crimson but which, against the scarlet of the bed, looked purple. On the walls on either side of the bed hung Turkish carpets whose background was an opulently dull, more ancient red – almost black where the canopy cast its shade.

I was moved by the sight. The girl called Mitzi was watching me as I stood in the kitchen doorway. 'Coffee?' she said.

'Whose room is that?'

'It's Frau Chef's room. She sleeps there.'

Now another girl, tall, lanky Gertha, with her humorous face and slightly comic answer to everything, skipped over to the bedroom door and said, 'We are instructed to keep the door closed,' and for a moment before closing it she drew open the door quite wide for me to see some more of the room. I caught sight of a tiled stove constructed of mosaic tiles that were not a local type; they were lustrous – ochre and green – resembling the tiles on the floors of Byzantine ruins. The stove looked like a temple. I saw a black lacquered cabinet inlaid with mother-of-pearl, and just before Gertha closed the door I noticed, standing upon the cabinet, a large ornamental clock, its case enamelled rosily with miniature inset pastel paintings; each curve and twirl in the case of this clock was overlaid with that gilded-bronze alloy which is known as ormolu. The clock twinkled in the early sunlight which slanted between the window hangings.

I went into the polished dining-room, and Mitzi brought my coffee there. From the window I could see Frau Lublonitsch in her dark dress, her black boots and wool stockings. She was plucking a chicken over a bucketful of feathers. Beyond her I could see the sulky figure of Herr Stroh standing collarless, fat and unshaven, in the open door of his hotel across the path. He seemed to be meditating upon Frau Lublonitsch.

It was that very day that the nuisance occurred. The double windows of my bedroom were directly opposite the bed-room windows of the Hotel Stroh, with no more than twenty feet between – the width of the narrow path that led up to the frontier.

It was a cold day. I sat in my room writing letters. I glanced out of the window. In the window directly opposite me stood Herr Stroh, gazing blatantly upon me. I was annoyed at his interest. I pulled down the blind and switched on the light to continue my writing. I wondered if Herr Stroh had seen me doing anything peculiar before I had noticed him, such as tapping my head with the end of my pen or scratch-ing my nose or pulling at my chin, or one of the things one might do while writing a letter. The drawn blind and the artificial light irritated me, and suddenly I didn't see why I shouldn't write my letters by daylight without being stared at. I switched off the light and released the blind. Herr Stroh had gone. I concluded that he had taken my action as a signal of disapproval, and I settled back to write.

I looked up a few moments later, and this time Herr Stroh was seated on a chair a little way back from the window. He was facing me squarely and holding to his eyes a pair of field-glasses.

I left my room and went down to complain to Frau Lub-lonitsch.

'She's gone to the market,' Gertha said. 'She'll be back in half an hour.'

So I lodged my complaint with Gertha.

'I shall tell Frau Chef,' she said.

Something in her manner made me ask, 'Has this ever happened before?'

'Once or twice this year,' she said. 'I'll speak to Frau Chef.'

And she added, with her music-hall grimace, 'He was probably counting your eyelashes.'

I returned to my room. Herr Stroh still sat in position, the field-glasses in his hands resting on his knees. As soon as I came within view, he raised the glasses to his eyes. I decided to stare him out until such time as Frau Lublonitsch should return and take the matter in hand.

For nearly an hour I sat patiently at the window. Herr Stroh rested his arms now and again, but he did not leave his seat. I could see him clearly, although I think I imagined the grin on his face as, from time to time, he raised the glasses to his eyes. There was no doubt that he could see, as if it were within an inch of his face, the fury on mine. It was too late now for one of us to give in, and I kept glancing down at the entrances to the Hotel Stroh, expecting to see Frau Lublonitsch or perhaps one of her sons or the yard hands going across to deliver a protest. But no one from our side approached the Stroh premises, from either the front or the back of the house. I continued to stare, and Herr Stroh continued to goggle through his glasses.

Then he dropped them. It was as if they had been jerked out of his hands by an invisible nudge. He approached close to the window and gazed, but now he was gazing at a point above and slightly to the left of my room. After about two minutes, he turned and disappeared.

Just then Gertha knocked at my door. 'Frau Chef has protested, and you won't have any more trouble,' she said.

'Did she telephone to his house?'

'No, Frau Chef doesn't use the phone; it mixes her up.'

'Who protested, then?'

'Frau Chef.'

'But she hasn't been across to see him. I've been watching the house.'

'No, Frau Chef doesn't visit with him. But don't worry, he knows all right that he mustn't annoy our guests.'

When I looked out of the window again, I saw that the

blind of Herr Stroh's room had been pulled down, and so it remained for the rest of my stay.

Meantime, I went out to post my letters in the box opposite our hotel, across the path. The sun had come out more strongly, and Herr Stroh stood in his doorway blinking up at the roof of the Guesthouse Lublonitsch. He was engrossed, he did not notice me at all.

I didn't want to draw his attention by following the line of his gaze but I was curious as to what held him staring so trancelike up at our roof. On my way back from the postbox I saw what it was.

Like most of the roofs in that province, the Lublonitsch roof had a railed ledge running several inches above the eaves, for the purpose of preventing the snow from falling in heavy thumps during the winter. On this ledge, just below an attic window, stood the gold-and-rose ormolu clock that I had seen in Frau Lublonitsch's splendid bedroom.

I turned the corner just as Herr Stroh gave up his gazing; he went indoors, sullen and bent. Two car-loads of people who had moved into the hotel that morning were now moving out, shifting their baggage with speed and the signs of a glad departure. I knew that his house was nearly empty.

Before supper, I walked past the Hotel Stroh and down across the bridge to the café. There were no other customers in the place. The proprietor brought the harsh gin that was the local speciality over to my usual table and I sipped it while I waited for someone to come. I did not have to wait long, for two local women came in and ordered ices, as many of them did on their way home from work in the village shops. They held the long spoons in their rough, knobbly hands and talked, while the owner of the café came and sat with them to exchange the news of the day.

'Herr Stroh has been defying Frau Lublonitsch,' one of the women said.

'Not again?'

'He's been offending her tourists.'

MURIEL SPARK

'Dirty old Peeping Tom.'

'He only does it to annoy Frau Lublonitsch.'

'I saw the clock on the roof. I saw—'

'Stroh is finished, he—'

'Which clock?'

'What she bought from him last winter when he was hard up. All red and gold, like an altarpiece. A beautiful clock – it was his grandfather's when things were different.'

'Stroh is finished. She'll have his hotel. She'll have—'

'She'll have the pants off him.'

'He'll have to go. She'll get the place at her price. Then she'll build down to the bridge. Just wait and see. Next winter she'll have the Hotel Stroh. Last winter she had the clock. It's two years since she gave him the mortgage.'

'It's only Stroh's place that's standing in her way. She'll pull it down.'

The faces of the two women and the man nearly met across the café table, hypnotized by the central idea of their talk. The women's spoons rose to their mouths and returned to their ices while the man clasped his hands on the table in front of him. Their voices went on like a litany.

'She'll expand down to the bridge.'

'Perhaps beyond the bridge.'

'No, no, the bridge will be enough. She's not so young.'

'Poor old Stroh!'

'Why doesn't she expand in the other direction?'

'Because there isn't so much trade in the other direction.'

'The business is down here, this side of the river.'

'Old Stroh is upset.'

'She'll build down to the bridge. She'll pull down his place and build.'

'Beyond the bridge.'

'Old Stroh. His clock stuck up there for everyone to see.'

'What does he expect, the lazy old pig?'

'What does he expect to see with his field-glasses?'

'The tourists.'

'I wish him joy of the tourists.'

160

They giggled, then noticed me sitting within earshot, and came out of their trance.

How delicately Frau Lublonitsch had sent her deadly message! The ormolu clock was still there on the roof ledge when I returned. It was thus she had told him that time was passing and the end of summer was near, and that his hotel, like his clock, would soon be hers. As I passed, Herr Stroh shuffled out to his front door, rather drunk. He did not see me. He was looking at the clock where it hung in the sunset, he looked up at it as did the quaking enemies of the Lord upon the head of Holofernes. I wondered if the poor man would even live another winter; certainly he had taken his last feeble stand against Frau Lublonitsch.

As for her, she would probably live till she was ninety or more. The general estimate of her age was fifty-three, fifty-four, five, six: a healthy woman.

Next day, the clock was gone. Enough was enough. It had gone back to that glamorous room behind the kitchen to which Frau Lublonitsch retired in the early hours of the morning to think up her high conceptions, not lying supine like a defeated creature but propped up on the white pillows, surrounded by her crimson, her scarlet, her gold-and-rosy tints, which, like a religious discipline, disturbed her spirit out of its sloth. It was from here she planted the palm tree and built the shops.

When, next morning, I saw her scouring the pots in the yard and plodding about in her boots among the vegetables, I was somewhat terrified. She could have adorned her own person in scarlet and gold, she could have lived in a turreted mansion rivalling that of the apothecary in the village. But like one averting the evil eye, or like one practising a pure disinterested art, she had stuck to her brown apron and her boots. And she would, without a doubt, have her reward. She would take the Hotel Stroh. She would march on the bridge, and beyond it. The café would be hers, the swimming pool, the cinema. All the market place would be hers before she died in the scarlet bed under the gold-fringed canopy, facing her ormolu clock, her deed boxes, and her ineffectual bottle of medicine.

Almost as if they knew it, the three tourists remaining in the Hotel Stroh came over to inquire of Frau Lublonitsch if there were any rooms available and what her terms were. Her terms were modest, and she found room for two of them. The third left on his motorcycle that night.

Everyone likes to be on the winning side. I saw the two new arrivals from the Hotel Stroh sitting secure under the Lublonitsch chestnut trees, taking breakfast, next morning. Herr Stroh, more sober than before, stood watching the scene from his doorway. I thought, Why doesn't he spit on us, he's got nothing to lose? I saw again, in my mind's eye, the ormolu clock set high in the sunset splendour. But I had not yet got over my fury with him for spying into my room, and was moved, all in one stroke, with high contempt and deep pity, feverish triumph and chilly fear.

DORIS LESSING

Flight

Above the old man's head was the dovecote, a tall wire-netted shelf on stilts, full of strutting, preening birds. The sunlight broke on their grey breasts into small rainbows. His ears were lulled by their crooning, his hands stretched up towards his favourite, a homing pigeon, a young plump-bodied bird which stood still when it saw him and cocked a shrewd bright eye.

'Pretty, pretty, pretty,' he said, as he grasped the bird and drew it down, feeling the cold coral claws tighten around his finger. Content, he rested the bird lightly on his chest, and leaned against a tree, gazing out beyond the dovecote into the landscape of a late afternoon. In folds and hollows of sunlight and shade, the dark red soil, which was broken into great dusty clods, stretched wide to a tall horizon. Trees marked the course of the valley; a stream of rich green grass the road.

His eyes travelled homewards along this road until he saw his grand-daughter swinging on the gate underneath a frangipani tree. Her hair fell down her back in a wave of sunlight, and her long bare legs repeated the angles of the frangipani stems, bare, shining-brown stems among patterns of pale blossoms.

She was gazing past the pink flowers, past the railway cottage where they lived, along the road to the village.

His mood shifted. He deliberately held out his wrist for the bird to take flight, and caught it again at the moment it spread its wings. He felt the plump shape strive and strain under his fingers; and, in a sudden access of troubled spite, shut the bird into a small box and fastened the bolt. 'Now you stay there,' he muttered; and turned his back on the shelf of birds. He moved warily along the hedge, stalking his grand-daughter, who was now looped over the gate, her head loose on her arms, singing. The light happy sound mingled with the crooning of the birds, and his anger mounted.

'Hey!' he shouted; saw her jump, look back, and abandon the gate. Her eyes veiled themselves, and she said in a pert neutral voice: 'Hullo, Grandad.' Politely she moved towards him, after a lingering backward glance at the road.

'Waiting for Steven, hey?' he said, his fingers curling like claws into his palm.

'Any objection?' she asked lightly, refusing to look at him.

He confronted her, his eyes narrowed, shoulders hunched, tight in a hard knot of pain which included the preening birds, the sunlight, the flowers. He said: 'Think you're old enough to go courting, hey?'

The girl tossed her head at the old-fashioned phrase and sulked, 'Oh, Grandad!'

'Think you want to leave home, hey? Think you can go running around the fields at night?'

Her smile made him see her, as he had every evening of this warm end-of-summer month, swinging hand in hand along the road to the village with that red-handed, red-throated, violent-bodied youth, the son of the postmaster. Misery went to his head and he shouted angrily: 'I'll tell your mother!'

'Tell away!' she said, laughing, and went back to the gate.

He heard her singing, for him to hear:

> *'I've got you under my skin,*
> *I've got you deep in the heart of . . .'*

'Rubbish,' he shouted. 'Rubbish. Impudent little bit of rubbish!'

Growling under his breath he turned towards the dove-cote, which was his refuge from the house he shared with his daughter and her husband and their children. But now the house would be empty. Gone all the young girls with their laughter and their squabbling and their teasing. He would be left, uncherished and alone, with that square-fronted, calm-eyed woman, his daughter.

He stooped, muttering, before the dovecote, resenting the absorbed cooing birds.

From the gate the girl shouted: 'Go and tell! Go on, what are you waiting for?'

Obstinately he made his way to the house, with quick, pathetic persistent glances of appeal back at her. But she never looked around. Her defiant but anxious young body stung him into love and repentance. He stopped. 'But I never meant . . .' he muttered, waiting for her to turn and run to him. 'I didn't mean . . .'

She did not turn. She had forgotten him. Along the road came the young man Steven, with something in his hand. A present for her? The old man stiffened as he watched the gate swing back, and the couple embrace. In the brittle shadows of the frangipani tree his grand-daughter, his darling, lay in the arms of the postmaster's son, and her hair flowed back over his shoulder.

'I see you!' shouted the old man spitefully. They did not move. He stumped into the little whitewashed house, hearing the wooden veranda creak angrily under his feet. His daughter was sewing in the front room, threading a needle held to the light.

He stopped again, looking back into the garden. The couple were now sauntering among the bushes, laughing. As he watched he saw the girl escape from the youth with a sudden mischievous movement, and run off through the flowers with him in pursuit. He heard shouts, laughter, a scream, silence.

'But it's not like that at all,' he muttered miserably. 'It's not like that. Why can't you see? Running and giggling, and kissing and kissing. You'll come to something quite different.'

He looked at his daughter with sardonic hatred, hating himself. They were caught and finished, both of them, but the girl was still running free.

'Can't you *see*?' he demanded of his invisible grand-daughter, who was at that moment lying in the thick green grass with the postmaster's son.

His daughter looked at him and her eyebrows went up in tired forbearance.

'Put your birds to bed?' she asked, humouring him.

'Lucy,' he said urgently. 'Lucy . . .'

'Well, what is it now?'

'She's in the garden with Steven.'

'Now you just sit down and have your tea.'

He stumped his feet alternatively, thump, thump, on the hollow wooden floor and shouted: 'She'll marry him. I'm telling you, she'll be marrying him next!'

His daughter rose swiftly, brought him a cup, set him a plate.

'I don't want any tea. I don't want it, I tell you.'

'Now, now,' she crooned. 'What's wrong with it? Why not?'

'She's eighteen. Eighteen!'

'I was married at seventeen and I never regretted it.'

'Liar,' he said. 'Liar. Then you should regret it. Why do you make your girls marry? It's you who do it. What do you do it for? Why?'

'The other three have done fine. They've three fine husbands. Why not Alice?'

'She's the last,' he mourned. 'Can't we keep her a bit longer?'

'Come, now, dad. She'll be down the road, that's all. She'll be here every day to see you.'

'But it's not the same.' He thought of the other three girls, transformed inside a few months from charming petulant spoiled children into serious young matrons.

'You never did like it when we married,' she said. 'Why not? Every time, it's the same. When I got married you made me feel like it was something wrong. And my girls the same. You get them all crying and miserable the way you go on. Leave Alice alone. She's happy.' She sighed, letting her eyes linger on the sunlit garden. 'She'll marry next month. There's no reason to wait.'

'You've said they can marry?' he said incredulously.

'Yes, dad, why not?' she said coldly, and took up her sewing.

His eyes stung, and he went out on to the veranda. Wet spread down over his chin and he took out a handkerchief and mopped his whole face. The garden was empty.

From around the corner came the young couple; but their faces were no longer set against him. On the wrist of the postmaster's son balanced a young pigeon, the light gleaming on its breast.

'For me?' said the old man, letting the drops shake off his chin. 'For me?'

'Do you like it?' The girl grabbed his hand and swung on it. 'It's for you, Grandad. Steven brought it for you.' They hung about him, affectionate, concerned, trying to charm away his wet eyes and his misery. They took his arms and directed him to the shelf of birds, one on each side, enclosing him, petting him, saying worldlessly that nothing would be changed, nothing could change, and that they would be with him always. The bird was proof of it, they said, from their lying happy eyes, as they thrust it on him. 'There, Grandad, it's yours. It's for you.'

They watched him as he held it on his wrist, stroking its soft, sun-warmed back, watching the wings lift and balance.

'You must shut it up for a bit,' said the girl intimately. 'Until it knows this is its home.'

'Teach your grandmother to suck eggs,' growled the old man.

Released by his half-deliberate anger, they fell back, laughing at him. 'We're glad you like it.' They moved off, now serious and full of purpose, to the gate, where they hung, backs to him, talking quietly. More than anything could, their grown-up seriousness shut him out, making him alone; also, it quietened him, took the sting out of their tumbling like puppies on the grass. They had forgotten him again. Well, so they should, the old man reassured himself, feeling his throat clotted with tears, his lips trembling. He held the new bird to his face, for the caress of its silken feathers. Then he shut it in a box and took out his favourite.

'Now you can go,' he said aloud. He held it poised, ready for flight, while he looked down the garden towards the boy and the girl. Then, clenched in the pain of loss, he lifted the bird on his wrist, and watched it soar. A whirr and a spatter of wings, and a cloud of birds rose into the evening from the dovecote.

At the gate Alice and Steven forgot their talk and watched the birds.

On the veranda, that woman, his daughter, stood gazing, her eyes shaded with a hand that still held her sewing.

It seemed to the old man that the whole afternoon had stilled to watch his gesture of self-command, that even the leaves of the trees had stopped shaking.

Dry-eyed and calm, he let his hands fall to his sides and stood erect, staring up into the sky.

The cloud of shining silver birds flew up and up, with a shrill cleaving of wings, over the dark ploughed land and the darker belts of trees and the bright folds of grass, until they floated high in the sunlight, like a cloud of motes of dust.

They wheeled in a wide circle, tilting their wings so there was flash after flash of light, and one after another they dropped from the sunshine of the upper sky to shadow, one after another, returning to the shadowed earth over trees and grass and field, returning to the valley and the shelter of night.

The garden was all a fluster and a flurry of returning birds. Then silence, and the sky was empty.

The old man turned, slowly, taking his time; he lifted his eyes to smile proudly down the garden at his granddaughter. She was staring at him. She did not smile. She was wide-eyed, and pale in the cold shadow, and he saw the tears run shivering off her face.

ELSPETH DAVIE

Pedestrian

A great patch of scoured and gravelly land at either end marked the approach to the motorway café. Beyond that were flat fields and a long horizon line broken here and there by distant clumps of trees. At no point on this line was there a sign of building. A glass-sided, covered bridge joined the car park to the café, and people if they wished could stand in the middle and look down onto the road below. The four lanes of the motorway carried every sort of traffic. The long vehicles were the most spectacular and there was no limit to their loads – lorries carrying sugar and cement and tanks of petrol went past, carrying building cranes and wooden planks, barrels of beer, cylinders of gas, sheep and horses, bulls in boxes, hens, furniture and parts of aeroplanes. There were lorries carrying cars and lorries carrying lorries.

The café itself was filled day and night with a periodic inrush of people and changed its whole appearance from half-hour to half-hour throughout the twenty-four. It had its empty time and its time of chaos. Habitual tough travellers of the road mixed here with couples stopping for the first time for morning coffee. Here buses disgorged football fans and concert parties, and stuffed family cars laboriously unloaded parents, children, grandparents, for their evening meal. The cars far outnumbered other vehicles. And no pedestrian, as opposed to hitchhiker, was ever seen here, for it would be nearly impossible to arrive by foot. Any person unattached to a vehicle was as unlikely as a being dropped from the skies. There was no place for him on the motorway.

Nevertheless there were still pedestrians in everyday life.

A married couple who were queueing at the counter of this café one evening found themselves standing beside a man who admitted to being one himself. The couple had been discussing car mileage with one another and they kindly brought him into it. 'And how about you?' asked the wife. 'How much have you done?' The other smiled but said nothing. He had obviously missed out on their discussion, and she didn't repeat the question. From his blank look she might have just as easily been asking how much time he had done in jail. Behind the counter a woman with a long-armed trowel was shovelling chips from a shelf, while her companion dredged up sausages from a trough of cooling fat. 'Sorry,' said the man suddenly, 'I didn't pick you up just now. No. I'm not in a car. I'm in the bus out there. Long distance to Liverpool.'

'Good idea,' said the woman's husband. 'Good idea to leave it at home once in a while. No fun on the roads these days. No fun at all!'

'No, I haven't got a car.'

'You don't run one?'

'No, never had one.'

'Then you're probably a lot luckier than the rest of us,' said the man after only the slightest pause, at the same time giving him a quick look up and down. He saw a well set-up fellow, well-dressed and about his own age. Not a young man. This look, however, cost him an outsize scoopful of thick, unwanted gravy on his plate. He slid cautiously on towards a bucket of bright peas. His wife, who had kept her eye on her plate, now bent forward and asked politely: 'Have you ever thought about it?'

'Thought about . . . ?'

'Getting one.'

'No, I can't say I have.'

The woman nodded wisely, blending in a bit of compassion in case there was some good reason for it – a physical or even a mental defect. For a moment the hiss of descending orange and lemonade prevented further talk. The three

170

moved across to a table which had just been vacated by the window. From this point they had a straight view of the bridge and a glimpse of the road beneath. Every now and then, in the momentary silence of noisy places, they could hear the regular swish of passing traffic. On the far side of the bridge glittering ranks of cars filled one end of the parking space with lorries at the other. Long red-and-green buses were waiting near an exit for their passengers.

'You don't mind if I go ahead?' said the man on the bus. 'There's only twenty minutes or so to eat.'

'No, go right on. Don't wait for us,' said the woman. The couple were occupied with some problem about the engine of their car and the unfamiliar sound it had been making for ten miles back. They discussed what kind of sound – tick or rattle or thump – and with almost musicianlike exactitude queried the type of beat – regular or irregular? There was the question of whether to look into it themselves, have it looked into or go straight on. Even now they were careful to include the other in the talk in case he should feel left out. They let him into the endless difficulties of parking, of visiting friends in narrow streets, or of visiting friends in any street, wide or narrow, because of the meter. They told him how much for twenty minutes, how much for forty minutes, how much if you were to talk for an hour. They discussed the price of petrol and of garage repairs and the horrors of breakdown on the road.

'And the hard shoulder can be a very lonely place on the motorway,' said the woman. 'All those cars rushing past you. Have you ever had to pull over yourself?'

'No, I haven't,' the man said, with a hint of apology in his voice.

'Oh no, no – of course you haven't! I absolutely forgot for the moment that you haven't got . . . Excuse me. I am being so stupid.'

The man said no, there was nothing to excuse. It was easy to forget. He added that the hard shoulder did indeed sound a very unsympathetic place to rest on in the night.

The three of them had now finished their first course and had turned towards the door to watch the next group entering. Half a dozen families were coming in, and a carload of men carrying trumpets. Two policemen were moving slowly about among the tables. At the far end of the room a waitress was mopping up the floor where someone had let a plate slide from a tray. The policemen bent and spoke to a man at a table, then sat down, one on either side of him while he put ketchup on a last wedge of steak pie and ate it with seeming relish. The three of them left the café together. 'This is where you find them,' remarked the car-owner to his wife and the passenger from the bus. They had now started on their squares of yellow sponge cake with a custard layer between. The custard too had been sliced into neat and solid squares, and their plates when they had finished were as dry and clean as when they had started. 'One job less for the staff, I suppose,' said the husband examining his dish with distrust.

The other man – seeing they had confided in him – began to tell them what it felt like to walk along the edge of an ordinary country road while the cars went by. The husband looked vaguely aside. It was not a believable thing for a grown man to do and he did not hear it beyond the first sentence. But the woman said: 'You mean hitch-hiking?'

'No, no – just getting about from one place to another, sometimes by bus and train, naturally, and sometimes walking.'

'As a pedestrian?'

'Yes, I suppose so. In cities naturally one walks a good deal.'

'Yes, I see – a pedestrian,' said the woman, looking at him with a vague interest.

Her husband had now brought coffee for the three of them and the man drank his quickly, for the time was up.

'I'm sorry to rush,' he said, 'but the bus leaves in eight minutes, and they don't wait long. Thanks for the coffee – and a very good journey!'

'And the same to you!' They watched him go, weaving between the tables, and a few minutes later saw him hurrying down the glass bridge and starting to run as he reached the far end.

'A pedestrian,' murmured the woman musingly.

'Well, a bus-traveller.'

'But he tells me he walks a lot of the time, in country as well as city.'

After a while her husband looked at his watch. 'Shall we get on then?'

'Might as well. We can take our time.' They wandered slowly away from the windows, looking back to see one of the buses moving off. '*His* bus, I expect,' said the woman. 'Careful and don't slip on that chip,' she added as they passed the spot where the plate had fallen.

The glass bridge over the motorway was the only viewing-point for miles. The man and woman paused in the middle and looked down onto the great streams below. Four or five chains of long vehicles happened to be coming up on one side with a second line going down on the other. Great grey roofs slid beneath them in opposition like extra roads moving along on top of the others. At this time of day the cars too were coming one after the other with scarcely a second between them, and – seen from above – scarcely an inch.

'I can't say I've met many non-drivers in my time,' said the man broodingly, 'but there's usually a perfect legitimate reason for it. Certainly not money in his case though.'

'Physical disablement, maybe,' said his wife. 'Remember Harry Ewing. *He* didn't drive. He had one short leg.'

'You'd never have known. Anyway, with all the dash-board gadgets these days, what's a short leg, or arm for that matter?'

'Some people have bad eyes,' suggested the woman.

'Funny thing, but I've seen cross-eyed people driving about and nobody stopped them yet. And as for one eye at the wheel – that's common enough, believe me!'

Watchers on the bridge, or any persons not in a hurry, invariably attracted others. Something about the static bridge, sealed in above the speed, made company acceptable. So, before long, the two who had been standing there found that another couple had joined them – a man in a blue summer jacket and his wife in a cream coat. For a while the four of them stood comfortably together, silently watching. Then the first man said, 'My wife and I were speaking about non-drivers – their reasons, I mean, for not having a car. Most disabilities can be overcome, you know.'

'Maybe it's nerves,' said the man in the blue jacket. 'Or more likely psychological.'

'You mean,' said his wife, 'like that woman who'd never let her boy touch a machine – not even a child's scooter. So he never had a car all his life, not even when she was dead. Well, I suppose he loved his mother.'

'Well, I've heard that story the other way,' said her husband. 'His mother *wants* him to own this super-car since ever he opened his eyes. Nagged him all his life. And he won't do it, not even when she's dead.'

'Sure,' said the other man, 'because he *doesn't* love his mother.'

They turned and sauntered slowly along the bridge together like old acquaintances, looking down at the motorway to the left and right of them as though it was still a long, long way off.

'That man in the café – maybe he just didn't want one,' said the first wife. Her husband looked aside again with his vague and unbelieving smile. The four of them now seemed reluctant to reach the end of the bridge. They began to walk more and more slowly as they neared the opening. In front the great gravelled space was, if anything, more closely packed than ever – some cars edging out, others slowly burrowing in like beetles into hidden corners. The two couples paused and stared intently at this space, searching for their own. 'Well, nice to have met you,' they said to one another, 'very nice indeed to have the pleasure . . .' For one more moment they hesitated on the sloping ramp of the bridge. An overpowering whiff of loneliness reached them from the fumy air beyond. Then they stepped down and out into the narrow lanes between the cars and the glittering maze of metal divided them.

Who Killed Baker?

Wakefield was attending a series of philosophy lectures at London University, and for the past ten minutes his fellow-guests at Haldane's had been mutely enduring a *précis* of the lecturer's main contentions.

'What it amounts to, then,' said Wakefield, towards what they hoped was the close of his peroration, 'is that philosophy deals not so much with the answers to questions about Man and the Universe as with the problem of *what questions may properly be asked*. Improper questions' – here a little man named Fielding, whom no one knew very well, choked suddenly over his port and had to be led out – 'improper questions can only confuse the issue. And it's this aspect of philosophy which in my opinion defines its superiority to other studies, such as – such as' – Wakefield's eye lighted on Gervase Fen, who was stolidly cracking walnuts opposite – 'such as, well, criminology, for instance.'

Fen roused himself.

'Improper questions,' he said reflectively. 'I remember a case which illustrates very clearly how—'

'Defines,' Wakefield repeated at a higher pitch, 'it's superiority to—'

But at this point, Haldane, perceiving that much more of Wakefield on epistemology would certainly bring the party to a premature end, contrived adroitly to upset his port into Wakefield's lap, and in the mêlée which ensued it proved possible to detach the conversational initiative from Wakefield and confer it on Fen.

'*Who killed Baker?*' With this rather abrupt query Fen established a foothold while Wakefield was still scrubbing ineffectually at his damp trousers with a handkerchief. 'The situation which resulted in Baker's death wasn't in itself specially complicated or obscure, and in consequence the case was solved readily enough.'

'Yes, it would be, of course,' said Wakefield sourly, 'if you were solving it.'

'Oh, but I wasn't.' Fen shook his head decisively, and Wakefield, shifting about uncomfortably in the effort to remove wet barathea from contact with his skin, glowered at him. 'The case was solved by a very able Detective Inspector of the County CID, by name Casby, and it was from him that I heard of it, quite recently, while we were investigating the death of that Swiss schoolmaster at Cotten Abbas. As nearly as I can, I'll tell it to you the way he told me. And I ought to warn you in advance that it's a case in which the mode of telling is important – as important, probably, as the thing told. . . .

'At the time of his death Baker was about forty-five, a self-important little man with very black, heavily-brilliantined hair, an incipient paunch, dandified clothes, and a twisted bruiser's nose which was the consequence not of pugnacity but of a fall from a bicycle in youth. He was not, one gathers, at all a pleasing personality, and he had crowned his dislikeable qualities by marrying, and subsequently bullying, a wife very much younger and more attractive than himself. For a reason which the sequel will make obvious, there's not much evidence as to the form this bullying took, but it was real enough – no question about that – and three years of it drove the wretched woman, more for consolation than for passion, into the arms of the chauffeur, a gloomy, sallow young man named Arnold Snow. Since Snow had never read D. H. Lawrence, his chief emotion in the face of Mary Baker's advances was simple surprise, and to do him justice, he seems never to have made the smallest attempt to capitalize his position in any of the obvious ways.

But, of course, the neighbours talked; there are precedents enough for such a relationship's ending in disaster.'

Haldane nodded. 'Rattenbury,' he suggested, 'and Stoner.'

'That sort of thing, yes. It wasn't a very sensible course for Mary Baker to adopt, the more so as for religious reasons she had a real horror of divorce. But she was one of those warm, good-natured, muddle-headed women – not, in temperament, unlike Mrs Rattenbury – to whom a man's affection is overwhelmingly necessary, as much for emotional as for physical reasons; and three years of Baker had starved that side of her so effectively that when she did break out, she broke out with a vengeance. I've seen a photograph of her, and can tell you that she was rather a big woman (though not fat), as dark as her husband or her lover, with a large mouth and eyes, and a Rubensish figure. Why she married Baker in the first place I really can't make out. He was well-to-do – or, anyway, seemed so – but Mary was the sort of woman to whom money quite genuinely means nothing; and oddly enough, Snow seems to have been as indifferent to it as she.

'Baker was a manufacturer. His factory just outside Twelford made expensive model toys – ships, aeroplanes, cars, and so forth. The demand for such things is strictly limited – people who know the value of money very properly hesitate before spending fifteen guineas on a toy which their issue are liable to sit on, or drop into a pond, an hour later – and when Philip Eckerson built a factory in Ruislip for producing the same sort of thing, only more cheaply, Baker's profits dropped with some abruptness to rather less than half what they'd been before. So for five years there was a price-war – a price-war beneficial to the country's nurseries, but ruinous to Baker and Eckerson alike. When eventually they met, to arrange a merger, both of them were close to bankruptcy.

'It was on 10 March of this year they met – not on neutral territory, but in Baker's house at Twelford, where Eckerson was to stay the night. Eckerson was an albino, which is uncommon, but apart from that the only remarkable thing about him was obstinacy, and since he confined this trait to business, the impression he made on Mary Baker during his visit to her house was in every respect colourless. She was aware, in a vague, general way, that he was her husband's business rival, but she bore him not the least malice on that account; and as to Snow, the mysteries of finance were beyond him, and from first to last he never understood how close to the rocks his employer's affairs had drifted. In any case, neither he nor Mary Baker had much attention to spare for Eckerson, because an hour or two before Eckerson arrived Baker summoned the pair of them to his study, informed them that he knew of their liaison, and stated that he would take steps immediately to obtain a divorce.

'It's doubtful, I think, if he really intended to do anything of the kind. He didn't sack Snow, he didn't order his wife out of the house, and apparently he had no intention of leaving the house himself – all of which would amount, in law, to condoning his wife's adultery and nullifying the suit. No, he was playing cat-and-mouse, that was all; he knew his wife's horror of divorce, and wished quite simply to make her miserable for as long as the pretence of proceedings could be kept up; but neither Mary nor Snow had the wit to see that he was duping them for his own pleasure, and they assumed in consequence that he meant every word he said. Mary became hysterical – in which condition she confided her obsession about divorce to Snow. And Snow, a remarkably naïve and impressionable young man, took it all *au grand sérieux*. He had not, up to now, displayed any notable animus against Baker, but Mary's terror and wretchedness fanned hidden fires, and from then on he was implacable. They were a rather pitiful pair, these two young people cornered by an essentially rather trivial issue, but their very ignorance made them dangerous, and if Baker had had more sense he'd never have played such an imbecile trick on them. Psychologically, he was certainly in a morbid condition, for apparently he was prepared to let the relationship go on, provided he could indulge his sadistic instincts in this weird and preposterous fashion. What the end of it all would have been, if death hadn't intervened, one doesn't, of course, know.

'Well, in due course Eckerson arrived, and Mary entertained him as well as her emotional condition would allow, and he sat up with Baker till the small hours, talking business. The two men antagonized one another from the start; and the more they talked, the more remote did the prospect of a merger become, until in the latter stages all hope of it vanished, and they went to their beds on the very worst of terms, with nothing better to look forward to than an extension of their present cut-throat competition, and eventual ruin. You'd imagine that self-interest would be strong enough, in a case like that, to compel them to some sort of agreement, but it wasn't – and of course the truth of the matter is that each was hoping that, if competition continued, the other would crack first, leaving a clear field. So they parted on the landing with mutual, and barely concealed, ill-will; and the house slept.

'The body was discovered shortly after nine next morning, and the discoverer was Mrs Blaine, the cook. Unlike Snow, who lived in, Mrs Blaine had a bed-sitting-room in the town; and it was as she was making her way round to the back door of Baker's house, to embark on the day's duties, that she glanced in at the drawing-room window and saw the gruesome object which lay in shadow on the hearth-rug. Incidentally, you mustn't waste any of your energy suspecting Mrs Blaine of the murder; I can assure you she had nothing to do with it, and I can assure you, too, that her evidence, for what little it was worth, was the truth, the whole truth, and nothing but the truth. . . .

'Mrs Blaine looked in at the window, and her first thought, to use her own words, "was that 'e'd fainted". But the streaks of blood on the corpse's hair disabused her of this notion without much delay, and she hurried indoors to rouse the household. Well, in due course Inspector Casby arrived, and in due course assembled such evidence as there was. The body lay prone on a rug soaked with dark venous blood, and the savage cut which had severed the internal jugular vein had obviously come from behind, and been wholly unexpected. Nearby, and innocent of fingerprints, lay the sharp kitchen knife which had done the job. Apart from these things, there was no clue.

'No clue, that is, of a positive sort. But there *had* been an amateurish attempt to make the death look like a consequence of burglary – or rather, to be more accurate, of housebreaking. The pane of a window had been broken, with the assistance of flypaper to prevent the fragments from scattering, and a number of valuables were missing. But the breakfast period is not a time usually favoured by thieves, there were no footprints or marks of any kind on the damp lawn and flower bed beneath the broken window (which was not, by the way, the window through which Mrs Blaine had looked, but another, at right angles to it, on a different side of the house), and finally – and in Inspector Casby's opinion, most conclusive of all – one of the objects missing was a tiny but very valuable bird-study by the Chinese emperor Hui Tsung, which Baker, no connoisseur or collector of such things, had inherited from a great-uncle. The ordinary thief, Casby argued, would scarcely give a Chinese miniature a second glance, let alone remove it. No, the burglary was bogus; and unless you postulated an implausibly sophisticated double-bluff, then the murder had been done by one of the three people sleeping in the house. As to motive – well, you know all about that already; and one way and another it didn't take Inspector Casby more than 24 hours to make his arrest.'

Somewhat grudgingly, Fen relinquished the walnuts and applied himself to stuffed dates instead. His mouth full, he looked at the company expectantly; and with equal expectancy the company looked back at him. It was Wakefield who broke the silence.

'But that can't be *all*,' he protested.

'Certainly it's all,' said Fen. 'I've told you the story as Inspector Casby told it to me, and I now repeat the question he asked me at the end of it – and which I was able to answer, by the way: *Who killed Baker?*'

Wakefield stared mistrustfully. 'You've left something out.'

'Nothing, I assure you. If anything, I've been rather more generous with clues than Inspector Casby was. But if you still have no idea who killed Baker, I'll give you another hint: he died at 9 a.m. Does that help?'

They thought about this. Apparently it didn't help in the least.

'All right,' Wakefield said sulkily at last. 'We give up. Who killed Baker?'

And Fen replied blandly, 'The public executioner killed him – after he had been tried and convicted for the murder of Eckerson.'

For a moment Wakefield sat like one stupefied; then he emitted a howl of rage. 'Unfair!' he shouted, banging on the table. 'Trickery!'

'Not at all.' Fen was unperturbed. 'It's a trick story, admittedly, but you were given ample warning of that. It arose out of a discussion about the propriety of asking certain questions; and there was only one question – *Who killed Baker?* – which I asked. What's more, I emphasized at the outset that the mode of telling was as important as the thing told.

'But quite apart from all that, you had your clue. Mrs Blaine, looking in through a window at a figure lying in shadow, concluded that violence had been done for the reason that she saw blood on the hair. Now that blood, as I mentioned, was dark venous blood; and I mentioned also that Baker had black, heavily-brilliantined hair. Is it conceivable that dark blood would be *visible* on such hair – visible, that is, when the body was in shadow and the observer outside the window of the room in which it lay? Of course not. Therefore, the body was not Baker's. But it couldn't have been Mary Baker's, or Snow's, since they too were black-haired – and that leaves only Eckerson. Eckerson was an albino, which means that his hair was white; and splotches of blood would show up on white hair all right – even though it was in shadow, and Mrs Blaine some distance away. Who, then, would want to kill Eckerson? Baker, obviously, and Baker alone – I emphasized that both Snow and Mary were quite indifferent to the visitor. And who, after the arrest, would be likely to kill (notice, please, that I never at any time said 'murder') Baker? There's only one possible answer to that. . . .'

'And what happened to the wife?' Haldane asked. 'Did she marry Snow?'

'No. He melted,' said Fen complacently, 'away. She married someone else, though, and according to Inspector Casby is very happy now. Baker's and Eckerson's businesses both collapsed under heavy debts, and no longer exist.'

There was a pause; then: 'The nature of existence,' said Wakefield suddenly, 'has troubled philosophers in all ages. What are the sensory and mental processes which cause us to assert that this table, for instance, is *real*? The answer given by the subjective idealists—'

'Will have to wait,' said Haldane firmly, 'till we meet again.' He pushed back his chair. 'Let's go and see what the women are up to, shall we?'

GEORGE MACKAY BROWN
The Wireless Set

The first wireless ever to come to the valley of Tronvik in
Orkney was brought by Howie Eunson, son of Hugh the
fisherman and Betsy.

Howie had been at the whaling in the Antarctic all winter,
and he arrived back in Britain in April with a stuffed wallet
and jingling pockets. Passing through Glasgow on his way
home he bought presents for everyone in Tronvik – fiddle-
strings for Sam down at the shore, a bottle of malt whisky for
Mansie of the hill, a secondhand volume of Spurgeon's
sermons for Mr Sinclair the missionary, sweeties for all the
bairns, a meerschaum pipe for his father Hugh and a portable wireless set for his mother Betsy.

There was great excitement the night Howie arrived home
in Tronvik. Everyone in the valley – men, women, children,
dogs, cats – crowded into the but-end of the croft, as Howie
unwrapped and distributed his gifts.

'And have you been a good boy all the time you've been
away?' said Betsy anxiously. 'Have you prayed every night,
and not sworn?'

'This is thine, mother,' said Howie, and out of a big cardboard box he lifted the portable wireless and set it on the
table.

For a full two minutes nobody said a word. They all stood
staring at it, making small round noises of wonderment, like
pigeons.

'And mercy,' said Betsy at last, 'what is it at all?'

'It's a wireless set,' said Howie proudly. 'Listen.'

He turned a little black knob and a posh voice came out of

the box saying that it would be a fine day tomorrow over England, and over Scotland south of the Forth–Clyde valley, but that in the Highlands and in Orkney and Shetland there would be rain and moderate westerly winds.

'If it's a man that's speaking', said old Hugh doubtfully, 'where is he standing just now?'

'In London,' said Howie.

'Well now,' said Betsy, 'if that isn't a marvel! But I'm not sure, all the same, but what it isn't against the scriptures. Maybe, Howie, we'd better not keep it.'

'Everybody in the big cities has a wireless,' said Howie. 'Even in Kirkwall and Hamnavoe every house has one. But now Tronvik has a wireless as well, and maybe we're not such clodhoppers as they think.'

They all stayed late, listening to the wireless. Howie kept twirling a second little knob, and sometimes they would hear music and sometimes they would hear a kind of loud half-witted voice urging them to use a particular brand of tooth-paste.

At half past eleven the wireless was switched off and everybody went home. Hugh and Betsy and Howie were left alone.

'Men speak,' said Betsy, 'but it's hard to know sometimes whether what they say is truth or lies.'

'This wireless speaks the truth,' said Howie.

Old Hugh shook his head. 'Indeed,' he said, 'it doesn't do that. For the man said there would be rain here and a westerly wind. But I assure you it'll be a fine day, and a southerly wind, and if the Lord spares me I'll get to the lobsters.'

Old Hugh was right. Next day was fine, and he and Howie took twenty lobsters from the creels he had under the Gray Head.

It was in the spring of the year 1939 that the first wireless set came to Tronvik. In September that same year war broke out, and Howie and three other lads from the valley joined the minesweepers.

That winter the wireless standing on Betsy's table became the centre of Tronvik. Every evening folk came from the crofts to listen to the nine o'clock news. Hitherto the wireless had been a plaything which discoursed Scottish reels and constipation advertisements and unreliable weather forecasts. But now the whole world was embattled and Tronvik listened appreciatively to enthusiastic commentators telling them that General Gamelin was the greatest soldier of the century, and he had only to say the word for the German Siegfried Line to crumble like sand. In the summer of 1940 the western front flared into life, and then suddenly no more was heard of General Gamelin. First it was General Weygand who was called the heir of Napoleon, and then a few days later Marshal Petain.

France fell all the same, and old Hugh turned to the others and said, 'What did I tell you? You can't believe a word it says.'

One morning they saw a huge grey shape looming along the horizon, making for Scapa Flow. 'Do you ken the name of that warship?' said Mansie of the hill. 'She's the *Ark Royal*, an aircraft carrier.'

That same evening Betsy twiddled the knob of the wireless and suddenly an impudent voice came drawling out. The voice was saying that German dive bombers had sunk the *Ark Royal* in the Mediterranean. 'Where is the *Ark Royal*?' went the voice in an evil refrain. 'Where is the *Ark Royal*? Where is the *Ark Royal*?'

'That man,' said Betsy 'must be the Father of Lies.'

Wasn't the *Ark Royal* safely anchored in calm water on the other side of the hill?

Thereafter the voice of Lord Haw-Haw cast a spell on the inhabitants of Tronvik. The people would rather listen to him than to anyone, he was such a great liar. He had a kind of bestial joviality about him that at once repelled and fascinated them; just as, for opposite reasons, they had been repelled and fascinated to begin with by the rapturous ferocity of Mr Sinclair's Sunday afternoon sermons, but had grown quite pleased with them in time.

They never grew pleased with William Joyce, Lord Haw-Haw. Yet every evening found them clustered round the portable radio, like awed children round a hectoring schoolmaster.

'Do you know,' said Sam of the shore one night, 'I think that man will come to a bad end?'

Betsy was frying bloody-puddings over a primus stove, and the evil voice went on and on against a background of hissing, sputtering, roaring and a medley of rich succulent smells.

Everyone in the valley was there that night. Betsy had made some new ale and the first bottles were being opened. It was good stuff, right enough; everybody agreed about that.

Now the disembodied voice paused, and turned casually to a new theme, the growing starvation of the people of Britain. The food ships were being sunk one after the other by the heroic U-boats. Nothing was getting through, nothing, nor a cornstalk from Saskatchewan nor a tin of pork from Chicago. Britain was starving. The war would soon be over. Then there would be certain pressing accounts to meet. The ships were going down. Last week the Merchant Navy was poorer by a half million gross registered tons. Britain was starving –

At this point Betsy, who enjoyed her own ale more than anyone else, thrust the hissing frying pan under the nose – so to speak – of the wireless, so that its gleam was dimmed for a moment or two by a rich blue tangle of bloody-pudding fumes.

'Smell that, you brute,' cried Betsy fiercely, 'smell that!'

The voice went on, calm and vindictive.

'Do you ken,' said Hugh, 'he canna hear a word you're saying.'

'Can he not?' said Sandy Omand, turning his taurine head from one to the other. 'He canna hear?'

Sandy was a bit simple.

'No,' said Hugh, 'nor smell either.'

After that they switched off the wireless, and ate the bloody-puddings along with buttered bannocks, and drank more ale, and told stories that had nothing to do with war, till two o'clock in the morning.

One afternoon in the late summer of that year the island postman cycled over the hill road to Tronvik with a yellow corner of telegram sticking out of his pocket.

He passed the shop and the manse and the schoolhouse, and went in a wavering line up the track to Hugh's croft. The wireless was playing music inside, Joe Loss and his orchestra.

Betsy had seen him coming and was standing in the door.

'Is there anybody with you?' said the postman.

'What way would there be?' said Betsy. 'Hugh's at the lobsters.'

'There should be somebody with you,' said the postman.

'Give me the telegram,' said Betsy, and held out her hand. He gave it to her as if he was a miser parting with a twenty-pound note.

She went inside, put on her spectacles, and ripped open the envelope with brisk fingers. Her lips moved a little, silently reading the words.

Then she turned to the dog and said, 'Howie's dead.' She went to the door. The postman was disappearing on his bike round the corner of the shop and the missionary was hurrying towards her up the path.

She said to him, 'It's time the peats were carted.'

'This is a great affliction, you poor soul,' said Mr Sinclair the missionary. 'This is bad news indeed. Yet he died for his country. He made the great sacrifice. So that we could all live in peace, you understand.'

Betsy shook her head. 'That isn't it at all,' she said. 'Howie's sunk with torpedoes. That's all I know.'

They saw old Hugh walking up from the shore with a pile of creels on his back and a lobster in each hand. When he came to the croft he looked at Betsy and the missionary standing together in the door. He went into the outhouse and set down the creels and picked up an axe he kept for chopping wood.

Betsy said to him, 'How many lobsters did you get?'

He moved past her and the missionary without speaking into the house. Then from inside he said, 'I got two lobsters.'

'I'll break the news to him,' said Mr Sinclair.

From inside came the noise of shattering wood and metal.

'He knows already,' said Betsy to the missionary. 'Hugh knows the truth of a thing generally before a word is uttered.'

Hugh moved past them with the axe in his hand.

'I got six crabs forby,' he said to Betsy, 'but I left them in the boat.'

He set the axe down carefully inside the door of the out-house. Then he leaned against the wall and looked out to sea for a long while.

'I got thirteen eggs,' said Betsy. 'One more than yester-day. That old Rhode Islander's laying like mad.'

The missionary was slowly shaking his head in the door-way. He touched Hugh on the shoulder and said, 'My poor man –'

Hugh turned and said to him, 'It's time the last peats were down from the hill. I'll go in the morning first thing. You'll be needing a cart-load for the Manse.'

The missionary, awed by such callousness, walked down the path between the cabbages and potatoes. Betsy went into the house. The wireless stood, a tangled wreck, on the dresser. She brought from the cupboard a bottle of whisky and glasses. She set the kettle on the hook over the fire and broke the peats into red and yellow flames with a poker. Through the window she could see people moving towards the croft from all over the valley. The news had got round. The mourners were gathering.

Old Hugh stood in the door and looked up at the drift of clouds above the cliff. 'Yes,' he said, 'I'm glad I set the creels where I did, off Yesnaby. They'll be sheltered there once the wind gets up.'

'That white hen,' said Betsy, 'has stopped laying. It's time she was in the pot, if you ask me.'

FRANCIS KING
The Puppets

The old man, Kanjiro Fujiyama, lay huddled on a *tatami*-grass mat in a narrow room, lit only by a skylight, behind the stage of the 'Grand Salon' night-club. His mind hovering in that twilight between sleep and waking which it now increasingly inhabited, he from time to time muttered to himself, sighed, chuckled or emitted a stifled groan. His three assistants and his young second wife, playing a Japanese version of gin rummy, paid no attention to him. He was in his eighty-sixth year.

Periodically Haruko's peasant body, draped in a hand-woven silk kimono which the old man had chosen for her, jerked in rhythm to the music being blared out from the stage. Suddenly she jumped up, threw down her cards and began to twist before the three men. The youngest of the trio, a boy of seventeen, first scowled at her in disapproval behind his thick, heavy-rimmed glasses and then looked down in pretence of adjusting his *haori*, the half-length coat of heavy black silk which all the men were wearing; but the other two grinned their enthusiasm and clapped when she resumed her seat. Haruko, panting and flushed from the exertion, looked at the watch on her plump wrist: 'They're behind schedule,' she said.

A moment later the old man's son, Jun-ichiro, came in, dressed in the same heavy black silk. The upper part of his face shared his father's leonine good looks, but his mouth was small and petulant and his chin receded beneath it. 'Haven't they brought the beer yet?' he demanded.

'No,' the taller of the assistants replied.

'Not even the old man's tea,' Haruko said.

'Go and remind them,' Jun-ichiro ordered the young boy. 'Tell them we've waited for twenty minutes.'

'They have so many customers tonight,' the shortest of the assistants said.

'And what brought them here?' Jun-ichiro retorted. 'They've come here to see us. Haven't they?'

The old man stirred and then heaved himself up on to an elbow, his white hair and beard dishevelled and his face blotchy and damp with sweat. 'Where is my tea?' he asked fretfully.

'It's coming,' Haruko said.

'Coming, coming,' the old man repeated. 'Give me my pipe.'

'You must not smoke now,' Jun-ichiro said. 'It is bad for your breathing.'

'Do as I say. Give me my pipe. My pipe.'

Haruko and Jun-ichiro exchanged glances; then the girl jumped up and began to prepare the old man's Japanese pipe, packing it with tobacco which looked like nicotine-stained cotton wool.

'When do we begin?' the old man demanded, kicking off the blanket which covered his legs.

'Soon,' said Jun-ichiro.

'So much noise,' the old man said. 'What is all this noise? You must complain to the theatre manager.'

'This is not a theatre, *oji-san*,' the shorter assistant explained. 'Don't you remember? This is the "Grand Salon" night-club.' He spoke as to a child.

'The "Grand Salon" night-club!' Momentarily the old man was bewildered. Then he smiled, patting his knees with arthritic hands: 'Ah, yes. Yes. Of course. The night-club. For the first time we shall play Bunraku at a night-club.'

'For the first time in history,' Jun-ichiro said.

Haruko picked up the cards, shuffled them and began to set them out for telling her fortune. 'What are you asking the cards?' the taller assistant queried.

'Sh! Be quiet. Leave me alone. I must think hard.'

'About our journey to the West?'

'Possibly.'

After the music had come to an end, they were all so intent on listening to the voice of the *nisei* who announced each turn first in Japanese and then in English that they failed to notice that the young assistant had returned, carrying a tray which he proceeded to set down on a table in the corner. 'Just in time,' Jun-ichiro exclaimed, when eventually he saw him. He seized a glass of beer and gulped at it. 'Where's the master's tea?' he asked, his upper lip white with foam.

'Here you are, sir,' one of the waiters from the night-club, a pert youth whose glossy black hair made a beehive around his face, sang out as he flounced into the room and banged down the tea-tray.

'This way, this way!' the old man commanded, but the waiter pretended not to hear. 'Bring my tea over here to me.'

In the end it was the youthful assistant who poured out the tea and carried it to his master, going down on his knees, bowing deeply in respect, and watching him affectionately while he sucked and gulped with the noises, at once repellent and pitiful, of a baby at the bottle.

Soon the *nisei*, wearing a dinner-jacket and an extravagantly pleated and embroidered white dress-shirt above a purple cummerbund, appeared in the doorway. 'All ready?' he exploded his smile at them like a flashlight bulb, leaving them open-mouthed and blinking. 'Five minutes to go.' The band outside was playing 'Don't Step on my Blue Suede Shoes'; the singer was a male high-school student in levis and sweatshirt, a crucifix dangling around his scrawny neck and the emaciated fingers of his left hand clicking noiselessly in time to the music.

'Come along, *oji-san!*'

The young assistant and Haruko began between them to drag the old man to his feet and to support him out of the room. Haruko was humming to the music from the stage and as she gripped the old man's arm with her right hand, the fingers of her own left hand were also rhythmically clicking.

Barbara James and her friend Enid Weatherby belonged to that species of elderly American women, philanthropic and cultivated, which so often becomes the butt of undeserved mockery in Europe. Barbara's husband, a company president, had dropped dead of a heart-attack two years before, leaving her childless and rich. Enid had recently been forced by ill-health to retire from the post of senior Teacher of Classics at the same Women's College at which the two of them had first met some forty years before. They were now consoling each other on a Far Eastern tour at Barbara's expense.

The pert waiter had just attempted, unasked, to refill Enid's glass with Scotch; but she raised a small, freckled hand and shook her head. 'Maybe we should order something else,' she suggested nervously.

'Some fruit,' said Barbara.

'Fruit, yes madam, fruit.' The waiter whirled off, his silver tray high. Against fruit on the menu appeared no price but merely the words 'According to Season'; whatever the season, the price was invariably exhorbitant.

'Dreadful this noise,' Enid said.

'But if we hadn't taken this table out in front, we shouldn't be able to see the puppets. It's bad luck that they're not performing in a theatre. But I'm determined that you should see them.'

'Thank you, dear,' said Enid, who was feeling both exhausted and ill.

'This old man's marvellous. George and I saw him, oh, six or seven years ago. He was already eighty then, just imagine. He's been designated a National Cultural Treasure or Asset or Property or something like that.'

'Well, isn't that pretty!' The fruit, set down by the waiter on a huge silver platter, had been cut with the most delicate artistry. Bananas had become fish, with pistachio nuts for the eyes; oranges had blossomed into roses; apples were pigs – or were they dogs? 'It seems a shame actually to *eat* anything.'

Others had felt the same and much of the fruit had in fact come untouched from the tables of previous customers.

'So much artistry goes into their daily lives,' Barbara said. 'Beautiful.'

'You'll find these puppets a little odd at first, I imagine. There's no attempt to conceal the manipulators – except that they wear hoods over their faces. And even then the face of the chief manipulator is left uncovered.' Barbara, who enjoyed instructing her friend just as she enjoyed herself being instructed, went on to explain the two kinds of puppet – those not more than one foot high and those two-thirds of life size. 'We shall see the big ones.'

'And this is the first time this troop has appeared in a night-club?'

'This is the first time *any* troop has appeared in a night-club. Rather sad, really. They can't attract the spectators for a show lasting several hours in a theatre of their own. But as a turn between some German conjurors and an English strip-show – well, as you see, the place is full.'

The band, to Enid's relief, had momentarily stopped its din; but now it once again struck up, whining out the Japanese folk-song 'Soran bushi' at a funereal pace, as though it were a Blues. The *nisei* came forward, sleeked down his already sleek hair with both hands, cleared his throat and exploded his smile in all directions. Then he announced in English: 'Good evening, ladies and gentlemen – to those of you to whom I haven't had the privilege of saying good evening already. I hope that you're enjoying Osaka and this glorious weather of ours.' One or two people laughed and a few more smiled; the rainy season had already lasted for more than a month. 'Well, now we have something extra special for you – very Japanese, very high-class, very beautiful. I don't mean that those English ladies weren't very high-class and very beautiful, don't get me wrong –' he waited for the laugh which barely came – 'but, well, this is maybe a little more *cultural*. You've heard, I guess, of the famous Japanese puppets – or Bunraku, as we call them here. . . .' He spoke for several minutes to an increasingly restive audience, explaining first the history of the puppet theatre, then the history of the old man's troup, and finally the theme of the play 'Dojoji', which they were now going to witness. 'There's this young priest – his name is Anchin – and when he's travelling on a pilgrimage, he stays at a house where there's this young girl, and he – well, I guess that young people are the same the world over – he falls for the lovely Kiyohime. . . .'

Barbara glanced apprehensively at her friend. She wanted her to enjoy her first view of the Bunraku as much as she herself and George had enjoyed theirs, so many years ago; but might not this all-pervasive vulgarity spoil it for her even before it had started? As she thought this, she saw, with horror, that the eight girls billed outside the nightclub as 'The Grand Salon Gardenias' had begun to prance out in front of the curtain, four of them dressed as priests and four as women of the Heian period, to perform a dance which approximated no more closely to a folk-dance than the music of the orchestra approximated to the original 'Soran bushi'. Wagging their heads from side to side and raising their hands to the audience as though in a half-hearted attempt to halt oncoming traffic, they maintained fixed smiles on faces which reflected a macabre greenish pallor from the lights overhead. Enid's face had the same pallor; Barbara supposed, wrongly, that her own had it too.

After the girls had twirled off to either side of the stage the five musicians for the Bunraku filed self-consciously on to a platform specially erected for them over what was, on other nights, a small bar. They cleared their throats, mopped at their faces and necks with handkerchiefs drawn out of the recesses of their voluminous Japanese clothes, and exchanged whispers and nervous giggles. Barbara explained the role of each to Enid; she had made a study of the

Japanese theatre. Enid smiled and nodded and directed her quick, bird-like glances from one performer to another; but all this brisk interest was merely the automatism of habit and in fact she felt a deadly weariness, not merely of the flesh and bones but of the spirit itself.

Kanjiro Fujiyama, the old master, was the chief manipulator of the doll Kiyohime; his son was in charge of Anchin, the priest. Each had two assistants, shrouded in black velvet robes and with black velvet hoods drawn down over their faces. The black accented the white of the old man's skin, and the added stature given to the assistants by their hoods made him seem even more diminutive. Barbara was shocked to see how much he had changed in six years: he had been an old man then, now he was ancient, like some mummy galvanised into a momentary approximation to life. It was cruel, she thought, horribly cruel, as he shuffled on to the stage, his mouth sagging downwards at one corner and his eyes almost closed against the glare of the footlights. His wrists looked incredibly thin: his arms, when the sleeves of his kimono slipped back, of a skeletal fragility. Under his domed forehead and the aristocratically high bridge of his nose his nostrils were vast, boring back deep into his skull. He should be in bed, she thought, or at least huddled in a chair and no longer obliged to exact from his dwindling physique the effort required to manipulate the doll. This figure, gorgeous in its stiff brocades, seemed larger than its master; and at first – even Enid was aware of this – he had difficulty in making it go through its movements. Fortunately that first encounter between Anchin and Kiyohime made few demands, but Barbara, who knew the play well, wondered how the old man would manage in the tremendous scene when Kiyohime, spurned by Anchin, transforms herself into a serpent and pursues him to his temple where he takes refuge in its great bell.

The curtain swished across. Again the Grand Salon Gardenias jigged and gyrated back and forth, while behind the stage a saxophone resumed the melody of 'Soran bushi'.

Barbara leant across to whisper to Enid: 'Pathetic, wasn't it? He was marvellous once. But now. . . . They shouldn't let him do it. I wonder if he's going on the American tour.'

'I hope not.' Enid gave a small, involuntary shudder. 'Lazarus must have looked like that.'

But in the next scene an extraordinary change took place. At first the old man continued to shuffle and falter as in the scene before; until suddenly, by some macabre reversal of roles, it was as if the doll, the baleful Kiyohime maddened by unrequited love, first struggled with him for mastery and then took complete control of him, to drag him helplessly hither and thither across the stage like some inanimate object. Furiously she worked his arms; the small, delicate body was hurled now this way, now that; the face became a vague smudge of white, an incompetently fashioned mask beside her distinct and cruelly expressive one. The transformation of the girl into a snake, the pursuit into the bell, the destruction of priest and bell together, after which the serpent-girl glides away into the Hadaka River to vanish forever: all these events were intended to produce awe and horror in the spectator, but the awe and horror which the two American women felt had their sources elsewhere. As the curtain closed, this time to a blaring-out of the folk-song by the whole band, Enid exclaimed: 'Marvellous! But, oh, how spooky. It terrified me.'

'He was better even than the last time I saw him. And didn't you feel –'

'That the doll was manipulating him and not he the doll! It had a life of its own. A gruesome life.'

Barbara pushed back her chair and took her hand-bag. 'Let's go back stage.'

'Is that possible?'

'Of course. I told you, I know the old man; I met him last time. And even if he's forgotten me, as I'm sure he has, I telephoned earlier to his son, Jun-ichiro. I think that they'll probably come and stay with me on their visit to Cambridge.'

'I'll wait for you, shall I?'

'Wait for me!' Barbara usually had to push Enid, who was naturally timid. 'But you must come and meet him. You may never have the chance again.'

'All right, dear. If you think it'll be all right.'

When the two American women entered the narrow, high-ceilinged room, the *nisei* accompanying them, they found the old man once again curled up on his *tatami*-grass mat, like a child, his knees drawn up almost to his chin and one hand under his cheek. From time to time a shudder moved through his whole body. Haruko, kneeling beside him, was wiping his face and hands with a cloth which she periodically dipped in a bowl of water beside her. The three assistants who had been with him before had now been joined by the remaining two, all of them squatting in a circle. Junichiro had stripped off his heavy silk upper garments and was standing, his thin torso in nothing but a sweat-dampened singlet, under the naked light-bulb.

'These two American ladies say that they know you,' the *nisei* announced in Japanese. 'I am sure that you enjoyed the beautiful performance,' he said to Barbara and Enid, as though they were children who needed prompting. Junichiro had started to give them a series of jerky bows.

'Oh, yes, we did. It was wonderful,' Barbara said. The youngest of the assistants rose to his feet; the others remained on the floor, staring up at her. 'Are we disturbing you? Would Fujiyama-san like to be left alone?'

'Please, please,' Jun-ichiro said, smiling as he bowed yet again.

'He must be exhausted,' Barbara said. 'We enjoyed it so much. Better even than I remember it. I'm Barbara James and this is my friend, Miss Weatherby. Miss Weatherby is on her first visit to Japan.' Barbara always said this when she introduced Enid. 'I telephoned you this morning, remember?'

'Yes, yes,' said Jun-ichiro. 'Please.' He pointed to the chairs around the table.

'We only came for a moment. Just to congratulate you all—

and thank you. When you come to the States, I'm sure that you'll have a tremendous success. Mr Ginsberg' – this was the impresario who was to present them – 'is a friend of mine and I'm going to write and tell him just how wonderful the show was tonight.'

Jun-ichiro nodded, smiled and said nothing. The *nisei* translated.

'You know Mr Ginsberg?' Jun-ichiro then asked, on a note of vague incredulity.

'Yes. I sometimes managed to persuade my husband to put money into his shows. He usually lost it.' The *nisei* translated again.

At this Jun-ichiro at once sent the younger assistant to fetch two glasses of Scotch for the women, even though they both insisted that they wanted nothing to drink. 'Fujiyama-san is tired, very tired,' he said. 'He is old man. Eighty-six.'

'Yes,' said Barbara. 'I know.'

'He is most famous Bunraku performer in all Japan.'

'Yes.'

'He perform for Emperor Meiji.'

The two women were appropriately astonished.

'Once, when I was a young boy, I met Lafcadio Hearn.' The two women started and turned simultaneously as the voice, so resonant and so meticulous in its pronunciation of English, came from the corner behind the still kneeling girl. Was it possible? Barbara totted up the years. 'He was at the house of Mr Chamberlain,' the old man added.

'The English Prime Minister, Mr Neville Chamberlain!' exclaimed the *nisei*.

'No, no,' Barbara said impatiently. 'He must mean Basil Hall Chamberlain – the scholar.'

'Mr Basil Hall Chamberlain,' said the old man. Then he muttered fretfully to Haruko in Japanese: 'Enough, enough, woman. Leave me alone.'

'Have you ever visited the West?' asked Barbara. Unself-consciously she went over to the old man and knelt down on the *tatami*-mat beside him, where Haruko had just been kneeling. It was something which Enid realized that she herself could never have done and, tired though she was, she felt a pang of admiration for them as she saw them there, face to face, each so handsome and each possessing a kind of aristocratic grandeur which had nothing to do with the wealth of the one or the distinction of the other. The old man took one of Barbara's large, capable hands in both of his as he replied: 'Yes. Many, many years ago I visited England— I met the poet William Butler Yeats and Fenellosa and — and . . .' He released her hand; suddenly a look of despair crossed his face. 'I have forgotten their names. I am old. I forget everything.'

'And America?' she prompted.

'Yes,' he said, 'Yes.' There was a long silence during which the large eyes in his wasted face seemed to grow even duller, as though a film were thickening over them. 'Yes, America,' he said at last. 'America. Washington . . . St Louis . . . Yes . . . Yale and Harvard.'

'And you're going to visit Harvard again. Will you come and stay with me? My house is in Cambridge.'

'Your house is in Cambridge,' he repeated.

'Not Cambridge, England! Cambridge, Massachussets.'

Suddenly she was aware that Jun-ichiro and Haruko were both standing above them.

'Yes, I will stay with you. Thank you.'

Jun-ichiro intervened; he spoke rapidly and softly as though he thought that in this way the old man, whose English was so much superior to his own, would be prevented from understanding. 'Fujiyama-san will not accompany us. The doctor say that health does not permit. We tell him many times, but he forget.'

'I intend to go to America,' the old man said in Japanese. 'That is enough.'

All at once the three of them were arguing. Barbara got to her feet: although she did not understand what they were saying, she knew that something had gone wrong and guessed that probably she was to blame for it. The old man's voice became high and querulous; Haruko stooped and put an arm round his shoulders, but he gave her a little push and then a harder one. Red spots appeared on Jun-ichiro's usually sallow cheeks, as with agitated hands he kept tying and untying the knot of his *obi*. The *nisei* grinned at the two American women. 'Family troubles,' he said. He glanced at his watch. 'I must go back in front to introduce those krauts.'

Barbara stepped between the old man and Jun-ichiro and Haruko. 'We must leave you,' she said. 'But I'll come again – perhaps tomorrow or the night after. You'll be here for a week, won't you?'

With difficulty Jun-ichiro coaxed his small, petulant mouth into a smile. 'Please, come and see us tonight, after second performance is over. Fujiyama-san must go sleep, but we can visit bar for drink. Please.'

'But that will be terribly late,' Barbara said.

'Twelve o'clock, quarter past twelve.'

'How about it, Enid?'

Enid hesitated. 'I must go to bed, dear. All that sightseeing has worn me out. But you stay.'

'Well, we'll see,' said Barbara. 'We'll come if we can. Is that all right?'

The old man held out a hand, which Barbara stooped to take. 'Please come,' he said. 'They always wish me to sleep, sleep, always sleep. We will talk about Cambridge. A church – a church. . . .' He looked desperately round him as though for something he had lost. Then he smiled, revealing teeth still peerlessly white: 'King's College Church,' he said. 'Do you know it?'

Barbara nodded.

'Well, dear, if it's all the same to you, I think that I'll go back to the hotel. I'm just about ready for bed.'

'Are you sure that you're feeling all right?'

'Yes of course. Why?'

'You look . . .'

'I guess the old man has depressed me a little. He – he smelled of death. Did you notice?'

'All old people smell a little musty! He's still pretty tough.'

'Then it's Nara tomorrow?'

'That's right. Or will that be too much for you?'

'No, dear. Of course not. I just need some sleep.'

'Shall I give the usual call?'

'Yes, do that, dear.'

Alone, Barbara also began to feel despondent. Old age was dreadful! Humiliating! That argument between the old man, his son and that girl (Barbara did not guess that she was Fujiyama's wife): it was like a child arguing with his parents about his bed-time. But he certainly was a darling, no doubt about that. At their last meeting he had treated her and George with a certain well-bred disdain; not impolite, unfriendly only in the subtlest and most imperceptible of ways. Well, it had been so soon after the occupation when everyone had had more than enough of Americans. But this evening – Yeats, Fenellosa, even Hearn! She must try to have a quiet hour alone with him, to get him really talking. . . .

'More fruit, madam?'

'No thank you.' It was the pert waiter.

'Another drink?'

'No thank you.'

The waiter ostentatiously removed from the table everything except her still unfinished glass of Scotch. He would have taken that too if she had not said: 'No, leave that, please.' She was too old and too much travelled to be intimidated.

This time the old man was even better than before; but Barbara found herself watching his performance with an unease which slowly deepened into an acute, almost physical distress. No, no, no, she wanted to cry out in protest when, at some moment of more then usually tumultuous movement, the imperious doll dragged the limp old man back and forth and up and down the stage. Barbara felt that, if subjected to such continued violence, one of his arms or legs would break off. It was a relief when it was over. She had, she realized, been increasingly terrified throughout: terrified for him, terrified of – well, what? The doll?

Without waiting for the *nisei* she hurried round back stage alone. Passing one of the dressing-rooms, its door left ajar, she could hear a vaguely Cockney voice: '. . . and that ruddy electric-fire has conked out . . .' Farther on was the door to the narrow room to which the *nisei* had led her, but her knock received no answer and when she looked in, she found no one there. Then, ahead of her, down the long, murky corridor, she saw them approaching. First came two of the assistants, black-robed and with their hoods still shrouding their faces like mediaeval executioners or members of some diabolical Ku-Klux klan. Then, behind them, shuffled the old man, still clutching the doll, while his son supported him on one side and Haruko on the other. The doll no longer had any life in it; it flopped limply against him, its dangling legs getting entangled from time to time with his own, and its mouth hanging ajar to reveal the two cords which connected its jaws to its cheeks. In the rear walked the remaining assistants and then the musicians. One of these last was gently rapping with the fingers of one hand on his drum.

The old man looked up and smiled faintly as he saw Barbara, the heavy folds creasing on either side of his eyes and his nostrils dilating. His face was greenish and clammy, his head trembled slightly from side to side. 'One moment,' he muttered. He turned, swaying, into a room, as Jun-ichiro opened the door to reveal to Barbara a glimpse of boxes, some lacquered and some of plain, unvarnished wood, in which reposed, as in coffins, innumerable dolls. Other dolls sprawled on the floor in ungainly postures and one sat, legs crossed, in a chair, his head fallen forward so that his beard swept his knees. The old man lifted up the puppet he was carrying.

Then all at once, it seemed to Barbara's horrified gaze as if the limp bundle of wood, plaster and wire again took possession of him. It stiffened, it filled out, it rose up in his arms. A sound, half gurgle and half scream, came from one or other of them. The doll sprang into the air, dragging the old man with it, and then both of them crashed downwards onto one of the open boxes. The sagging half of the old man's mouth twitched and his eyes rolled frantically from side to side. Then his gaze met Barbara's terrified gaze. He tried to say something, he choked. One of his legs was dangling outside the box, the back of his right hand was starting to bleed from a graze. The doll lay on top of him. His tongue came out from between his lips and moved from side to side, but the only sound which followed was a strange wooden click.

NADINE GORDIMER
Happy Event

There were so many things in life you couldn't ever imagine
yourself doing, Ella Plaistow told herself. Once or twice she
had said it aloud, too, to Allan. But mostly it grew, forced its
way up out of the silences that fell upon her like a restraining
hand during those first few days after she had come home
from the nursing home. It seemed to burst through her
mouth in a sudden irresistible germination, the way a
creeper shoots and uncurls into leaf and stem in one of those
films which telescope plant growth into the space of a few
terrifying vital seconds.

 Silence followed it again. In her mind, if she had spoken
inwardly, to herself; in the room, if she had spoken aloud.
The silence that covers the endless inward activity of
shuffling for a foothold, making out of a hundred-and-one
past justifications and pressures the accommodations of a
new position for oneself. It was true, of course. You start off
as a child, pretending to think the blonde doll prettier than
the brunette, so that your loved sister may fall into the trap of
choosing the one you don't want for yourself. You go on by
one day finding your own tongue glibly acquiescing to a
discussion of your best friend's temperament with someone
whom you know to be her disliked enemy. And before you
know where you are, you have gone through all the sidlings
and inveiglings of taking somebody's work for less than it is
worth, throwing someone into an agony of jealousy for the
sake of a moment's vanity, pretending not to see an old lover
lest he should not seem impressive enough in the eyes of the
new one. It is impossible to imagine yourself doing any of

these; but once done . . . Like ants teeming to repair a broken anthill, like white corpuscles rushing to a wound, all the forces that protect oneself from oneself have already begun their quick, sure, furtive, uneasy juggling for a new stance, a rearrangement for comfort into which amorphous life seems to have edged you.

It's your *body* that objects,' said Allan. 'Remember that. That's all. There's some sort of physical protest that's got nothing to do with you at all, really. You must expect it. It'll pass off in a week or so.'

And of course he was quite right. She certainly didn't have any regrets. They had two children, a girl and a boy (the wrong way round, as they said – the girl was the elder – but it's dangerous to have everything too much the way you want it!) who were just old enough to be left with their grandmother. Allan's new partner was thoroughly reliable, the bond on the house was almost paid off; at last there was nothing to stop Allan and Ella: they had booked to go to Europe, in the spring of next year. So to have allowed themselves to be stopped by this – ! To be, instead, this time next year, caught up in chemists' bills and napkins and wakeful nights all over again! No, they had brought up their babies, had loved and resented them and were content with them, and all through eight years had planned for this time when they would suddenly lift themselves clear of whatever it was that their lives had settled into, and land, free of it, lightly in another country.

Because it was something that Ella could never have dreamed she would ever do, in a week or two the trip to the nursing home slipped away into the unimportance of things that might never have happened. She was busy planning next winter's clothes for the children – it would be winter in South Africa while she and Allan were in spring in Europe – and getting the garden into shape because they hoped to let the house for the period they were to be away, and if they wanted a decent tenant the place must look attractive. She was just beginning to feel really strong again – undoubtedly that business had left her a little weak – and it was just as well, since she had so much to do, when, of course, servant trouble started.

The old house-cum-garden boy, Thomasi, began quarrelling with Lena, the native maid whom Ella had thought herself lucky to engage two months ago. Lena, a heavy, sullen, light-coloured Basuto, represented in her closed-in solemnity something that challenged irritation in Thomasi. Thomasi was a Basuto himself – Ella had the vague conviction that it was best to have servants who belonged to the same tribe, rather as she would have felt that it would be better to have two Siamese cats instead of one Siamese and one tabby, or two fan-tailed goldfish rather than one plain and one fancy. She always felt puzzled and rather peevish, then, when, as had happened often before, she found that her two Basutos or two Zulus or two Xhosas did not necessarily get on any better than one would have expected two Frenchman to get on simply because both were French, or two Englishmen simply because both were English.

Now Thomasi, barely five feet tall and with that charming, ancient, prehuman look of little dark-skinned men with bandy legs, was maddened by the very presence of Lena, like an insect circling angrily around the impassive head of some great slow animal. He quarrelled with her over dusters, over the state of the kitchen sink, over the bones for the dog; he went about his work shaking his head and rumbling with volcanic mutterings.

'If you've got anything to say, come out and say it,' Ella said to him, irritated herself. 'What's the matter now?'

'That woman is too lazy, madam,' he said in his high, philosophical, exasperated voice.

It was difficult to think of old Thomasi as something quite like oneself, when he rose to his hind legs. (Yes, one had the feeling that this was *exactly* what happened when he got up from polishing the floor. Of course, if he had been dressed in a tailored American-drape hopsack instead of the regulation 'kitchen boy' outfit that was a cross between a small boy's cotton sailor suit and a set of underwear, he might not have looked any funnier than any of the small, middle-aged Johannesburg men behind their directors' desks.) 'Look, Thomasi, she does her work. I'm satisfied with her. I don't want you to go making trouble. I'm the missus, and she works for me, not you, you understand?'

Then, later in the day, Ella would relent. Having shown Thomasi the hand of authority, she could approach him on the other level of their association: that of common concern for the house that they had 'run' together for nearly six years, and whose needs and prices and inanimate quirks both understood perfectly.

'Thomasi?'

'Missus?' She might be strolling in the garden, pretending that she was not seeking him out. He would go on wielding the grass shears, widening and snapping like the sharp bill of some great bird imprisoned in his hands.

'What has she done?'

'Well, I tell her the dog he mustn't have the small bone. Yesterday I tell her. Now she doesn't say nothing when I tell her. This morning I see she give the chicken bone to the dog. All that small bone, you know, the missus keep for the cats. Now when I say why you give that bone to the dog, the dog he's going to get sick, she just look me . . .'

The coffee cups left unwashed from the night before.

The iron left switched on while she went to her room after lunch.

And too many friends in her room at night, too many.

'I think she makes the kaffir beer,' said Thomasi.

But at this complaint Ella was ready to discredit all the others, again. This was Thomasi trying to cook something up. If the girl brewed kaffir beer in her room, Thomasi would be her first customer, not the informant seeking to get her into trouble.

'Listen, Thomasi, I don't want to hear any more of these tales and grumbles, you understand? I'll see if Lena works properly or not, and I don't want you interfering with her.'

As she would give her children a handful of sweets each to equalize some difference between them, Ella cleared out a cupboard that needed clearing anyway, and gave Thomasi an old shirt of Allan's, Lena a cheap blue satin nightgown that she had bought to take to the nursing home and that she somehow felt she didn't want to wear again. 'I must keep the peace,' she said to Allan. 'I'm not going to go training another new girl now. I must stick it out with this one until we go. She's a perfectly nice girl, really – a bit sulky, that's all. But you know what an old devil he can be when he wants to. I shouldn't be surprised if what's behind it is that he fancies her, and she's not interested. Shame, he looks such a little old wizened imp of a thing next to her, she's such a hulking, big-breasted Juno.'

But the gifts did not quiet for long whatever it was that inflamed Thomasi's malice. The following month, on a Monday morning, Ella found Thomasi alone in the kitchen, cooking the greasy, metallic-tasting fried eggs that were his idea of a white man's breakfast. Lena, he said, bearing his message from across that neat stretch of grass and crisscross washing line that was the no-man's-land between the lives of the white people in the house and the black people in their back-yard quarters, said she was sick this morning. She would do the washing tomorrow.

'Are those for the master . . . ?' Ella indicated the eggs but lacked the courage to complain. 'What's wrong with Lena?'

Over the frying pan, Thomasi gave a great shrug of disbelief and contempt.

'What does she say?'

Thomasi turned around to the young woman in the soiled pink dressing-gown, the dark line of her plucked and dyed white-woman's eyebrows showing like pen strokes on the pastel of her fair-skinned face, unmade-up, faintly greasy with the patina of sleep. His brow drew in, intricately lined, over his little yellowish eyes; he said with exaggerated poise and indifference, 'I don't know how she's sick. I can't say

how a person she's sick when there's noise in her room all
night. When people is talking there, late. Sometimes I think:
She got someone staying there, or something? Talking, and
late, late, a baby crying.'

Ella went out, over the stones and the grass, across the
yard to the native girl's room. The grass was crisp with dew
and the chill struck through the old sandals she liked to wear
instead of slippers; long threads of spider-web danced between the clothes-line. She knocked on the door of the little
brick room; the window was closed and curtained. She
knocked again and called softly, 'Lena?'

'Ma'am?' The voice came after a pause.

Ella opened the door with difficulty – natives usually tam-
pered with the doorknobs in their rooms, making them
removable as an added protection against intruders – and,
finding it would open only halfway, edged her way in. The
room had a warm animal smell, like the inside of the cupboard where old Lixi, the tabby, lay with her kittens at her
belly, purring and licking, purring and licking. The air in
here had nothing to do with that other air, wet and sharp
with morning, just outside: it was a creature air, created by
breathing beings. Although the room was small, Lena in her
bed seemed far away. The bed was raised high on bricks,
and it was half-curtained, like a homemade four-poster.
Some sort of design worked in red and purple thread trailed
round the hems of the material. Lena lay, her head turned to
the angle of her raised arm on the pillow. She seemed to be
taking some communion of comfort from her own tender
exposed armpit, close to her face.

'Are you sick, Lena?' said the white woman gently.

The black woman turned her head back and forth once,
quickly on the pillow. She swallowed and said, 'Yes.'

'What do you feel?' said Ella, still at the door, which she
now saw could not open properly because of a cupboard
made of boxes which was pushed half against it.

'My stomach, ma'am.' She moved under the fringed
travelling rug that was her blanket.

'Do you think you've eaten something that's made you sick?' said Ella.

The girl did not answer. Ella saw her big slow eyes and the white of her teeth come out of the gloom.

'Sometimes I've got a cold in my stomach,' the girl said at last.

'Is it pain?' said Ella.

'I can do the washing tomorrow,' said the voice from the great, hemmed-in agglomerate of the bed.

'Oh, it doesn't matter,' said Ella. 'I'll send Thomasi out with something for you to take. And do you want something to eat?'

'Only tea, thank you, ma'am.'

'All right then.'

She felt the woman's slow eyes watching her out of that room, which curiously, despite its poverty, its soapbox cupboards fretted with cut-out newspaper edgings, the broken china ducks, and the sword-fern draped in stained crêpe paper (the ornaments and the fern were discards from the house), had something of the richly charged air of grand treasure-filled rooms of old houses heavy with association, rooms much used, thick with the overlaid echoes of human concourse. She thought, for some reason, of the kind of room in which one expects to find a Miss Havisham. And how ridiculous! These two whitewashed servants' rooms neatly placed out of the way between the dustbin and the garage! What had they to do with Dickens or flights of fancy or anything else, in fact, except clean, weatherproof, and fairly decent places for the servants to sleep? They belonged to nothing and nobody, merely were thrown in along with the other conditions of work.

On the kitchen step Ella stopped and shook each foot like a cat; her feet were sopping. She made a little exclamation of irritation with herself.

And when she had dressed, she sent Thomasi out to the room with a dose of chlorodyne ready-mixed with water in one of the old kitchen-glasses. She got her younger child Pip ready for Allan to take to nursery school and saw that her daughter Kathie had some cake to take for her school lunch in place of the sandwiches Lena usually made.

'Darned nuisance, mmh?' Allan said (suppressing a belch, with distaste, after the eggs).

'Can't be helped, I suppose,' Ella said. 'I wouldn't mind so much if only it wasn't Monday. You know how it is when the washing isn't done on the right day. It puts the whole of the rest of the week out. Anyway, she should be all right by tomorrow.'

The next morning when Ella got up, Lena was already doing the washing. 'Girl appeared again?' called Allan from the bathroom. Ella came in, holding one of Pip's vests to her cheek to see if it was quite dry. 'She doesn't look too good, poor thing. She's moving terribly slowly between the tub and the line.'

'Well she's never exactly nimble is she?' murmured Allan, concentrating on the slight dent in his chin, always a tricky place to shave. They smiled at each other; when they smiled at each other these days, they had the conspiring look of children who have discovered where the Christmas presents are hidden: Europe, leisure, and the freedom of the money they had saved up were unspoken between them.

Ella and Allan Plaistow lived in one of the pleasantest of Johannesburg suburbs: gently rolling country to the north of the city, where the rich had what amounted to country estates, and the impecunious possessors of good taste had small houses in an acre or two of half-cultivated garden. Some of the younger people, determined not to be forced back into real suburbia through lack of money, kept chickens or bred dogs to supplement the upkeep of their places, and one couple even had a small Jersey herd. Ella was one of their customers, quite sure she could taste the difference between their, and what she called 'city' milk.

One morning about a week after the native girl Lena had delayed Ella's wash-day, the milk delivery cart was bowling along the ruts it had made for itself along the track between the dairy and the houses in the Plaistow's direction, when the horse swerved and one wheel bowed down the tall grasses at the side of the track. There was a tinny clang; the wheel slithered against something. Big Charlie, the milk 'boy', growled softly at the horse, and climbed down to see. There, as if it had made a bed for itself in the long grass the way an animal turns round and round before sinking to rest, was a paraffin tin. Big Charlie stubbed at it once with his boot, as if to say, oh, well, if that's all . . . But it gave back the resistance of a container that has something inside it; through his toes, there came to him the realization that this was not merely an empty tin. It was upside down, the top pressed to the ground. He saw an edge of blue material, stained with dew and earth, just showing. Still with his foot, he pushed hard – too hard, for whatever was inside was light – and the tin rocked over. There spilled out of it a small bundle, the naked decaying body of what had been a new-born child, rolled, carelessly as one might roll up old clothing, in a blue satin nightgown.

It did not seem for a moment to Big Charlie that the baby was dead. He gave a kind of aghast cluck, as at some gross neglect – one of his own five doubled up with a bellyache after eating berries, or the youngest with flies settling on his mouth because the mother had failed to wipe the milk that trickled down his chin from her abundance when she fed him – and knelt down to make haste to do whatever it was that the little creature needed. And then he saw that this was hardly a child at all; was now closer to those kittens he was sometimes ordered by his employers to drown in a bucket of water or closer still to one of those battered fledglings found lying beneath the mimosa trees the night after a bad summer storm.

So now he stood back and did not want to touch it. With his mouth lifted over his teeth in a superstitious horror at the coldness of what had been done, he took the crumpled satin in the tips of his fingers and folded it over the body again, then dropped the bundle back into the paraffin tin and lifted the tin onto the cart beside him.

As he drove, he looked down now and then, swiftly, in dismay to see it there still beside him. The bodice of the nightgown was uppermost and lifted in the firm currents of the morning air. It was inside out, and showed a sewn-on laundry label. Big Charlie could neither read or write so he did not know that it said in the neat letters devised for the nursing home, E. PLAISTOW.

That, of course, was how Ella came to find herself in court.

When she opened the door to the plainclothes detective that afternoon, she had the small momentary start, a kind of throb in some organ one didn't know one had, of all people who do not steal and who have paid their taxes: an alarm at the sight of a policeman that is perhaps rooted in the memory, of childhood threats. The man was heavily built and large-footed and he had a very small, well-brushed moustache, smooth as the double flick of a paintbrush across his broad lip. He said in Afrikaans, *'Goeie middag. Mevrou Plaistow?'* And when she answered in English, he switched to slow, stilted English. She led him into the living room with a false air of calm and he sat on the edge of the sofa. When he told her that the Evans's milk boy had found a dead native baby in a paraffin tin on the veld, she made a polite noise of horror and even felt a small shudder, just back of her jaws, at the idea, but her face kept its look of strained patience: what had this gruesome happening to do with *her*? Then he told her that the child was found wrapped in a blue satin nightgown bearing her name, and she rose instantly from her chair in alarm, as if there had been a sudden jab inside her.

'In my nightgown?' she accused, standing over the man.

'Yes, I'm afraid so, lady.'

'But are you sure?' she said, withdrawing into anger and hauteur.

He opened a large brief-case he had brought with him and which she had imagined as much a part of his equipment as his official English or the rolled-gold signet ring on his little finger. Carefully he spread out the blue satin, which still kept, all refracted by creases, the sheen of satin, despite the earth stains and some others caused by something that had dried patchily – perhaps that birth fluid, *vernix caseosa*, in which a baby is coated when it slips into the world. The sight filled her with revulsion: 'Oh, put it away!' she said with difficulty.

'You recognize it?' he said – pronouncing the word as if it were spelled 'racognize'.

'It's mine all right,' she said. 'It's the one I gave to Lena a few weeks ago. But good God – ?'

'It's a native girl, of course, the one you gave it to?' He had taken out his notebook.

Now all sorts of things were flooding into her mind. 'That's right! She was sick, she stayed in bed one day. The boy said he heard a baby cry in the night –' She appealed to the policeman: 'But it couldn't be!'

'Now if you'll just tal me, lady, what was the date when you gave the girl the nightgown . . .' Out of the disorder of her quicker mind, his own slow one stolidly sorted this recollection from that; her confused computation of dates and times through the measure of how much time had passed between the day Pip chipped a tooth at nursery school (that, she remembered distinctly, happened on the same day that she had given Thomasi a shirt and Lena the nightgown) and the morning the washing had not been done, became a statement. Then she went, haltingly because of her nervousness, into the kitchen to call Lena and Thomasi. 'Thomasi!' she called. And then, after a pause: 'Lena'. And she watched for her, coming across the yard.

But the two Africans met the fact of the policeman far more calmly than she herself had done. For Africans there is no stigma attached to any involvement with the forces of the law; the innumerable restrictions by which their lives are hedged from the day they are born make transgressions commonplace and punishment inevitable. To them a few days in prison is no more shaming than an attack of the measles. After all, there are few people who could go through a lifetime without at least once forgetting to carry the piece of paper which is their 'pass' to free movement about the town, or without getting drunk, or without sitting on a bench which looks just like every other bench but happens to be provided exclusively for the use of people with a pale skin. All these things keep Africans casually going in and out of prison, hardly the worse – since it is accepted that this is the ways things are – for a cold, buggy night in the cells or a kick from a warder.

Lena has not a pleasant face, thought Ella, but thought too that perhaps she was merely reading this into the face, now. The woman simply stood there, answering, in an obedient Afrikaans, the detective's questions about her identity. The detective had hitched his solid rump onto the kitchen table, and his manner had changed to the impatient one customarily used for Africans by all white persons in authority. The woman appeared weary, more than anything else; she did not look at the detective when he spoke to her or she answered. And she spoke coldly, as was her custom; just as she said, 'Yes madam no madam,' when Ella reproached her for some neglected chore. She was an untidy woman, too; now she had on her head a woollen *doek* again, instead of the maid's cap Ella provided for her to wear. Ella looked at her, from the *doek* to the coloured sandals with the cut thongs where they caught the toes; looked at her in a kind of fascination, and tried to fit with her the idea of the dead baby, rolled in a nightgown and thrust into a paraffin tin. It was neither credible nor did it inspire revulsion. Because she is not a *motherly* figure, Ella thought – that is it. One cannot imagine her mother to anything. She is the sort of woman, white or black, who is always the custodian of other people's children; she washes their faces and wipes their noses, but they throw their arms around somebody else's neck.

And just then the woman looked at her, suddenly, directly, without a flicker of escape, without dissimulation or appeal, not as a woman looks to another woman, or even a human being to another human being; looked at her out of those wide-set, even-lidded eyes and did not move a muscle of her face.

Oh, but I don't know her, I know nothing about her . . . Ella recoiled, retracting to herself.

'She'll have to come along with me,' the detective was saying, and as the woman stood a moment, as if awaiting some permission, he told her in Afrikaans that she could go to her room if she wanted anything, but she must be quick.

Ella stood near the door watching her servant go slowly across the yard to the little brick room. Her own heart was pounding slowly. She felt a horrible conflict of agitation and shame – for what, she did not know. But if I go after her, she seemed to answer herself, what can I say to her? Behind Ella, the detective was questioning Thomasi, and Thomasi was enjoying it; she could hear from the quick, meaningful, confidential tones of Thomasi's voice that he was experiencing all the relish of a gossip who finds himself at last in the powerful position of being able to influence the lives of those who have forced him out into the cold of a vicarious recorder.

Ella said suddenly to the detective, 'Will you excuse me now, please –' and went away through the house to her bedroom. She was standing there still, some minutes later, when the detective called from the front door, 'Thank you very much, lady, hey? We'll let you know –' and she did not come out but called back, as if she were at some task she could not leave for a moment, 'I'm sorry – will you find your way out . . .'

But she could not forbear to bend apart the slats of the venetian blind in time to see the back of Lena, in one of those cheap short coats – jeep coats, they were called, beloved of suburban African girls – getting into the police car. It's unbelievable, she told herself; she didn't look any fatter than she does now . . . And she did the whole week's washing . . .

The moment Ella heard the car drive away, she went to

telephone Allan. As she dialled, she noticed that her fingers were fumbling and damp. I'm really upset, she thought; I'm really upset about this thing.

By the time the court case came to be heard, the quiet, light-coloured Lena lying in her bed that day with her head turned to her arm for comfort, standing obediently before the questioning of the detective in the kitchen, was changed in Ella Plaistow's mind into the ghoulish creature who emerged out of discussion of the affair with friends and neighbours. A woman who could kill her own baby! A murderer, nothing less! It's quite awful to think that she handled Pip and Kathie, other women sympathized. It just shows you, you never know who you're taking into your home . . . You never know, with *them* . . . You can send them to a doctor to make sure you aren't harbouring some-one who's diseased, but you've no way of finding out what sort of person a servant is. Well, Thomasi didn't like her from the first, you know, Ella always said at this point. Ah, Thomasi, someone would murmur, now he's a good old thing.

So that when Ella saw the woman Lena in court, there was something disquieting and unexpected about the ordinari-ness, the naturalness of her appearance: this was simply the woman who had stood so often at the stove in Ella's red-and-white kitchen. And where was the other, that creature who had abandoned her own newborn child to the cold of the veld?

Embarrassment precluded all other feelings, once the white woman found herself in the witness stand. Ella had never, she said again and again afterward, felt such a fool in her whole life.

'You are, of course, a married woman?' said the magis-trate.

'Yes,' said Ella.

'How long have you been married?'

'Eight years.'

'I see. And you have children?'

'Yes, two children.'

'Mrs Plaistow, am I to understand that you, a woman who has been married for eight years and has herself borne two children, were not aware that this woman in your employ was on the point of giving birth to a child?'

Of course, the man must have thought her quite moronic! But how to explain that one didn't go measuring one's servant's waistline, that she was a very big well-built woman in any case, and that since she must have been well into her pregnancy when she started work, any further changes in her figure were not noticed?

He made such a *fool* of me, Ella protested; you can't imagine how *idiotic* I felt.

The case dragged on through two days. The woman herself said that the child had been born dead, and that since no one knew that she was pregnant, she had been 'frightened' and had hidden the body and then left it on the veld, but post-mortem findings showed strong evidence that the child might have lived some hours after birth, and had not died naturally. Then there was Thomasi's statement that he had heard an infant cry in the night.

'In your opinion, Doctor,' the magistrate asked the government medical officer, in an attempt to establish how much time had elapsed between the birth and death of the infant, 'would it be possible for a woman to resume her normal day's work thirty-six hours after confinement? This women did her employer's household washing the following day.'

The doctor smiled slightly. 'Were the woman in question a European, I should, of course, say this would be most unlikely. Most unlikely. But of a native woman, I should say yes – yes, it would be possible.' In the silence of the court, the reasonableness, the validity of this statement had the air of clinching the matter. After all, everyone knew, out of a mixture of hearsay and personal observation, the physical stamina of the African. Hadn't everyone heard of at least one native who had walked around for three days with a fractured skull, merely complaining of a headache? And of one who had walked miles to a hospital, carrying, Van Gogh-like, in a piece of newspaper, his own ear – sliced off in a faction fight?

Lena got six months' hard labour. Her sentence coincided roughly with the time Ella and Allan spent in Europe, but though she was out of prison by the time they returned, she did not go back to work for them again.

GEORGE MACDONALD FRASER
The General Danced at Dawn

Friday night was always dancing night. On the six other evenings of the week the officers' mess was informal, and we had supper in various states of uniform, mufti and undress, throwing bits of bread across the table and invading the kitchen for second helpings of caramel pudding. The veranda was always open, and the soft, dark night of North Africa hung around pleasantly beyond the screens.

Afterwards in the ante-room we played cards, or ludo, or occasional games of touch rugby, or just talked the kind of nonsense that subalterns talk, and whichever of these things we did our seniors either joined in or ignored completely; I have seen a game of touch rugby in progress, with the chairs and tables pushed back against the wall, and a heaving mass of Young Scotland wrestling for a 'ball' made of sock stuffed with rags, while less than a yard away the Adjutant, two company commanders, and the M.O. were sitting round a card table holding an inquest on five spades doubled. There was great toleration.

Friday night was different. On that evening we dressed in our best tartans and walked over to the mess in two's and three's as soon as the solitary piper, who had been playing outside the mess for about twenty minutes broke into the slow, plaintive 'Battle of the Somme' – or, as it is known colloquially, 'See's the key, or I'll roar up yer lobby.'

In the mess we would have a drink in the ante-room, the captains and the majors sniffing at their Talisker and Glengrant, and the rest of us having beer or orange juice – I have known messes where subalterns felt they had to drink hard stuff for fear of being thought cissies, but in a Highland mess nobody presses anybody. For one thing, no senior officer with a whisky throat wants to see his single malt being wasted on some pink and eager one-pipper.

Presently the Colonel would knock his pipe out and limp into the dining-room, and we would follow in to sit round the huge white table. I never saw a table like it, and never expected to; Lord Mayors' banquets, college dinners, and American conventions at 100 dollars a plate may surpass it in spectacular grandeur, but when you sat down at this table you were conscious of sitting at a dinner that had lasted for centuries.

The table was a mass of silver: the horse's-hoof snuff-box that was a relic of the few minutes at Waterloo when the regiment broke Napoleon's cavalry, and Wellington himself took off his hat and said, 'Thank you, gentlemen'; the set of spoons from some forgotten Indian palace with strange gods carved on the handles; the great bowl, magnificently engraved, presented by an American infantry regiment in Normandy, and the little quaich that had been found in the dust at Magersfontein; loot that had come from Vienna, Moscow, Berlin, Rome, the Taku Forts, and God knows where, some direct and some via French, Prussian, Polish, Spanish, and other regiments from half the countries on earth – stolen, presented, captured, bought, won, given, taken, and acquired by accident. It was priceless, and as you sat and contemplated it you could almost feel the shades elbowing you round the table.

At any rate, it enabled us to get through the tinned tomato soup, rissoles and jam tart, which seemed barely adequate to such a splendid setting, or to the sonorous grace which the padre had said beforehand ('I say, padre, can you say it in Gaelic?' 'Away, a' he talks is Glesca.' 'Wheesht for the minister'). And when it was done and the youth who was vice-president had said, 'The King', passed the port in the wrong direction, giggled, upset his glass, and been sorrowfully rebuked from the table head, we lit up and waited for the piper. The voices, English of Sandhurst and Scottish of Kelvinside, Perthshire, and Peterhead, died away, and the pipe-major strode in and let us have it.

A twenty-minute pibroch is no small thing at a range of four feet. Some liked it, some affected to like it, and some buried their heads in their hands and endured it. But in everyone the harsh, keening siren-sound at least provoked thought. I can see them still, the faces round the table; the sad padre, tapping slowly to 'The Battle of the Spoiled Dyke'; the junior subaltern, with his mouth slightly open, watching the tobacco smoke wreathing in low clouds over the white cloth; the signals officer, tapping his thumb-nail against his teeth and shifting restlessly as he wondered if he would get away in time to meet that Ensa singer at the club; the Colonel, chin on fist like a great bald eagle with his pipe clamped between his teeth and his eyes two generations away; the men, the boys, the dreamer's eyes and the boozer's melancholy, all silent while the music enveloped them.

When it was over, and we had thumped the table, and the pipe-major had downed his whisky with a Gaelic toast, we would troop out again, and the Colonel would grin and rub tobacco between his palms, and say:

'Right, gentlemen, shall we dance?'

This was part of the weekly ritual. We would take off our tunics, and the pipers would make preparatory whines, and the Colonel would perch on a table, swinging his game leg which the Japanese had broken for him on the railway, and would say:

'Now, gentlemen, as you know there is Highland dancing as performed when ladies are present, and there is Highland dancing. We will have Highland dancing. In Valetta in '21 I saw a Strip the Willow performed in eighty-nine seconds, and an Eightsome reel in two minutes twenty-two seconds. These are our targets. All right, pipey.'

We lined up and went at it. You probably know both the dances referred to, but until you have seen Highland subalterns and captains giving them the treatment you just don't appreciate them. Strip the Willow at speed is lethal; there is much swinging round, and when fifteen stone of heughing humanity is whirled at you at close range you have to be wide awake to sidestep, scoop him in, and hurl him back again. I have gone up the line many times, and it is like being bounced from wall to wall of a long corridor with heavy weights attached to your arms. You just have to relax and concentrate on keeping upright.

Occasionally there would be an accident, as when the padre, his Hebridean paganism surging up through his Calvinistic crust, swung into the M.O., and the latter, his constitution undermined by drink and peering through microscopes, mistimed him and received him heavily amidships. The padre simply cried: 'The sword of the Lord and of Gideon!' and danced on, but the M.O. had to be carried to the rear and his place taken by the second-in-command, who was six feet four and a danger in traffic.

The Eightsome was even faster, but not so hazardous, and when it was over we would have a breather while the Adjutant, a lanky Englishman who was transformed by pipe music into a kind of Fred Astaire, danced a 'ragged trousers' and the cooks and mess waiters came through to watch and join in the gradually mounting rumble of stamping and applause. He was the clumsiest creature in everyday walking and moving, but out there, with his fair hair falling over his face and his shirt hanging open, he was like thistledown on the air; he could have left Nijinsky frozen against the cushion.

The pipe-sergeant loved him, and the pipe-sergeant had skipped nimbly off with prizes uncounted at gatherings and games all over Scotland. He was a tiny, india-rubber man, one of your technically perfect dancers who had performed before crowned heads, viceroys, ambassadors, 'and all sorts of wog presidents and the like of that'. It was to mollify him that the Colonel would encourage the Adjutant to perform, for the pipe-sergeant disliked 'wild' dancing of the Strip the

Willow variety, and while we were on the floor he would stand with his mouth primly pursed and his glengarry pulled down, glancing occasionally at the Colonel and sniffing.

'What's up, pipe-sarnt,' the Colonel would say, 'too slow for you?'

'Slow?' the pipe-sergeant would say. 'Fine you know, sir, it's not too slow for me. It's a godless stramash is what it is, and shouldn't be allowed. Look at the unfortunate Mr Cameron, the condition of him; he doesn't know whether it's Tuesday or breakfast.'

'They love it; anyway, you don't want them dancing like a bunch of old women.'

'No, not like old women, but chust like proper Highlandmen. There is a form, and a time, and a one-two-three, and a one-two-three, and thank God it's done and here's the lovely Adjutant.'

'Well, don't worry,' said the Colonel, clapping him on the shoulder. 'You get 'em twice a week in the mornings to show them how it ought to be done.'

This was so. On Tuesdays and Thursdays batmen would rouse officers with malicious satisfaction at 5.30, and we would stumble down, bleary and unshaven, to the M.T. sheds, where the pipe-sergeant would be waiting, skipping in the cold to put us through our session of practice dancing. He was in his element, bounding about in his laced pumps, squeaking at us while the piper played and we galumphed through out eightsomes and foursomes. Unlovely we were, but the pipe-sergeant was lost in the music and the mists of time, emerging from time to time to rebuke, encourage and commend.

'Ah, the fine sound,' he would cry, pirouetting among us. 'And a one, two, three, and a one, two, three. And there we are, Captain MacAlpine, going grand, going capital! One, two, three and oh, observe the fine feet of Captain MacAlpine! He springs like a startled ewe, he does! And a one, two, three, Mr Elphinstone-Hamilton, and a pas-de-bas, and, yes, Mr Cameron, once again. But now a one, two, three, four, Mr Cameron, and a one, two, three, four, and the rocking-step. Come to me, Mr Cameron, like a full-rigged ship. But, oh, dear God, the horns of the deer! Boldly, proudly, that's the style of the masterful Mr Cameron; his caber feidh is wonderful, it is fit to frighten Napoleon.'

He and Ninette de Valois would have got on a fair treat. The Colonel would sometimes loaf down, with his greatcoat over his pyjamas, and lean on his cromach, smoking and smiling quietly. And the pipe-sergeant, carried away, would skip all the harder and direct his running commentary at his audience of one.

'And a one, two, three, good morning to you, sir, see the fine dancing, and especially of Captain MacAlpine! One, two, three, and a wee bit more, Mr Cameron, see the fine horns of the deer, colonel sir, how he knacks his thoos, God bless him. Ah, yes, that is it, Mr Elphinstone-Hamilton, a most proper appearance, is it not, Colonel?'

'I used to think,' the Colonel would say later, 'that the pipe-sergeant must drink steadily from 3 a.m. to get into that elevated condition. Now I know better. The man's bewitched.'

So we danced, and it was just part of garrison life, until the word came of one of our periodic inspections, which meant that a general would descend from Cairo and storm through us, and report to G.H.Q. on our condition, and the Colonel, Adjutant, Regimental Sergeant Major and so on would either receive respective rockets or pats on the back. Especially the Colonel. And this inspection was rather more than ordinarily important to the old boy, because in two months he and the battalion would be going home, and soon after that he would be retiring. He should by rights have retired long before, but the war had kept him on, and he had stayed to the last possible minute. After all it was his life: he had gone with this battalion to France in '14 and hardly left it since; now he was going for good, and the word went round that his last inspection on active service must be something for him to remember in his old age, when he could look back on a battalion so perfect that the inspecting general had not been able to find so much as a speck of whitewash out of place. So we hoped.

Now, it chanced that, possibly in deference to the Colonel, the Very Senior Officer who made this inspection was also very Highland. The pipe-sergeant rubbed his hands at the news. 'There will be dancing,' he said, with the air of the Creator establishing land and sea. 'General MacCrimmon will be enchanted; he was in the Argylls, where they dance a wee bit. Of course, being an Argyll he is chust a kind of Campbell, but it will have to be right dancing for him, I can assure you, one, two, three, and no lascivious jiving.'

Bursting with zeal, he worked our junior officers' dancing class harder than ever, leaping and exhorting until he had us exhausted; meanwhile, the whole barracks was humming with increased activity as we prepared for inspection. Arab sweepers brushed the parade ground with hand brushes to free it of dust, whitewash squads were everywhere with their buckets and stained overalls; every weapon in the place, from dirks and revolvers to the three-inch mortars, was stripped and oiled and cleaned three times over; the cookhouses, transport sheds, and even the little church, were meticulously gone over; Private McAuslan, the dirtiest soldier in the world, was sent on leave, squads roamed the barrack grounds continually, picking up paper, twigs, leaves, stones, and anything that might offend military symmetry; the Colonel snapped and twisted his handkerchief and broke his favourite pipe; sergeants became hoarse and fretful, corporals fearful, and the quarter-masters and company clerks moved uneasily in the dark places of their stores, sweating in the knowledge of duty ill-done and judgment at hand. But, finally, we were ready; in other words we were clean. We were so tired that we couldn't have withstood an attack by the Tiller Girls, but we were clean.

The day came, and disaster struck immediately. The sentry at the main gate turned out the guard at the approach of the General's car, and dropped his rifle in presenting arms. That was fairly trivial, but the General commented on it as he stepped out to be welcomed by the Colonel, and that put everyone's nerves on edge; matters were not improved by the obvious fact that he was pleased to have found a fault so early, and was intent on finding more.

He didn't have far to look. He was a big, beefy man, turned out in a yellowing balmoral and an ancient, but beautifully cut kilt, and his aide was seven feet of sideways invisibility in one of the Guards regiments. The General announced that he would begin with the men's canteen ('men's welfare comes first with me; should come first with every officer'), and in the panic that ensued on this unexpected move the canteen staff upset a swill-tub in the middle of the floor five seconds before he arrived; it had been a fine swill-tub, specially prepared to show that we had such things, and he shouldn't have seen it until it had been placed at a proper distance from the premises.

The General looked at the mess, said 'Mmh', and asked to see the medical room ('always assuming it isn't rife with bubonic plague'); it wasn't, as it happened, but the M.O.'s terrier had chosen that morning to give birth to puppies, beating the Adjutant to it by a short head. Thereafter a fire broke out in the cookhouse, a bren-gun carrier broke down, an empty cigarette packet was found in 'B' company's garden, and Private McAuslan came back off leave. He was tastefully dressed in shirt and boots, but no kilt, and entered the main gate in the company of three military policemen who had foolishly rescued him from a canal into which he had fallen. The General noted his progress to the guardroom with interest; McAuslan was alternately singing the Twenty-third Psalm and threatening to write to his Member of Parliament.

So it went on; anything that could go wrong, seemed to go wrong, and by dinner-time that night the General was wearing a sour and satisfied expression, his aide was silently contemptuous, the battalion was boiling with frustration and resentment, and the Colonel was looking old and ill. Only once did he show a flash of spirit, and that was when the junior subaltern passed the port the wrong way again, and the General sighed, and the Colonel caught the subaltern's eye and said loudly and clearly: 'Don't worry, Ian; it doesn't matter a damn.'

That finally froze the evening over, so to speak, and when we were all back in the ante-room and the senior major remarked that the pipe-sergeant was all set for the dancing to begin, the Colonel barely nodded, and the General lit a cigar and sat back with the air of one who was only mildly interested to see how big a hash we could make of this too.

Oddly enough, we didn't. We danced very well, with the pipe-sergeant fidgeting on the outskirts, hoarsely whispering, 'One, two, three,' and afterwards he and the Adjutant and two of the best subalterns danced a foursome that would have swept the decks at Braemar. It was good stuff, really good, and the General must have known it, but he seemed rather irritated than pleased. He kept moving in his seat, frowning, and when we had danced an eightsome he finally turned to the Colonel.

'Yes, it's all right,' he said. 'But, you know, I never cared much for the set stuff. Did you never dance a sixteensome?'

The Colonel said he had heard of such a thing, but had not, personally, danced it.

'Quite simple,' said the General, rising. 'Now, then. Eight more officers on the floor. I think I remember it, although it's years now . . .'

He did remember; a sixteensome is complicated, but its execution gives you the satisfaction that you get from any complex manoeuvre; we danced it twice, the General calling the changes and clapping (his aide was studying the ceiling with the air of an archbishop at a cannibal feast), and when it was over the General actually smiled and called for a large whisky. He then summoned the pipe-sergeant, who was looking disapproving.

'Pipe-sergeant, tell you what,' said the General. 'I have

been told that back in the 'nineties the First Black Watch sergeants danced a thirty-twosome. Always doubted it, but suppose it's possible. What do you think? Yes, another whisky, please.'

The pipe-sergeant, flattered but slightly outraged, gave his opinion. All things were possible; right, said the General, wiping his mouth, we would try it.

The convolutions of an eightsome are fairly simple; those of a sixteensome are difficult, but a thirty-twosome is just murder. When you have thirty-two people weaving and circling it is necessary that each one should move precisely right, and that takes organization. The General was an organizer; his tunic came off after half an hour, and his voice hoarsely thundered the time and the changes. The mess shook to the crash of feet and the skirling of the pipes, and at last the thirty-twosome rumbled, successfully, to its ponderous close.

'Dam' good! Dam' good!' exclaimed the General, flushed and applauding. 'Well danced, gen'men. Good show, pipe-sarn't! Thanks, Tom, don't mind if I do. Dam' fine dancing. Thirty-twosome, eh? That'll show the Black Watch!'

He seemed to sway a little as he put down his glass. It was midnight, but he was plainly waking up.

'Thirty-twosome, by Jove! Wouldn't have thought it possible.' A thought seemed to strike him. 'I say, pipe-sarn't, I wonder . . . d'you suppose that's as far as we can go? I mean is there any reason . . . ?'

He talked, and the pipe-sergeant's eyes bulged. He shook his head, the General persisted, and five minutes later we were all outside on the lawn and trucks were being sent for so that their headlights could provide illumination, and sixty-four of us were being thrust into our positions, and the General was shouting orders through cupped hands from the veranda.

'Taking the time from me! Right, pipers? It's p'fickly simple. S'easy. One, two, an' off we go!'

It was a nightmare, it really was. I had avoided being in the sixty-four; from where I was standing it looked like a crowd scene from 'The Ten Commandments', with the General playing Cecil de Mille. Officers, mess-waiters, batmen, swung into the dance as the pipes shrilled, setting to partners, circling forwards and back, forming an enormous ring, and heughing like things demented. The General bounded about the veranda, shouting; the pipe-sergeant hurtled through the sets, pulling, directing, exhorting; those of us watching clapped and stamped as the mammoth dance surged on, filling the night with its sound and fury.

It took, I am told, one hour and thirteen minutes by the Adjutant's watch, and by the time it was over the Fusiliers from the adjoining barracks were roused and lined along the wall, assorted Arabs had come to gaze on the wonders of civilization, and the military police mobile patrol was also on hand. But the General was tireless; I have a vague memory of him standing on the tailboard of a truck, addressing the assembled mob; I actually got close enough to hear him exhorting the pipe sergeant in tones of enthusiasm and entreaty:

'Pipe-sarn't! Pipey! May I call you Pipey? . . . never been done . . . three figures . . . think of it . . . hunner'n-twenty-eightsome . . . never another chance . . . try it . . . rope in the Fusiliers . . . massed pipers . . . regimental history . . . please, Pipey, for me . . .'

Some say that it actually happened, that a one hundred and twenty-eightsome reel was danced on the parade ground that night, General Sir Roderick McGrimmon, K.C.B., D.S.O., and bar, presiding; that it was danced by Highlanders, Fusiliers, Arabs, military police, and three German prisoners of war; that it was danced to a conclusion, all figures. It may well have been; all I remember is a heaving, rushing crowd, like a mixture of Latin Carnival and Scarlett's uphill charge at Balaclava, surging ponderously to the sound of the pipes; but I distinctly recall one set in which the General, the pipe-sergeant, and what looked like a genuine Senussi in a burnous, swept by roaring, 'One, two, three,' and I know, too, that at one point I personally was part of a swinging human chain in which my immediate partners were the Fusiliers' cook-sergeant and an Italian café proprietor from down the road. My memory tells me that it rose to a tremendous crescendo just as the first light of dawn stole over Africa, and then all faded away, silently, in the tartan-strewn morning.

No one remembers the General leaving later in the day, although the Colonel said he believed he was there, and that the General cried with emotion. It may have been so, for the inspection report later congratulated the battalion, and highly commended the pipe-sergeant on the standard of the officers' dancing. Which was a mixed pleasure to the pipe-sergeant, since the night's proceedings had been an offence to his orthodox soul.

'Mind you,' he would say, 'General McGrimmon had a fine agility at the pas-de-bas, and a decent sense of the time. Och, aye, he wass not bad, not bad . . . for a Campbell.'

R. PRAWER JHABVALA
Desecration

It is more than ten years since Sofia committed suicide in the hotel room in Mohabbatpur. At the time, it was a great local scandal, but now almost no one remembers the incident or the people involved in it. The Raja Sahib died shortly afterwards – people said it was of grief and bitterness – and Bakhtawar Singh was transferred to another district. The present Superintendent of Police is a mild-mannered man who likes to spend his evenings at home playing card games with his teenage daughters.

The hotel in Mohabbatpur no longer exists. It was sold a few months after Sofia was found there, changed hands several times, and was recently pulled down to make room for a new cinema. This will back on to the old cinema, which is still there, still playing ancient Bombay talkies. The Raja Sahib's house also no longer exists. It was demolished because the land on which it stood has become very valuable, and has been declared an industrial area. Many factories and workshops have come up in recent years.

When the Raja Sahib had first gone to live there with Sofia, there had been nothing except his own house, with a view over the ruined fort and the barren plain beyond it. In the distance there was a little patch of villagers' fields and, huddled out of sight, the village itself. Inside their big house, the Raja Sahib and Sofia had led very isolated lives. This was by choice – his choice. It was as if he had carried her away to this spot with the express purpose of having her to himself, of feasting on his possession of her.

Although she was much younger than he was – more than

233

thirty years younger – she seemed perfectly happy to live there alone with him. But in any case she was the sort of person who exudes happiness. No one knew where the Raja Sahib had met and married her. No one really knew anything about her, except that she was a Muslim (he, of course, was a Hindu) and that she had had a good convent education in Calcutta – or was it Delhi? She seemed to have no one in the world except the Raja Sahib. It was generally thought that she was partly Afghan, perhaps even with a dash of Russian. She certainly did not look entirely Indian; she had light eyes and broad cheekbones and a broad brow. She was graceful and strong, and at times she laughed a great deal, as if wanting to show off her youth and high spirits, not to mention her magnificent teeth.

Even then, however, during their good years, she suffered from nervous prostrations. At such times the Raja Sahib sat by her bedside in a darkened room. If necessary, he stayed awake all night and held her hand (she clutched his). Sometimes this went on for two or three weeks at a time, but his patience was inexhaustible. It often got very hot in the room; the house stood unprotected on that barren plain, and there was not enough electricity for air-conditioning – hardly even enough for the fan that sluggishly churned the hot air. Her attacks always seemed to occur during the very hot months, especially during the dust storms, when the landscape all around was blotted out by a pall of desert dust and the sky hung down low and yellow.

But when the air cleared, so did her spirits. The heat continued, but she kept all the shutters closed, and sprinkled water and rose essence on the marble floors and on the scented grass mats hung around the verandas. When night fell, the house was opened to allow the cooler air to enter. She and the Raja Sahib would go up on the roof. They lit candles in coloured glass chimneys and read out the Raja Sahib's verse dramas. Around midnight the servants would bring up their dinner, which consisted of many elaborate dishes, and sometimes they would also have a bottle of

French wine from the Raja Sahib's cellar. The dark earth below and the sky above were both silver from the reflection of the moon and the incredible number of stars shining up there. It was so silent that the two of them might as well have been alone in the world – which of course was just what the Raja Sahib wanted.

Sitting on the roof of his house, he was certainly monarch of all he surveyed, such as it was. His family had taken possession of this land during a time of great civil strife some hundred and fifty years before. It was only a few barren acres with some impoverished villages thrown in, but the family members had built themselves a little fort and had even assumed a royal title, though they weren't much more than glorified landowners. They lived like all the other land-owners, draining what taxes they could out of their tenant villagers. They always needed money for their own living, which became very sophisticated, especially when they began to spend more and more time in the big cities like Bombay, Calcutta, or even London. At the beginning of the century, when the fort became too rough and dilapidated to live in, the house was built. It was in a mixture of Mogul and Gothic styles, with many galleries and high rooms closed in by arched verandas. It had been built at great cost, but until the Raja Sahib moved in with Sofia it had usually remained empty except for the ancestral servants.

On those summer nights on the roof, it was always she who read out the Raja Sahib's plays. He sat and listened and watched her. She wore coloured silks and the family jewelry as an appropriate costume in which to declaim his blank verse (all his plays were in English blank verse). Sometimes she couldn't understand what she was declaiming, and sometimes it was so high-flown that she burst out laughing. He smiled with her and said, 'Go on, go on.' He sat cross-legged smoking his hookah, like any peasant; his clothes were those of a peasant too. Anyone coming up and seeing him would not have thought he was the owner of this house, the husband of Sofia – or indeed the author of all that romantic blank verse. But he was not what he looked or pretended to be. He was a man of considerable education, who had lived for years abroad, had loved the opera and theatre, and had had many cultivated friends. Later – whether through general disgust or a particular disappointment, no one knew – he had turned his back on it all. Now he liked to think of himself as just an ordinary peasant landlord.

The third character in this story, Bakhtawar Singh, really did come from a peasant background. He was an entirely self-made man. Thanks to his efficiency and valour, he had risen rapidly in the service and was now the district Superintendent of Police (known as the S.P.). He had been responsible for the capture of some notorious dacoits. One of these – the uncrowned king of the countryside for almost twenty years – he had himself trapped in a ravine and shot in the head with his revolver, and he had taken the body in his jeep to be displayed outside police headquarters. This deed and others like it had made his name a terror among dacoits and other proscribed criminals. His own men feared him no less, for he was known as a ruthless disciplinarian. But he had a softer side to him. He was terribly fond of women and, wherever he was posted, would find himself a mistress very quickly – usually more than one. He had a wife and family, but they did not play much of a role in his life. All his interests lay elsewhere. His one other interest besides women was Indian classical music, for which he had a very subtle ear.

Once a year the Raja Sahib gave a dinner party for the local gentry. These were officials from the town – the District Magistrate, the Superintendent of Police, the Medical Officer, and the rest – for whom it was the greatest event of the social calendar. The Raja Sahib himself would have gladly dispensed with the occasion, but it was the only company Sofia ever had, apart from himself. For weeks beforehand, she got the servants ready – cajoling rather than commanding them, for she spoke sweetly to everyone always – and had all the china and silver taken out. When the great night came, she sparkled with excitement. The guests were provincial, dreary, unrefined people, but she seemed not to notice that. She made them feel that their presence was a tremendous honour for her. She ran around to serve them and rallied her servants to carry in a succession of dishes and wines. Inspired by her example, the Raja Sahib also rose to the occasion. He was an excellent raconteur and entertained his guests with witty anecdotes and Urdu couplets, and sometimes even with quotations from the English poets. They applauded him not because they always understood what he was saying but because he was the Raja Sahib. They were delighted with the entertainment, and with themselves for having risen high enough in the world to be invited. There were not many women present, for most of the wives were too uneducated to be brought out into society. Those that came sat very still in their best georgette saris and cast furtive glances at their husbands.

After Bakhtawar Singh was posted to the district as the new S.P., he was invited to the Raja Sahib's dinner. He came alone, his wife being unfit for society, and as soon as he entered the house it was obvious that he was a man of superior personality. He had a fine figure, intelligent eyes, and a bristling moustache. He moved with pride, even with some pomp – certainly a man who knew his own value. He was not put out in the least by the grand surroundings but enjoyed everything as if he were entirely accustomed to such entertainment. He also appeared to understand and enjoy his host's anecdotes and poetry. When the Raja Sahib threw in a bit of Shakespeare, he confessed frankly that he could not follow it, but when his host translated and explained, he applauded that too, in real appreciation.

After dinner, there was musical entertainment. The male guests adjourned to the main drawing-room, which was an immensely tall room extending the entire height of the house with a glass rotunda. Here they reclined on Bokhara rugs and leaned against silk bolsters. The ladies had been sent home in motorcars. It would not have been fitting for them to be present, because the musicians were not from a respectable class. Only Sofia was emancipated enough to overlook this restriction. At the first party that Bakhtawar Singh attended, the principal singer was a well-known prostitute from Mohabbatpur. She had a strong, well-trained voice, as well as a handsome presence. Bakhtawar Singh did not take his eyes off her. He sat and swayed his head and exclaimed in rapture at her particularly fine modulations. For his sake, she displayed the most delicate subtleties of her art, laying them out like bait to see if he would respond to them, and he cried out as if in passion or pain. Then she smiled. Sofia was also greatly moved. At one point, she turned to Bakhtawar Singh and said, 'How good she is.' He turned his face to her and nodded, unable to speak for emotion. She was amazed to see tears in his eyes.

Next day she was still thinking about those tears. She told her husband about it, and he said, 'Yes, he liked the music, but he liked the singer, too.'

'What do you mean?' Sofia asked. When the Raja Sahib laughed, she cried, 'Tell me!' and pummelled his chest with her fists.

'I mean,' he said, catching her hands and holding them tight, 'that they will become friends.'

'She will be his mistress?' Sofia asked, opening her eyes wide.

The Raja Sahib laughed with delight. 'Where did you learn such a word? In the convent?'

'How do you know?' she pursued. 'No, you must tell me! Is he that type of man?'

'What type?' he said, teasing her.

The subject intrigued her, and she continued to think about it to herself. As always when she brooded about anything, she became silent and withdrawn and sat for hours on the veranda, staring out over the dusty plain. 'Sofia, Sofia, what are you thinking?' the Raja Sahib asked her. She smiled and shook her head. He looked into her strange, light eyes. There was something mysterious about them. Even when she was at her most playful and affectionate, her eyes seemed always to be looking elsewhere, into some different and distant landscape. It was impossible to tell what she was thinking. Perhaps she was not thinking about anything at all, but the distant gaze gave her the appearance of keeping part of herself hidden. This drove the Raja Sahib crazy with love. He wanted to pursue her into the innermost recesses of her nature, and yet at the same time he respected that privacy of hers and left her to herself when she wanted. This happened often; she would sit and brood and also roam around the house and the land in a strange, restless way. In the end, though, she would always come back to him and nestle against his thin, gray-matted chest and seem to be happy there.

For several days after the party, Sofia was in one of these moods. She wandered around the garden, though it was very hot outside. There was practically no shade, because nothing could be made to grow, for lack of water. She idly kicked at pieces of stone, some of which were broken garden statuary. When it got too hot, she did not return to the house but took shelter in the little ruined fort. It was very dark inside there, with narrow underground passages and winding steep stairs, some of which were broken. Sometimes a bat would flit out from some crevice. Sofia was not afraid; the place was familiar to her. But one day, as she sat in one of the narrow stone passages, she heard voices from the roof. She raised her head and listened. Something terrible seemed to be going on up there. Sofia climbed the stairs, steadying herself against the dank wall. Her heart was beating as loudly as those sounds from above. When she got to the top of the stairs and emerged on to the roof, she saw two men. One of them was Bakhtawar Singh. He was beating the other man, who was also a policeman, around the neck and head with his fists. When the man fell, he kicked him and then hauled him up and beat him more. Sofia gave a cry. Bakhtawar Singh turned his head and saw her. His eyes looked into hers for a moment, and how different they were from that other time when they had been full of tears!

'Get out!' he told the policeman. The man's sobs continued to be heard as he made his way down the stairs. Sofia did not know what to do. Although she wanted to flee, she stood and stared at Bakhtawar Singh. He was quite calm. He put on his khaki bush jacket, careful to adjust the collar and sleeves so as to look smart. He explained that the man had been derelict in his duties and, to escape discipline, had run away and hidden here in the fort. But Bakhtawar Singh had tracked him down. He apologized for trespassing on the Raja Sahib's property and also – here he became courtly and inclined his body toward Sofia – if he had in any way upset and disturbed her. It was not a scene he would have wished a lady to witness.

'There is blood on your hand,' she said.

He looked at it. He made a wry face and then wiped it off. (Was it his own or the other man's?) Again he adjusted his jacket, and he smoothed his hair. 'Do you often come here?' he asked, indicating the stairs and then politely standing aside to let her go first. She started down, and looked back to see if he was following.

'I come every day,' she said.

It was easy for her to go down the dark stairs, which were familiar to her. But he had to grope his way down very carefully, afraid of stumbling. She jumped down the last two steps and waited for him in the open sunlight.

'You come here all alone?' he asked. 'Aren't you afraid?'

'Of what?'

He didn't answer but walked round the back of the fort. Here his horse stood waiting for him, grazing among nettles. He jumped on its back and lightly flicked its flanks, and it cantered off as if joyful to be bearing him.

That night Sofia was very restless, and in the morning her face had the clouded, suffering look that presaged one of her attacks. But when the Raja Sahib wanted to darken the room and make her lie down, she insisted that she was well. She got up, she bathed, she dressed. He was surprised– usually she succumbed very quickly to the first signs of an attack – but now she even said that she wanted to go out. He was very pleased with her and kissed her, as if to reward her for her pluck. But later that day, when she came in again, she did have an attack, and he had to sit by her side and hold her hand and chafe her temples. She wept at his goodness. She kissed the hand that was holding hers. He looked into her strange eyes and said, 'Sofia, Sofia, what are you thinking?' But she quickly covered her eyes, so that he could not look into them. Then he had to soothe her all over again.

Whenever he had tried to make her see a doctor, she had resisted him. She said all she needed was him sitting by her and she would get well by herself, and it did happen that way. But now she told him that she had heard of a very good doctor in Mohabbatpur, who specialized in nervous diseases. The drive was long and wearying, and she insisted that there was no need for the Raja Sahib to go there with her; she could go by herself, with the car and chauffeur. They had a loving quarrel about it, and it was only when she said very well, in that case she would not go at all, would not take medical treatment, that he gave way. So now once a week she was driven to Mohabbatpur by herself.

The Raja Sahib awaited her homecoming impatiently, and the evenings of those days were like celebrations. They sat on the roof, with candles and wine, and she told him about her drive to Mohabbatpur and what the doctor had said. The Raja Sahib usually had a new passage from his latest blank-verse drama for her to read. She would start off well enough, but soon she would be overcome by laughter and have to hide her face behind the pages of his manuscript. And he would smile with her and say, 'Yes, I know, it's all a lot of nonsense.'

'No, no!' she cried. Even though she couldn't understand a good deal of what she was reading, she knew that it expressed his romantic nature and his love for her, which were both as deep as a well. She said, 'It is only I who am stupid and read so badly.' She pulled herself together and went on reading, till made helpless with laughter again.

There was something strange about her laughter. It came bubbling out, as always, as if from an overflow of high spirits, but now her spirits seemed almost too high, almost hysterical. Her husband listened to these new notes and was puzzled by them. He could not make up his mind whether the treatment was doing her good or not.

The Raja Sahib was very kind to his servants, but if any of them did anything to offend him, he was quick to dismiss him. One of his bearers, a man who had been in his employ for twenty years, got drunk one night. This was by no means an unusual occurrence among the servants; the house was in a lonely spot, with no amusements, but there was plenty of cheap liquor available from the village. Usually the servants slept off the effects in their quarters, but this bearer came staggering up on the roof to serve the Raja Sahib and Sofia. There was a scene. He fell and was dragged away by the other servants, but he resisted violently, shouting frightful obscenities, so that Sofia had to put her hands over her ears. The Raja Sahib's face was contorted with fury. The man was dismissed instantly, and when he came back the next day, wretchedly sober, begging pardon and pleading for reinstatement, the Raja Sahib would not hear him. Everyone felt sorry for the man, who had a large family and was, except for these occasional outbreaks, a sober, hardworking person. Sofia felt sorry for him too. He threw himself at her feet, and so did his wife and many children. They all sobbed, and Sofia sobbed with them. She promised to try and prevail upon the Raja Sahib.

She said everything she could – in a rushed, breathless voice, fearing he would not let her finish – and she did not take her eyes off her husband's face as she spoke. She was horrified by what she saw there. The Raja Sahib had very thin lips, and when he was angry he bit them in so tightly that they quite disappeared. He did it now, and he looked so stern and unforgiving that she felt she was not talking to her husband at all but to a gaunt and bitter old man who cared nothing for her. Suddenly she gave a cry, and just as the servant had thrown himself at her feet, so she now prostrated herself at the Raja Sahib's. 'Forgive !' she cried. 'Forgive!' It was as if she were begging forgiveness for everyone who was weak and had sinned. The Raja Sahib tried to make her rise, but she lay flat on the ground, trying over and over again to bring out the word 'Forgive' and not succeeding because of her sobs. At last he managed to help her up; he led her to the bed and waited there till she was calm again. But he was so enraged by the cause of this attack that the servant and his family had to leave immediately.

She always dismissed the car and chauffeur near the doctor's clinic. She gave the chauffeur quite a lot of money – for his food, she said – and told him to meet her in the same place in the evening. She explained that she had to spend the day under observation at the clinic. After the first few times, no explanation was necessary. The chauffeur held out his hand for the money and disappeared until the appointed time. Sofia drew up her sari to veil her face and got into a cycle rickshaw. The place Bakhtawar Singh had chosen for them was a rickety two-storey hotel, with an eating shop downstairs. It was in a very poor, outlying, forgotten part of town, where there was no danger of ever meeting an acquaintance. At first Sofia had been shy about entering the hotel, but as time went on she became bolder. No one ever looked at her or spoke to her. If she was the first to arrive, the key was silently handed to her. She felt secure that the hotel people knew nothing about her, and certainly had never seen her face, which she kept veiled till she was upstairs and the door closed behind her.

In the beginning, he sometimes arrived before her. Then he lay down on the bed, which was the only piece of furniture besides a bucket and a water jug, and was at once asleep. He always slept on his stomach, with one cheek pressed into the pillow. She would come in and stand and look at his dark, muscular, naked back. It had a scar on it, from a knife wound. She lightly ran her finger along this scar, and if that did not wake him, she unwound his loosely tied dhoti, which was all he was wearing. That awakened him immediately.

He was strange to her. That scar on his back was not the only one; there were others on his chest and an ugly long one on his left thigh, sustained during a prison riot. She wanted to know all about his violent encounters, and about his boyhood, his upward struggle, even his low origins. She often asked him about the woman singer at the dinner party. Was it true what the Raja Sahib had said – that he had liked her? Had he sought her out afterwards? He did not deny it, but laughed as at a pleasant memory. Sofia wanted to know more and more. What it was like to be with a woman like that? Had there been others? How many, and what was it like with all of them? He was amused by her curiosity and did not mind satisfying it, often with demonstrations.

Although he had had many women, they had mostly been prostitutes and singers. Sometimes he had had affairs with the wives of other police officers, but these too had been rather coarse, uneducated women. Sofia was his first girl of good family. Her refinement intrigued him. He loved watching her dress, brush her hair, treat her skin with lotions. He liked to watch her eat. But sometimes it seemed as if he deliberately wanted to violate her delicacy. For instance, he knew that she hated the coarse, hot lentils that he loved from his boyhood. He would order great quantities, with coarse bread, and cram the food into his mouth and then into hers, though it burned her palate. As their intimacy progressed, he also made her perform acts that he had learned from prostitutes. It seemed that he could not reach far enough into her, physically and in every other way. Like the Raja Sahib, he was intrigued by the look in her foreign eyes, but he wanted to seek out that mystery and expose it, as all the rest of her was exposed to him.

The fact that she was a Muslim had a strange fascination for him. Here too he differed from the Raja Sahib who, as an educated nobleman, had transcended barriers of caste and community. But for Bakhtawar Singh these were still strong. All sorts of dark superstitions remained embedded in his mind. He questioned her about things he had heard whispered in the narrow Hindu alleys he came from – the rites of circumcision, the eating of unclean flesh, what Muslims did with virgin girls. She laughed, never having heard of such things. But when she assured him that they could not be true, he nodded as if he knew better. He pointed to one of his scars, sustained during a Hindu-Muslim riot that he had suppressed. He had witnessed several such riots and knew the sort of atrocities committed in them. He told her what he had seen Muslim men do to Hindu women. Again she would not believe him. But she begged him not to go on; she put her hands over her ears, pleading with him. But he forced her hands down again and went on telling her, and laughed at her reaction. 'That's what they did,' he assured her. '*Your* brothers. It's all true.' And then he struck her, playfully but quite hard, with the flat of his hand.

All week, every week, she waited for her day in Mohabbatpur to come round. She was restless and she began to make trips into the nearby town. It was the usual type of district town, with two cinemas, a jail, a church, temples and mosques, and a Civil Lines, where the government officers lived. Sofia now began to come here to visit the officers' wives whom she had been content to see just once a year at her dinner party. Now she sought them out frequently. She played with their children and designed flower patterns for them to embroider. All the time her thoughts were elsewhere; she was waiting for it to be time to leave. Then, with hurried farewells, promises to come again soon, she climbed into her car and sat back. She told the chauffeur – the same man who took her to Mohabbatpur every week – to drive her through the Police Lines. First there were the policemen's barracks – a row of hutments, where men in vests and shorts could be seen oiling their beards and winding their turbans; they looked up in astonishment from these tasks as her saloon car drove past. She leaned back so as not to be seen, but when they had driven beyond the barracks and had reached the Police Headquarters, she looked eagerly out of the window again. Every time she hoped to get a glimpse of him, but it never happened; the car drove through and she did not dare to have it slow down. But there was one further treat in store, for beyond the offices were the residential houses of the police officers – the Assistant Deputy S.P., the Deputy S.P., the S.P.

One day, she leaned forward and said to the chauffeur, 'Turn in.'

'In here?'

'Yes, yes!' she cried, mad with excitement.

It had been a sudden impulse – she had intended simply to drive past his house, as usual – but now she could not turn back, she had to see. She got out. It was an old house, built in the times of the British for their own S.P., and now evidently inhabited by people who did not know how to look after such a place. A cow was tethered to a tree on what had once been a front lawn; the veranda was unswept and empty except for some broken crates. The house too was practically unfurnished. Sofia wandered through the derelict rooms, and it was only when she had penetrated to the inner court-yard that the life of the house began. Here there were children and noise and cooking smells. A woman came out of the kitchen and stared at her. She had a small child riding on her hip; she was perspiring, perhaps from the cooking fire, and a few strands of hair stuck to her forehead. She wore a plain and rather dirty cotton sari. She might have been his servant rather than his wife. She looked older than he did, tired and worn out. When Sofia asked whether this was the house of the Deputy S.P., she shook her head wearily, without a smile. She told one of her children to point out the right house, and turned back into her kitchen with no further curiosity. A child began to cry.

At their next meeting, Sofia told Bakhtawar Singh what she had done. He was surprised and not angry, as she had feared, but amused. He could not understand her motives, but he did not puzzle himself about them. He was feeling terribly sleepy; he said he had been up all night (and didn't say why). It was stifling in the hotel room, and perspiration ran down his naked chest and back. It was also very noisy, for the room faced on to an inner yard, which was bounded on its opposite side by a cinema. From noon onward the entire courtyard boomed with the ancient sound track – it was a very poor cinema and could afford to play only very old films – filling their room with Bombay dialogue and music. Bakhtawar Singh seemed not to care about the heat or the noise. He slept through both. He always slept when he was tired; nothing could disturb him. It astonished Sofia, and so did his imperviousness to their surroundings – the horribly shabby room and smell of cheap oil frying from the eating shop downstairs. But now, after seeing his home, Sofia understood that he was used to comfortless surroundings; and she felt so sorry for him that she began to kiss him tenderly while he slept, as if wishing to make up to him for all his deprivations. He woke up and looked at her in surprise as she cried out, 'Oh, my poor darling!'

'Why?' he asked, not feeling poor at all.

She began for the first time to question him about his marriage. But he shrugged, bored by the subject. It was a marriage like every other, arranged by their two families when he and his wife were very young. It was all right; they had children – sons as well as daughters. His wife had plenty to do, he presumed she was content – and why shouldn't she be? She had a good house to live in, sufficient money for her household expenses, and respect as the wife of the S.P. He laughed briefly. Yes, indeed, if she had anything to complain of he would like to know what it was. Sofia agreed with him. She even became indignant, thinking of his wife

who had all these benefits and did not even care to keep a
nice home for him. And not just his home – what about his
wife herself? When she thought of that bedraggled figure,
more a servant than a wife, Sofia's indignation rose – and
with it her tender pity for him, so that again she embraced
him and even spilled a few hot tears, which fell on to his
naked chest and made him laugh with surprise.

A year passed, and it was again time for the Raja Sahib's
annual party. As always, Sofia was terribly excited and
began her preparations weeks beforehand. Only this time
her excitement reached such a pitch that the Raja Sahib was
worried. He tried to joke her out of it; he asked her whom
was she expecting, what terribly important guest. Had she
invited the President of India, or perhaps the King of
Afghanistan? 'Yes, yes, the King of Afghanistan!' she cried,
laughing but with that note of hysteria he always found so
disturbing. Also she lost her temper for the first time with a
servant; it was for nothing, for some trifle, and afterward she
was so contrite that she could not do enough to make it up to
the man.

The party was, as usual, a great success. The Raja Sahib
made everyone laugh with his anecdotes, and Bakhtawar
Singh also told some stories, which everyone liked. The
same singer from Mohabbatpur had been called, and she
entertained with the same skill. And again – Sofia watched
him – Bakhtawar Singh wept with emotion. She was deeply
touched; he was manly to the point of violence (after all, he
was a policeman), and yet what softness and delicacy there
was in him. She revelled in the richness of his nature. The
Raja Sahib must have been watching him too, because later,
after the party, he told Sofia, 'Our friend enjoyed the musical
entertainment again this year.'

'Of course,' Sofia said gravely. 'She is a very fine
singer.'

The Raja Sahib said nothing, but there was something in
his silence that told her he was having his own thoughts.

'If not,' she said, as if he had contradicted her, 'then why did you call for her again this year?'

'But of course,' he said. 'She is very fine.' And he chuckled to himself.

Then Sofia lost her temper with him—suddenly, violently, just as she had with the servant. The Raja Sahib was struck dumb with amazement, but the next moment he began to blame himself. He felt he had offended her with his insinuation, and he kissed her hands to beg her forgiveness. Her convent-bred delicacy amused him, but he adored it too.

She felt she could not wait for her day in Mohabbatpur to come round. The next morning, she called the chauffeur and gave him a note to deliver to the S.P. in his office. She had a special expressionless way of receiving them. She waited in the fort for Bakhtawar Singh to appear in answer to her summons, but the only person who came was the chauffeur, with her note back again. He explained that he had been unable to find the S.P., who had not been in his office. Sofia felt a terrible rage rising inside her, and she had to struggle with herself not to vent it on the chauffeur. When the man had gone, she sank down against the stone wall and hid her face in her hands. She did not know what was happening to her. It was not only that her whole life had changed; she herself had changed and had become a different person, with emotions that were completely unfamiliar to her.

Unfortunately, when their day in Mohabbatpur at last came around, Bakhtawar Singh was late (this happened frequently now). She had to wait for him in the hot little room. The cinema show had started, and the usual dialogue and songs came from the defective sound track, echoing through courtyard and hotel. Tormented by this noise, by the heat, and by her own thoughts, Sofia was now sure that he was with the singer. Probably he was enjoying himself so much that he had forgotten all about her and would not come.

But he did come, though two hours late. He was astonished by the way she clung to him, crying and laughing

249

and trembling all over. He liked it, and kissed her in return. Just then the sound track burst into song. It was an old favourite – a song that had been on the lips of millions; everyone knew it and adored it. Bakhtawar Singh recognized it immediately and began to sing, '*O my heart, all he has left you is a splinter of himself to make you bleed!*' She drew away from him and saw him smiling with pleasure under his moustache as he sang. She cried out, 'Oh, you pig!'

It was like a blow in the face. He stopped singing immediately. The song continued on the sound track. They looked at each other. She put her hand to her mouth with fear – fear of the depths within her from which that word had arisen (never, never in her life had she uttered or thought such abuse), and fear of the consequences.

But after that moment's stunned silence all he did was laugh. He took off his bush jacket and threw himself on the bed. 'What is the matter with you?' he asked. 'What happened?'

'Oh I don't know. I think it must be the heat.' She paused. 'And waiting for you,' she added, but in a voice so low she was not sure he had heard.

She lay down next to him. He said nothing more. The incident and her word of abuse wiped out of his mind completely. She was so grateful for this that she too said nothing, asked no questions. She was content to forget her suspicions – or at least to keep them to herself and bear with them as best she could.

That night she had a dream. She dreamed everything was as it had been in the first years of her marriage, and she and the Raja Sahib as happy as they had been then. But then one night – they were together on the roof, by candle- and moonlight – he was stung by some insect that came flying out of the food they were eating. At first they took no notice, but the swelling got worse and worse, and by morning he was tossing in agony. His entire body was discoloured; he had become almost unrecognizable. There were several people around his bed, and one of them took Sofia aside and told her that the Raja Sahib would be dead within an hour. Sofia screamed out loud, but the next morning she woke up, for the Raja Sahib had turned on the light and was holding her in his arms. Yes, that very same Raja Sahib about whom she had just been dreaming, only he was not discoloured, not dying, but as he was always – her own husband, with grey-stubbled cheeks and sunken lips. She looked into his face for a moment and, fully awake now, she said, 'It's all right. I had a nightmare.' She tried to laugh it off. When he wanted to comfort her, she said again, 'It's all right,' with the same laugh and trying to keep the irritation out of her voice. 'Go to sleep,' she told him, and pretending to do so herself, she turned on her side away from him.

She continued to be haunted by the thought of the singer. Then she thought, if with one, why not with many? She herself saw him for only those few hours a week. She did not know how he spent the rest of his time, but she was sure he did not spend much of it in his own home. It had had the look of a place whose master was mostly absent. And how could it be otherwise? Sofia thought of his wife – her neglected appearance, her air of utter weariness. Bakhtawar Singh could not be expected to waste himself there. But where did he go? In between their weekly meetings there was much time for him to go to many places, and much time for her to brood.

She got into the habit of summoning the chauffeur more frequently to take her into town. The ladies in the Civil Lines were always pleased to see her, and now she found more to talk about with them, for she had begun to take an interest in local gossip. They were experts on this, and were eager to tell her that the Doctor beat his wife, the Magistrate took bribes, and the Deputy S.P. had venereal disease. And the S.P.? Sofia asked, busy threading an embroidery needle. Here they clapped their hands over their mouths and rolled their eyes around, as if at something too terrible, too scandalous to tell. Was he, Sofia asked – dropping the needle, so that she had to bend down to pick it up again – was he known to be an . . . adventurous person? 'Oh! Oh! Oh!' they cried, and then they laughed because where to start, where to stop, telling of *his* adventures?

Sofia decided that it was her fault. It was his wife's fault first, of course, but now it was hers too. She had to arrange to be with him more often. Her first step was to tell the Raja Sahib that the doctor said she would have to attend the clinic several times a week. The Raja Sahib agreed at once. She felt so grateful that she was ready to give him more details, but he cut her short. He said that of course they must follow the doctor's advice, whatever it was. But the way he spoke – in a flat, resigned voice – disturbed her, so that she looked at him more attentively than she had for some time past. It struck her that he did not look well. Was he ill? Or was it only old age? He did look old, and emaciated too, she noticed, with his skinny, wrinkled neck. She felt very sorry for him and put out her hand to touch his cheek. She was amazed by his response. He seemed to tremble at her touch, and the expression on his face was transformed. She took him in her arms. He *was* trembling. 'Are you well?' she whispered to him anxiously.

'Oh yes!' he said in a joyful voice. 'Very, very well.'

She continued to hold him. She said, 'Why aren't you writing any dramas for me these days?'

'I will write,' he said. 'As many as you like.' And then he clung to her, as if afraid to be let go from her embrace.

But when she told Bakhtawar Singh that they could now meet more frequently, he said it would be difficult for him. Of course he wanted to, he said – and how much! Here he turned to her and with sparkling eyes quoted a line of verse which said that if all the drops of water in the sea were hours of the day that he could spend with her, still they would not be sufficient for him. 'But . . .' he added regretfully.

'Yes?' she asked, in a voice she tried to keep calm.

'Sh-h-h – Listen,' he said, and put his hand over her mouth.

There was an old man saying the Muhammedan prayers

in the next room. The hotel had only two rooms, one facing the courtyard and the other the street. This latter was usually empty during the day – though not at night – but today there was someone in it. The wall was very thin, and they could clearly hear the murmur of his prayers and even the sound of his forehead striking the ground.

'What is he saying?' Bakhtawar Singh whispered.

'I don't know,' she said. The usual – *la illaha il lallah* . . . I don't know.'

'You don't know your own prayers?' Bakhtawar Singh said, truly shocked.

She said, 'I could come every Monday, Wednesday, and Friday.' She tried to make her voice tempting, but instead it came out shy.

'You do it,' he said suddenly.

'Do what?'

'Like he's doing,' he said, jerking his head toward the other room, where the old man was. 'Why not?' he urged her. He seemed to want it terribly.

She laughed nervously. 'You need a prayer carpet. And you must cover your head.' (They were both stark naked.)

'Do it like that. Go on,' he wheedled. 'Do it.'

She laughed again, pretending it was a joke. She knelt naked on the floor and began to pray the way the old man was praying in the next room, knocking her forehead on the ground. Bakhtawar Singh urged her on, watching her with tremendous pleasure from the bed. Somehow the words came back to her and she said them in chorus with the old man next door. After a while, Bakhtawar Singh got off the bed and joined her on the floor and mounted her from behind. He wouldn't let her stop praying. 'Go on,' he said, and how he laughed as she went on. Never had he had such enjoyment out of her as on that day.

But he still wouldn't agree to meet her more than once a week. Later, when she tried ever so gently to insist, he became playful and said didn't she know that he was a very busy policeman. Busy with what, she asked, also trying to be playful. He laughed enormously at that and was very loving, as if to repay her for her good joke. But then after a while he grew more serious and said, 'Listen – it's better not to drive so often through Police Lines.'

'Why not?' Driving past his office after her visits to the ladies in the Civil Lines was still the highlight of her expeditions into town.

He shrugged. 'They are beginning to talk.'

'Who?'

'Everyone.' He shrugged again. It was only her he was warning. People talked enough about him anyway; let them have one more thing. What did he care?

'Oh nonsense,' she said. But she could not help recollecting that the last few times all the policemen outside their hutments seemed to have been waiting for her car. They had cheered her as she drove past. She had wondered at the time what it meant but had soon put it out of her mind. She did that now too; she couldn't waste her few hours with Bakhtawar Singh thinking about trivial matters.

But she remembered his warning the next time she went to visit the ladies in the Civil Lines. She wasn't sure then whether it was her imagination or whether there really was something different in the way they were with her. Sometimes she thought she saw them turn aside, as if to suppress a smile, or exchange looks with each other that she was not supposed to see. And when the gossip turned to the S.P., they made very straight faces, like people who know more than they are prepared to show. Sofia decided that it was her imagination; even if it wasn't, she could not worry about it. Later, when she drove through the Police Lines, her car was cheered again by the men in underwear lounging outside their quarters, but she didn't trouble herself much about that either. There were so many other things on her mind. That day she instructed the chauffeur to take her to the S.P.'s residence again, but at the last moment – he had already turned into the gate and now had to reverse – she changed her mind. She did not want to see his wife again; it was almost as if she were afraid. Besides, there was no need for it. The moment she saw the house, she realized that she had never ceased to think of that sad, bedraggled woman inside. Indeed, as time passed the vision had not dimmed but had become clearer. She found also that her feelings toward this unknown woman had changed completely, so that, far from thinking about her with scorn, she now had such pity for her that her heart ached as sharply as if it were for herself.

Sofia had not known that one's heart could literally, physically ache. But now that it had begun it never stopped; it was something she was learning to live with, the way a patient learns to live with his disease. And moreover, like the patient, she was aware that this was only the beginning and that her disease would get worse and pass through many stages before it was finished with her. From week to week she lived only for her day in Mohabbatpur, as if that were the only time when she could get some temporary relief from pain. She did not notice that, on the contrary, it was on that day that her condition worsened and passed into a more acute stage, especially when he came late, or was absent-minded, or – and this was beginning to happen too – failed to turn up altogether. Then, when she was driven back home, the pain in her heart was so great that she had to hold her hand there. It seemed to her that if only there were someone, one other living soul, she could tell about it, she might get some relief. Gazing at the chauffeur's stolid, impassive back, she realized that he was now the person who was closest to her. It was as if she had confided in him, without words. She only told him where she wanted to go, and he went there. He told her when he needed money, and she gave it to him. She had also arranged for several increments in his salary.

The Raja Sahib had written a new drama for her. Poor Raja Sahib! He was always there, and she was always with him, but she never thought about him. If her eyes fell on him, either she did not see or, if she did, she postponed consideration of it until some other time. She was aware that there was something wrong with him, but he did not speak of it, and she was grateful to him for not obtruding his own troubles. But when he told her about the new drama he wanted her to read aloud, she was glad to oblige him. She ordered a marvellous meal for that night and had a bottle of wine put on ice. She dressed herself in one of his grand-mother's saris, of a gold so heavy that it was difficult to carry. The candles in blue glass chimneys were lit on the roof. She read out his drama with all the expression she had been taught at her convent to put into poetry readings. As usual she didn't understand a good deal of what she was reading, but she did notice that there was something different about his verses. There was one line that read 'Oh, if thou didst but know what it is like to live in hell the way I do!' It struck her so much that she had to stop reading. She looked across at the Raja Sahib; his face was rather ghostly in the blue candlelight.

'Go on,' he said, giving her that gentle, self-deprecating smile he always had for her when she was reading his dramas.

But she could not go on. She thought, what does he know about that, about living in hell? But as she went on looking at him and he went on smiling at her, she longed to tell him what it *was* like.

'What is it, Sofia? What are you thinking?'

There had never been anyone in the world who looked into her eyes the way he did, with such love but at the same time with a tender respect that would not reach farther into her than was permissible between two human beings. And it was because she was afraid of changing that look that she did not speak. What if he should turn aside from her, the way he had when she had asked forgiveness for the drunken ser-vant?

'Sofia, Sofia, what are you thinking?'

She smiled and shook her head and, with an effort went on reading. She saw that she could not tell him but would have to go on bearing it by herself for as long as possible, though she was not sure how much longer that could be.

ALAN SILLITOE

Mr Raynor the School-teacher

Now that the boys were relatively quiet Mr Raynor looked out of the classroom window, across the cobbled road and into the window of Harrison's the draper's shop. With sight made keener by horn-rimmed spectacles he observed the new girl lift her arms above her head to reach some small drawers of cotton, an action which elongated the breasts inside the dark blue dress until she looked almost flat-chested. Mr Raynor rasped his shoes slightly on the bar of his tall stool, a stool once the subject of a common-room joke, which said that he had paid the caretaker well to put on longer legs so that he could see better out of the window and observe with more ease the girls in Harrison's shop across the road. Most of the boys before him had grown so used to his long periods of distraction – freedom for them – that they no longer found inclination or time to sneer at the well-known reason for it.

When the flat-chested girl went upstairs into the Men's Suits, another girl, small, heavy, and with a satisfyingly larger bosom, came into the centre span of the counter and spread out a box of coloured ties like wheel-spokes before a man who had just come in. But her appeal to his taste was still at an unpalatable extreme, and he again regretted the departure of a girl who had been, to him, perfect in every way. Against a background of road and shop, and movements between the two that his fixed stare kept easily in a state of insignificance, he recalled her image, a difficult thing because faces did not linger clearly for a long time in his memory, even though she had been dead only ten days.

Eighteen, he remembered her, and not too tall, with almost masculine features below short chestnut hair: brown eyes, full cheeks and proportionate lips, like Aphrodite his inward eye had commented time and time again, only a little sweeter. She wore brown sweater and brown cardigan, a union that gave only tormenting glimpses of her upper figure, until one summer's day when the cardigan was set aside, revealing breasts on the same classical style, hips a trifle broad, complementing nevertheless her somewhat stocky legs and fleshy redeeming calves. She had only to move from the counter to the foot of the stairs that led to the upper part of the shop, and Mr Raynor's maxims of common arithmetic became stale phrases of instruction to be given out quickly, leaving his delighted class with an almost free session.

What memory could not accomplish, imagination did, and he recreated a tangible image, moved by long-cultivated pre-occupations of sensuality in which his wife and family took no part. He adjusted his spectacles, rolled his tongue around the dry back of his teeth, and grated his feet once more on the bar of the chair. As she walked she had carried her whole body in a sublime movement conducive to the attraction of every part of it, so that he was even aware of heels inside her shoes and finger-tips buried perhaps beneath a bolt of opulent cloth. A big trolley-bus bundled its green-fronted track along the road, and carried his vision away on the coloured advertisements decorating the band between top and bottom deck.

Deprived so suddenly he felt for a cigarette, but there was half an hour yet for the playtime break. And he still had to deal with the present class before they went to geography at ten o'clock. The noise broke into him, sunk him down to reality like cold water entering a ship. They were the eldest rag-mob of the school, and the most illiterate, a C stream of fourteen-year-old louts rearing to leave and start work at the factories round about. Bullivant the rowdiest subsided only after his head was well turned from the window; but the noise went on. The one feasible plan was to keep them as quiet as possible for the remaining months, then open the gates and let them free, allow them to spill out into the big wide world like the young animals they were, eager for fags and football, beer and women and a forest of streets to roam in. The responsibility would be no longer his, once they were packed away with the turned pages of his register into another, more incorrigible annexe than the enclave of jungle he ruled for his living. He would have done whatever could be done with such basically unsuitable and unwilling scholars.

'All right,' he called out in a loud clear voice, 'let's have a little quietness in the room.' Though the noise persisted, an air of obedience reigned. Mr Raynor was not a strict disciplinarian, but he had taught for twenty-five years, and so acquired a voice of authority that was listened to. Even if he didn't hit them very often, it was realized that he was not a young man and could easily do so. And it was consciously felt that there was more force behind a middle-aged fist than a young and inexperienced one. Consequently when he told them to keep quiet, they usually did.

'Take out your Bibles,' he said, 'and open them at Exodus, chapter six.'

He watched forty-five hands, few of them clean, unaccountably opening the Bible, as they did all books, from the back and working to the front. Now and again he caught the flicker of brightly coloured illustrations at different points in the class, on their way through a welter of pages. He leaned forward on the high desk, one elbow supporting his forehead, seeing Bullivant whisper to the boy next to him, and hearing the boy giggle.

'Handley,' Mr Raynor demanded with a show of sternness, 'who was Aaron?'

A small boy from the middle of the class stood up: 'Aaron from the Bible, sir?'

'Yes. Who else, you ass?'

'Don't know, sir,' the boy answered, either because he

really didn't, Mr Raynor told himself, or by way of revenge for being called an ass.

'Didn't you read the chapter yesterday I told you to read?'

Here was a question he could answer. 'Yes, sir,' came the bright response.

'Well then, who was Aaron?'

His face was no longer bright. It became clouded as he admitted: 'I've forgot, sir.'

Mr Raynor ran a hand slowly over his forehead. He changed tack. 'NO!' he yelled, so loudly that the boy jumped. 'Don't sit down yet, Handley.' He stood up again. 'We've been reading this part of the Bible for a month, so you should be able to answer my question. Now: Who was the brother of Moses?'

Bullivant chanted from behind:

> 'Then the Lord said unto Moses
> All the Jews shall have long noses
> Exceptin' Aaron
> He shall 'ave a square 'un
> And poor old Peter
> He shall 'ave a gas-meter!'

The low rumble reached Mr Raynor, and he saw several half-tortured faces around Bullivant trying not to laugh. 'Tell me, Handley,' he said again, 'who was the brother of Moses?'

Handley's face became happy, almost recognizable under the unfamiliar light of inspiration, for the significance of the chanted verse had eaten its way through to his understanding. 'Aaron, sir,' he said.

'And so' – Mr Raynor assumed he was getting somewhere at last – 'who was Aaron?'

Handley, who had considered his ordeal to be over on hearing a subdued cheer of irony from Bullivant, lifted a face blank in defeat. 'Don't know, sir.'

A sigh of frustration, not allowed to reach the boys, escaped Mr Raynor. 'Sit down,' he said to Handley, who did so with such alacrity that the desk lid rattled. Duty had been done as far as Handley was concerned, and now it was Robinson's turn, who stood up from his desk a few feet away. 'Tell us who Aaron was,' Mr Raynor ordered.

Robinson was a brighter boy, who had thought to keep a second Bible open beneath his desk lid for reference. 'A priest, sir,' he answered sharply, 'the brother of Moses.'

'Sit down, then,' Mr Raynor said. 'Now, remember that, Handley. What House are you in, Robinson?'

He stood up again, grinning respectfully. 'Buckingham, sir.'

'Then take a credit star.'

After the green star had been fixed to the chart he set one of the boys to read, and when the monotonous drone of his voice was well under way he turned again to span the distance between his high stool and the draper's window. By uniting the figures and faces of the present assistants, and then by dissolving them, he tried to recapture the carnal vision of the girl who had recently died, a practice of reconstruction that had been the mainstay of his sojourn at this school, a line of sight across the cobbled road into Harrison's shop, beamed on to the girls who went to work there when they were fifteen and left at twenty to get married. He had become a connoisseur of young suburban womanhood, and thus the fluctuating labour and marriage market made Mr Raynor a fickle lover, causing him too often to forget each great passion as another one walked in to take its place. Each 'good' one was credit-starred upon his mind, left behind a trail of memories when it went, until a new 'good' one came like a solid fiscal stamp of spiritual currency that drove the other one out. Each memory was thus renewed, so that none of them died.

But the last one was the best of all, an unexpected beauty back-dropped against the traffic artery of squalid streets. He had watched her work and talk or on wet afternoons stand at the counter as if in a trance. The boy on the front row was reading like a prophet, and an agitated muttering sea began

ALAN SILLITOE

to grow about him, and the curtain of Mr Raynor's memory
drew back upon the runners of a line recalled from
Baudelaire: *'Timide et libertine, et fragile et robuste'* – revealing
the secret of her classical beauty and nubility, which vanished when the blood-filled phrase was dragged away by the
top deck of a trolley-bus laden with rigid staring faces. A
tea-boy carrying a white jug slipped out of the estate agents'
offices, dodged deftly through a line of cars and lorries that
had stopped for the traffic-lights, and walked whistling a
tune into a café further down the road.

The sea of noise surrounding the prophet-like monotonous voice of the reading boy increased to a higher magnitude
than discipline would permit, until a wave carried his sonorous words away and another sound dominated the scene.
He looked, and saw Bullivant on his feet thumping the boy
at the desk in front with all his might. The boy raised his fists
to hit back.

Mr Raynor roared with such fury that there was instant
silence, his ageing pink face thrust over his desk towards
them. 'Come out, Bullivant,' he cried. *Libertine et robuste:* the
phrase fought and died, was given a white cross and packed
away.

Bullivant slouched out between rows of apprehensive
boys. ' 'e 'it me first,' he said, nearing the blackboard.

'And now I'm going to hit you,' Mr Raynor retorted, lifting
the lid of his desk and taking out a stick. His antagonist eyed
him truculently, displaying his contempt of the desperate
plight he was supposed to be in by turning around and
winking at his friends. He was a big boy of fourteen, wearing
long drainpipe trousers and a grey jersey.

'Y'aren't gooin' ter 'it me,' he said. 'I ain't dun owt ter get
'it, yer know.'

'Hold out your hand,' Mr Raynor said, his face turning a
deep crimson. *Timide*. No, he thought, not likely. This is the
least I can do. I'll get these Teddy-boy ideas out of his head
for a few seconds.

No hand was extended towards him as it should have

been. Bullivant stood still, and Mr Raynor repeated his order. The class looked on, and moving traffic on the road hid none of the smaller mutterings that passed for silence. Bullivant still wouldn't lift his hand, and time enough had gone by that could be justified by Mr Raynor as patience.

'Y'aren't gooin' ter 'it me wi' that,' Bullivant said again, a gleam just showing from his blue half-closed eyes.

Robust. An eye for an eye. The body of the girl, the bottom line of the sweater spreading over her hips, was destroyed in silence. His urge for revenge was checked, but was followed by a rage that nevertheless bit hard and forced him to action. In the passing of a bus he stepped to Bullivant's side and struck him several times across the shoulders with the stick, crashing each blow down with all his force. 'Take that,' he cried out, 'you stupid defiant oaf.'

Bullivant shied away, and before any more blows could fall, and before Mr Raynor realized that such a thing was possible, Bullivant lashed back with his fists, and they were locked in a battle of strength, both trying to push the other away, to get clear and strike. Mr Raynor took up a stance with legs apart, trying to push Bullivant back against the desks, but Bullivant foresaw such a move from his stronger adversary and moved his own body so that they went scuffling between the desks. 'Yo' ain't 'ittin' me like that,' Bullivant gasped between his teeth. 'Oo do yo' think yo' are?' He unscrewed his head that was suddenly beneath Mr Raynor's arms, threw out his fists that went wide of the mark, and leapt like a giraffe over a row of desks. Mr Raynor moved quickly and blocked his retreat, grabbed his arm firmly and glowered at him with blood-red face, twisted the captive limb viciously, all in a second, then pushed him free, though he stood with the stick ready in case Bullivant should come for him again.

But Bullivant recognized the dispensation of a truce, and merely said: 'I'll bring our big kid up to settle yo',' and sat down. Experience was Mr Raynor's friend; he saw no point in spinning out trouble to its logical conclusion, which meant only more trouble. He was content to warn Bullivant to behave himself, seeing that no face had been lost by either side in the equal contest. He sat again on the high stool behind his desk. What did it matter, really? Bullivant and most of the others would be leaving in two months, and he could keep them in check for that short time. And after the holidays more Bullivants would move up into his classroom from the scholastic escalator.

It was five minutes to ten, and to ensure that the remaining time was peaceful he took out his Bible and began reading in a clear steady voice:

'Then the Lord said unto Moses (titters here), now shalt thou see what I will do to Pharaoh: for with a strong hand shall he let them go, and with a strong hand shall he drive them out of his land.'

The class that came in at half past ten was for arithmetic, and they were told to open their books and do the exercises on page fifty-four. He observed the leaves of many books covered with ink-scrawls, and obscene words written across the illustrations and decorating the 'answer' margins like tattooing on the arms of veteran sailors, pages that would be unrecognizable in a month, but would have to last for another twelve. This was a younger class, whose rebellion had so far reached only the pages of their books.

But that, too, was only something to accept and, inclining his head to the right, he forgot the noise of his class and looked across the road at the girls working in the draper's shop. Oh yes, the last one had been the best he could remember, and the time had come when he decided to cure his madness by speaking to her one evening as she left the shop. It was a good idea. But it was too late, for a young man had begun meeting her and seeing her safely, it seemed, to the bus stop. Most of the girls who gave up their jobs at the shop did so because they met some common fate or other. ('*Timide et libertine, et fragile et robuste*' – he could not forget the phrase.) Some were married, others, he had noticed, became pregnant and disappeared; a few had quarrelled with the manager and appeared to have been sacked. But the last one, he had discovered, on opening the newspaper one evening by the traffic-lights at the corner, had been murdered by the young man who came to meet her.

Three double-decker trolley-buses trundled by in a line, but he still saw her vision by the counter.

'Quiet!' he roared, to the forty faces before him. 'The next one to talk gets the stick.'

And there was quiet.

WILLIAM TREVOR

Broken Homes

'I really think you're marvellous', the man said.

He was small and plump, with a plump face that had a greyness about it where he shaved; his hair was grey also, falling into a fringe on his forehead. He was untidily dressed, a turtle-necked red jersey beneath a jacket that had a ball-point pen and a pencil sticking out of the breast pocket. When he stood up his black corduroy trousers developed concertina creases. Nowadays you saw a lot of men like this, Mrs Malby said to herself.

'We're trying to help them,' he said, 'and of course we're trying to help you. The policy is to foster a deeper understanding.' He smiled, displaying small, evenly-arranged teeth. 'Between the generations', he added.

'Well, of course it's very kind,' Mrs Malby said.

He shook his head. He sipped the instant coffee she'd made for him and nibbled the edge of a pink wafer biscuit. As if driven by a compulsion, he dipped the biscuit into the coffee. He said:

'What age actually are you, Mrs Malby?'

'I'm eighty-seven.'

'You really are splendid for eighty-seven.'

He went on talking. He said he hoped he'd be as good himself at eighty-seven. He hoped he'd even be in the land of the living. 'Which I doubt', he said with a laugh. 'Knowing me.'

Mrs Malby didn't know what he meant by that. She was sure she'd heard him quite correctly, but she could recall nothing he'd previously stated which indicated ill-health.

266

She thought carefully while he continued to sip at his coffee and to attend to the mush of biscuit. What he had said suggested that a knowledge of him would cause you to doubt that he'd live to old age. Had he already supplied further knowledge of himself which, due to her slight deafness, she had not heard? If he hadn't, why had he left everything hanging in the air like that? It was difficult to know how best to react, whether to smile or to display concern.

'So what I thought', he said, 'was that we could send the kids on Tuesday. Say start the job on Tuesday morning, eh, Mrs Malby?'

'It's extremely kind of you.'

'They're good kids.'

He stood up. He remarked on her two budgerigars and the geraniums on her window-sill. Her sitting-room was as warm as toast, he said; it was freezing outside.

'It's just that I wondered', she said, having made up her mind to say it, 'if you could possibly have come to the wrong house?'

'Wrong? *Wrong?* You're Mrs Malby, aren't you?' he raised his voice. 'You're Mrs Malby, love?'

'Oh, yes, it's just that my kitchen isn't really in need of decoration.'

He nodded. His head moved slowly and when it stopped his dark eyes stared at her from beneath his grey fringe. He said, quite softly, what she'd dreaded he might say: that she hadn't understood.

'I'm thinking of the community, Mrs Malby. I'm thinking of you here on your own above a greengrocer's shop with your two budgies. You can benefit my kids, Mrs Malby; they can benefit you. There's no charge of any kind whatsoever. Put it like this, Mrs Malby: it's an experiment in community relations.' He paused. He reminded her of a picture there'd been in a history book, a long time ago, history classes with Miss Deacon, a picture of a Roundhead. 'So you see, Mrs Malby', he said, having said something else while he was reminding her of a Roundhead.

'It's just that my kitchen is really quite nice.'

'Let's have a little look, shall we?'

She led the way. He glanced at the kitchen's shell-pink walls, and at the white paintwork. It would cost her nearly a hundred pounds to have it done, he said; and then, to her horror, he began all over again, as if she hadn't heard a thing he'd been saying. He repeated that he was a teacher, from the school called the Tite Comprehensive. He appeared to assume that she wouldn't know the Tite Comprehensive, but she did: an ugly sprawl of glass and concrete buildings, children swinging along the pavements, shouting obsceneties. The man repeated what he said before about these children: that some of them came from broken homes. The ones he wished to send to her on Tuesday morning came from such homes, which was no joke for them. He felt, he repeated, that we all had a social duty where such children were concerned.

Mrs Malby again agreed that broken homes were to be deplored. It was just, she explained, that she was thinking of the cost of decorating a kitchen which didn't need decorating. Paint and brushes were expensive, she pointed out.

'Freshen it over for you,' the man said, raising his voice. 'First thing Tuesday, Mrs Malby.'

He went away, and she realized that he hadn't told her his name. Thinking she might be wrong about that, she went over their encounter in her mind, going back to the moment when her doorbell had sounded. 'I'm from Tite Comprehensive', was what he'd said. No name had been mentioned, of that she was positive.

In her elderliness Mrs Malby liked to be sure of such details. You had to work quite hard sometimes at eighty-seven, straining to hear, concentrating carefully in order to be certain. You had to make it clear you understood because people often imagined you didn't. Communication was what it was called nowadays, rather than conversation.

Mrs Malby was wearing a blue dress with a pattern of darker blue flowers on it. She was a woman who had been tall but had shrunk a little with age and had become slightly bent. Scant white hair crowned a face that was touched with elderly freckling. Large brown eyes, once her most striking feature, were quieter than they had been, tired behind spectacles now. Her husband George, the owner of the greengrocer's shop over which she lived, had died five years ago; her two sons, Eric and Roy, had been killed in the same month – January 1942 – in the same desert retreat.

The greengrocer's shop was unpretentious, in an unpretentious street in Fulham: Agnes Street. The people who owned it now, Jewish people called King, kept an eye on Mrs Malby. They watched for her coming and going and if they missed her one day they'd ring her doorbell to see that she was all right. She had a niece in Ealing who looked in twice a year, and another niece in Islington, who was crippled with arthritis. Once a week Mrs Grove and Mrs Halbert came round with Meals on Wheels. A social worker, Mrs Tingle, called; and the Reverend Bush called. Men came to read the meters.

In her elderliness, living where she'd lived since her marriage in 1920, Mrs Malby was happy. The tragedy in her life – the death of her sons – was no longer a nightmare, and the time that had passed since her husband's death had allowed her to come to terms with being on her own. All she wished for was to continue in these same circumstances until she died, and she did not fear death. She did not believe she would be reunited with her sons and her husband, not at least in a specific sense; but she could not believe, either, that she would entirely cease to exist the moment she ceased to breathe. Having thought about death, it seemed likely to her that after it came she'd dream, as in sleep Heaven and hell were surely no more than flickers of such pleasant dreaming, or flickers of a nightmare from which there was no waking release? No loving, omnipotent God, in Mrs Malby's view, doled out punishments and reward: human conscience, the last survivor, did that. The idea of a God, which had puzzled her for most of her life, made sense when she thought of it in terms like these, when she forgot about the mystic qualities claimed for a Church and for Jesus Christ. Yet fearful of offending the Reverend Bush, she kept such conclusions to herself when he came to see her.

All Mrs Malby dreaded now was becoming senile and being forced to enter the Sunset Home in Richmond, of which the Reverend Bush and Miss Tingle warmly spoke. The thought of a communal existence, surrounded by other elderly people, with sing-songs and card games, was anathema to her. All her life she had hated anything that smacked of communal jolliness, refusing even to go on coach trips. She loved the house above the greengrocer's shop. She loved walking down the stairs and out on to the street, nodding at the Kings as she went by the shop, buying birdseed and eggs and fire-lighters, and fresh bread from Len Skipps, a man of sixty-two whom she'd remembered being born.

The dread of having to leave Agnes Street ordered her life. With all her visitors she was careful, constantly on the look-out for signs in their eyes which might mean they were diagnosing her as senile. It was for this reason that she listened so intently to all that was said to her, that she concentrated, determined to let nothing slip by. It was for this reason that she smiled and endeavoured to appear agreeable and co-operative at all times. She was well aware that it wasn't going to be up to her to state that she was senile, or to argue that she wasn't, when the moment came.

After the teacher from Tite Comprehensive had left, Mrs Malby continued to worry. The visit from this grey-haired man had bewildered her from the start. There was the oddity of his not giving his name, and then the way he'd placed a cigarette in his mouth and had taken it out again, putting it back in the packet. Had he imagined the cigarette smoke would offend her? He could have asked, but in fact he hadn't even referred to the cigarette. Nor had he said where he'd heard about her: he hadn't mentioned the Reverend Bush, for instance, or Mrs Grove and Mrs Halbert, or Miss Tingle.

He might have been a customer in the greengrocer's shop, but he hadn't given any indication that that was so. Added to which, and most of all, there was the consideration that her kitchen wasn't in the least in need of attention. She went to look at it again, beginning to wonder if there were things about it she couldn't see. She went over in her mind what the man had said about community relations. It was difficult to resist men like that; you had to go on repeating yourself and after a while you had to assess if you were sounding senile or not. There was also the consideration that the man was trying to do good, helping children from broken homes.

'Hi', a boy with long blond hair said to her on the Tuesday morning. There were two other boys with him, one with a fuzz of dark curls all round his head, the other red-haired, a greased shock that hung to his shoulders. There was a girl as well, thin and beaky-faced, chewing something. Between them they carried tins of paint, brushes, cloths, a blue plastic bucket, and a transistor radio. 'We come to do your kitchen out', the blond boy said. 'You Mrs Wheeler then?'

'No, no. I'm Mrs Malby.'

'That's right, Billo', the girl said. 'Malby.'

'I thought he says Wheeler.'

'Wheeler's the geyser in the paint shop', the fuzzy-haired boy said.

'Typical Billo', the girl said.

She let them in, saying it was very kind of them. She led them to the kitchen, remarking on the way that strictly speaking it wasn't in need of decoration, as they could see for themselves. She'd been thinking it over, she added: she wondered if they'd just like to wash the walls down, which was a task she found difficult to do herself?'

They'd do whatever she wanted, they promised, no problem. They put their paint tins on the table. The red-haired boy turned on the radio. 'Welcome back to Open House', a cheery voice said and then reminded its listeners that it was the voice of Pete Murray. It said that a record was about to be played for someone in Upminster.

'Would you like some coffee?' Mrs Malby suggested above the noise of the transistor.

'Great', the blond boy said.

They all wore blue jeans with patches on them. The girl had a T-shirt with the words *I Lay Down With Jesus* on it. The others wore T-shirts of different colours, the blond boy's orange, the fuzzy one's light blue, the red-haired one's red. *Hot Jam-roll* a badge on the chest of the blond boy said; *Jaws* and *Bay City Rollers* other badges said.

Mrs Malby made them Nescafé while they listened to the music. They lit cigarettes, leaning about against the electric stove and against the edge of the table and against a wall. They didn't say anything because they were listening. 'That's a load of crap', the red-haired boy pronounced eventually, and the others agreed. Even so they went on listening. 'Pete Murray's crappy', the girl said.

Mrs Malby handed them the cups of coffee, drawing their attention to the sugar she'd put out for them on the table, and to the milk. She smiled at the girl. She said again that it was a job she couldn't manage any more, washing walls.

'Get that, Billo?' the fuzzy-haired boy said. 'Washing walls.'

'Who loves ya, baby?' Billo replied.

Mrs Malby closed the kitchen door on them, hoping they wouldn't take too long because the noise of the transistor was so loud. She listened to it for a quarter of an hour and then she decided to go out and do her shopping.

In Len Skipp's she said that four children from the Tite Comprehensive had arrived in her house and were at present washing her kitchen walls. She said it again to the man in the fish shop and the man was surprised. It suddenly occurred to her that of course they couldn't have done any painting because she hadn't discussed colours with the teacher. She thought it odd that the teacher hadn't mentioned colours and wondered what colour the paint tins contained. It worried her a little that all that hadn't occurred to her before.

'Hi, Mrs Wheeler,' the boy called Billo said to her in her

hall when she returned. He was standing there combing his hair, looking at himself in the mirror of the hall-stand. Music was coming from upstairs.

There were yellowish smears on the stair-carpet, which upset Mrs Malby very much. There were similar smears on the landing carpet. 'Oh, but please,' she cried, standing in the kitchen doorway. 'Oh, please, no!' she cried.

Yellow emulsion paint partially covered the shell-pink of one wall. Some had spilt from the tin on to the black-and-white vinyl of the floor and had been walked through. The boy with the fuzzy hair was standing on a draining-board applying the same paint to the ceiling. He was the only person in the kitchen.

He smiled at Mrs Malby, looking down at her. 'Hi, Mrs Wheeler,' he said.

'But I said only to wash them,' she cried.

She felt tired, saying that. The upset of finding the smears on the carpets and of seeing the hideous yellow plastered over the quiet shell-pink had already taken a toll. Her emotional outburst had caused her face and neck to become warm. She felt she'd like to lie down.

'Eh, Mrs Wheeler?' The boy smiled at her again, continuing to slap paint on to the ceiling. A lot of it dripped back on top of him, on to the draining-board and on to cups and saucers and cutlery, and on to the floor. 'D'you fancy the colour, Mrs Wheeler?' he asked her.

All the time the transistor continued to blare, a voice inexpertly singing, a tuneless twanging. The boy referred to this sound, pointing at the transistor with his paint-brush, saying it was great. Unsteadily she crossed the kitchen and turned the transistor off. 'Hey, sod it, missus', the boy protested angrily.

'I said to wash the walls. I didn't even choose that colour.'

The boy, still annoyed because she'd turned off the radio, was gesturing crossly with the brush. There was paint in the fuzz of his hair and on his T-shirt and his face. Every time he moved the brush about paint flew off it. It speckled the windows and the small dresser, and the electric stove and the taps and the sink.

'Where's the sound gone?' the boy called Billo demanded, coming into the kitchen and going straight to the transistor.

'I didn't want the kitchen painted', Mrs Malby said again. 'I told you.'

The singing from the transistor recommenced, louder than before. On the draining-board the fuzzy-haired boy began to sway, throwing his body and his head about.

'Please stop him painting', Mrs Malby shouted as shrilly as she could. 'Here', the boy called Billo said, bundling her out on to the landing and closing the kitchen door. 'Can't hear myself think in there.'

'I don't want it painted.'

'What's that, Mrs Wheeler?'

'My name isn't Wheeler. I don't want my kitchen painted. I told you.'

'Are we in the wrong house? Only we was told –'

'Will you please wash that paint off.'

'If we come to the wrong house –'

'You haven't come to the wrong house. Please tell that boy to wash off the paint he's put on.'

'Did a bloke from the Comp come in to see you, Mrs Wheeler? Fat bloke?'

'Yes, yes, he did.'

'Only he give instructions –'

'Please would you tell that boy?'

'Whatever you say, Mrs Wheeler.'

'And wipe up the paint where it's spilt on the floor. It's been trampled out, all over my carpets.'

'No problem, Mrs Wheeler.'

Not wishing to return to the kitchen herself she ran the hot tap in the bathroom on to the sponge-cloth she kept for cleaning the bath. She found that if she rubbed hard enough at paint on the stair-carpet and on the landing carpet it began to disappear. But the rubbing tired her and as she put away the sponge-cloth she had a feeling of not quite knowing

274

what was what. Everything that had happened in the last few hours felt like a dream; it also had the feeling of plays she had seen on television; the one thing it wasn't like was reality. As she paused in her bathroom, having placed the sponge-cloth on a ledge under the hand-basin, Mrs Malby saw herself standing there, as she often did in a dream; she saw her body hunched within the same blue dress she'd been wearing when the teacher called, and two touches of red in her pale face, and her white hair tidy on her head, and her fingers seeming fragile. In a dream anything could happen next: she might suddenly find herself forty years younger, Eric and Roy might be alive. She might even be younger, Dr Ramsey might be telling her she was pregnant. In a television play it would be different: the children who came to her house might kill her. What she hoped for from reality was that order would be restored in her kitchen, that all the paint would be washed away from her walls as she had wiped it from her carpets, that the misunderstanding would be over. For an instant she saw herself in her kitchen, making tea for the children, saying it didn't matter. She even heard herself adding that in a life as long as hers you became used to everything.

She left the bathroom; the blare of the transistor still persisted. She didn't want to sit in her sitting-room, having to listen to it. She climbed the stairs to her bedroom, imagining the coolness there, and the quietness.

'Hey', the girl protested when Mrs Malby opened the bedroom door.

'Sod off, you guys', the boy with the red hair ordered.

They were in her bed. Their clothes were all over the floor. Her two budgerigars were flying about the room. Protruding from sheets and blankets were the boy's naked shoulders and the back of his head. The girl poked her face up from under him. She gazed at Mrs Malby. 'It's not them', she whispered to the boy. 'It's the woman.'

'Hi there, missus.' The boy twisted his head round. From the kitchen, still loudly, came the noise of the transistor.

'Sorry', the girl said.

'Why are you up here? Why have you let my birds out? You've no right to behave like this.'

'We needed sex', the girl explained.

The budgerigars were perched on the looking-glass on the dressing-table, beadily surveying the scene.

'They're really great, them budgies', the boy said.

Mrs Malby stepped through their garments. The budgerigars remained where they were. They fluttered when she seized them but they didn't offer any resistance. She returned with them to the door.

'You had no right,' she began to say to the two in her bed, but her voice had become weak. It quivered into a useless whisper, and once more she thought that what was happening couldn't be happening. She saw herself again, standing unhappily with the budgerigars.

In her sitting-room she wept. She returned the budgerigars to their cage and sat in an armchair by the window that looked out over Agnes Street. She sat in sunshine, feeling its warmth but not, as she might have, delighting in it. She wept because she had intensely disliked the finding of the boy and girl in her bed. Images from the bedroom remained vivid in her mind. On the floor the boy's boots were heavy and black, composed of leather that did not shine. The girl's shoes were green, with huge heels and soles. The girl's underclothes were purple, the boy's dirty. There'd been an unpleasant smell of sweat in her bedroom.

Mrs Malby waited, her head beginning to ache. She dried away her tears, wiping at her eyes and cheeks with a handkerchief. In Agnes Street people passed by on bicycles, girls from the polish factory returning home to lunch, men from the brickworks. People came out of the greengrocer's with leeks and cabbages in baskets, some carrying paper bags. Watching these people in Agnes Street made her feel better, even though her headache was becoming worse. She felt more composed, and more in control of herself.

'We're sorry', the girl said again, suddenly appearing,

teetering on her clumsy shoes. 'We didn't think you'd come up to the bedroom.'

She tried to smile at the girl, but found it hard to do so. She nodded instead.

'The others put the birds in', the girl said. 'Meant to be a joke, that was.'

She nodded again. She couldn't see how it could be a joke to take two budgerigars from their cage, but she didn't say that.

'We're getting on with the painting now', the girl said. 'Sorry about that.'

She went away and Mrs Malby continued to watch the people in Agnes Street. The girl had made a mistake when she'd said they were getting on with the painting: what she'd meant was that they were getting on with washing it off. The girl had come straight downstairs to say she was sorry; she hadn't been told by the boys in the kitchen that the paint had been applied in error. When they'd gone, Mrs Malby said to herself, she'd open her bedroom window wide in order to get rid of the odour of sweat. She'd put clean sheets on her bed.

From the kitchen, above the noise of the transistor, came the clatter of raised voices. There was laughter and a crash, and then louder laughter. Singing began, attaching itself to the singing from the transistor.

She sat for twenty minutes and then she went and knocked on the kitchen door, not wishing to push the door open in case it knocked someone off a chair. There was no reply. She opened the door gingerly.

More yellow paint had been applied. The whole wall around the window was covered with it, and most of the wall behind the sink. Half of the ceiling had it on it; the woodwork that had been white was now a glossy dark blue. All four of the children were working with brushes. A tin of paint had been upset on the floor.

She wept again, standing there watching, unable to prevent her tears. She felt them running warmly on her cheeks and then becoming cold. It was in this kitchen that she had cried first of all when the two telegrams had come in 1942, believing when the second one arrived that she would never cease to cry. It would have seemed ridiculous at the time, to cry just because her kitchen was all yellow.

They didn't see her standing there. They went on singing, slapping the paint-brushes back and forth. There'd been neat straight lines where the shell-pink met the white of the woodwork, but now the lines were any old how. The boy with the red hair was applying the dark-blue gloss.

Again the feeling that it wasn't happening possessed Mrs Malby. She'd had a dream a week ago, a particularly vivid dream in which the Prime Minister had stated on television that the Germans had been invited to invade England since England couldn't manage to look after herself any more. That dream had been most troublesome because when she'd woken up in the morning she'd thought it was something she'd seen on television, that she'd actually been sitting in her sitting room the night before, listening to the Prime Minister saying that he and the Leader of the Opposition had decided the best thing for Britain was invasion. After thinking about it, she'd established that of course it hadn't been true; but even so she'd glanced at the headlines of newspapers when she went out shopping.

'How d'you fancy it?' the boy called Billo called out, smiling across the kitchen at her, not noticing that she was upset. 'Neat, Mrs Wheeler?'

She didn't answer. She went downstairs and walked out of her hall-door, into Agnes Street and into the green-grocer's that had been her husband's. It never closed in the middle of the day; it never had. She waited and Mr King appeared, wiping his mouth. 'Well then, Mrs Malby?' he said.

He was a big man with a well-kept black moustache and Jewish eyes. He didn't smile much because smiling wasn't his way, but he was in no way morose, rather the opposite.

'So what can I do for you?' he said.

She told him. He shook his head and repeatedly frowned as he listened. His expressive eyes widened. He called his wife.

While the three of them hurried along the pavement to Mrs Malby's open hall-door it seemed to her that the Kings doubted her. She could feel them thinking that she must have got it all wrong, that she'd somehow imagined all this stuff about yellow paint and pop music on a radio, and her birds flying around her bedroom while two children were lying in her bed. She didn't blame them; she knew exactly how they felt. But when they entered her house the noise from the transistor could at once be heard.

The carpet of the landing was smeared again with the paint. Yellow footprints led to her sitting-room and out again, back to the kitchen.

'You bloody young hooligans', Mr King shouted at them. He snapped the switch on the transistor. He told them to stop applying the paint immediately. 'What the hell d'you think you're up to?' he demanded furiously.

'We come to paint out the old ma's kitchen', the boy called Billo explained, unruffled by Mr King's tone. 'We was carrying out instructions mister.'

'So it was instructions to spill the blooming paint all over the floor? So it was instructions to cover the windows with it and every knife and fork in the place? So it was instructions to frighten the life of a poor woman by messing about in her bedroom?'

'No one frightens her, mister.'

'You know what I mean, son.'

Mrs Malby returned with Mrs King and sat in the cubby-hole behind the shop, leaving Mr King to do his best. At three o'clock he arrived back, saying that the children had gone. He telephoned the school and after a delay was put in touch with the teacher who'd been to see Mrs Malby. He made this telephone call in the shop but Mrs Malby could hear him saying that what had happened was a disgrace. 'A woman of eighty-seven,' Mr King protested, 'thrown to a state of misery. There'll be something to pay on this, you know.'

There was some further discussion on the telephone, and then Mr King replaced the receiver. He put his head into the cubbyhole and announced that the teacher was coming round immediately to inspect the damage. 'What can I entice you to?' Mrs Malby heard him asking a customer, and a woman's voice replied that she needed tomatoes, a cauliflower, potatoes and Bramleys. She heard Mr King telling the woman what had happened, saying that it had wasted two hours of his time.

She drank the sweet milky tea which Mrs King had poured her. She tried not to think of the yellow paint, and the dark-blue gloss. She tried not to remember the scene in the bedroom and the smell there'd been, and the new marks that had appeared on her carpets after she'd wiped off the original ones. She wanted to ask Mr King if these marks had been washed out before the paint had a chance to dry, but she didn't like to ask this because Mr King had been so kind and it might seem like pressing him.

'Kids nowadays', Mrs King said. 'I just don't know.'

'Birched they should be', Mr King said, coming into the cubbyhole and picking up a mug of the milky tea. 'I'd birch the bottoms off them.'

Someone arrived in the shop, Mr King hastened from the cubbyhole. 'What can I entice you to, sir?' Mrs Malby heard him politely enquiring and the voice of the teacher who'd been to see her replied. He said who he was and Mr King wasn't polite any more. An experience like that, Mr King declared thunderously, could have killed an eighty-seven-year-old stone dead.

Mrs Malby stood up and Mrs King came promptly forward to place a hand under her elbow. They went into the shop like that. 'Three and a half p,' Mr King was saying to a woman who'd asked the price of oranges. 'The larger ones at four.'

Mr King gave the woman four oranges of the smaller size

and accepted her money. He called out to a youth who was passing by on a bicycle, about to start an afternoon paper round. He was a youth who occasionally assisted him on Saturday mornings: Mr King asked him now if he would mind the shop for ten minutes since an emergency had arisen. Just for once, Mr King argued, it wouldn't matter if the evening papers were a little late.

'Well, you can't say they haven't brightened the place up, Mrs Malby', the teacher said in her kitchen. He regarded her from beneath his grey fringe. He touched one of the walls with the tip of a finger. He nodded to himself, appearing to be satisfied.

The painting had been completed, the yellow and the dark-blue gloss. Where the colours met there were untidily jagged lines. All the paint that had been spilt on the floor had been wiped away, but the black-and-white vinyl had become dull and grubby in the process. The paint had also been wiped from the windows and from other surfaces, leaving them smeared. The dresser had been wiped down and was smeary also. The cutlery and the taps and the cups and saucers had all been washed or wiped.

'Well, you wouldn't believe it!' Mrs King exclaimed. She turned to her husband. However had he managed it all? she asked him. 'You should have seen the place!' she said to the teacher.

'It's just the carpets', Mr King said. He led the way from the kitchen to the sitting-room, pointed at the yellow on the landing carpet and on the sitting-room one. 'The blooming stuff dried', he explained, 'before we could get to it. That's where compensation comes in.' He spoke sternly, addressing the teacher. 'I'd say she has a bob or two owing.'

Mrs King nudged Mrs Malby, drawing attention to the fact that Mr King was doing his best for her. The nudge suggested that all would be well because a sum of money would be paid, possibly even a larger sum than was merited. It suggested also that in this way Mrs Malby might find herself doing rather well.

'Compensation?' the teacher said, bending down and scratching at the paint on the sitting-room carpet. 'I'm afraid compensation's out of the question.'

'She's had her carpets ruined', Mr King snapped quickly. 'This woman's been put about, you know.'

'She got her kitchen done free', the teacher snapped back at him.

'They released her pets. They got up to tricks in her bed. You'd no damn right –'

'These kids come from broken homes, sir. I'll do my best with your carpets, Mrs Malby.'

'But what about my kitchen?' she whispered. She cleared her throat because her whispering could hardly be heard. 'My kitchen?' she whispered again.

'What about it, Mrs Malby?'

'I didn't want it painted.'

'Oh, don't be silly now.'

The teacher took his jacket off and threw it impatiently on to a chair. He left the sitting-room. Mrs Malby heard him running a tap in the kitchen.

'It was best to finish the painting, Mrs Malby', Mr King said. 'Otherwise the kitchen would have driven you mad, half done like that. I stood over them till they finished it.'

'You can't take paint off, dear', Mrs King explained, 'once it's on. You've done wonders, Leo', she said to her husband. 'Young devils.'

'We'd best be getting back', Mr King said.

'It's quite nice, you know', his wife added. 'Your kitchen's quite cheerful, dear.'

The Kings went away and the teacher rubbed at the yellow on the carpets with her washing-up brush. The landing carpet was marked anyway, he pointed out, poking a finger at the stains left behind by the paint she'd removed herself with the sponge-cloth from the bathroom. She must be delighted with the kitchen, he said.

She knew she mustn't speak. She'd known she mustn't when the Kings had been there; she knew she mustn't now.

She might have reminded the Kings that she'd chosen the original colours in the kitchen herself. She might have complained to the man as he rubbed at her carpets that the carpets would never be the same again. She watched him, not saying anything, not wishing to be regarded as a nuisance. The Kings would have considered her a nuisance too, agreeing to let children into her kitchen to paint it and then making a fuss. If she became a nuisance the teacher and the Kings would drift on to the same side, and the Reverend Bush would somehow be on that side also, and Miss Tingle, and even Mrs Grove and Mrs Halbert. They would agree between themselves that what had happened had to do with her elderliness, with her not understanding that children who brought paint into a kitchen were naturally going to use it.

'I defy anyone to notice that', the teacher said, standing up, gesturing at the yellow blurs that remained on her carpets. He put his jacket on. He left the washing-up brush and the bowl of water he'd been using on the floor of her sitting-room. 'All's well that ends well', he said. 'Thanks for your co-operation, Mrs Malby.'

She thought of her two sons, Eric and Roy, not knowing quite why she thought of them now. She descended the stairs with the teacher, who was cheerfully talking about community relations. You had to make allowances, he said, for kids like that; you had to try and understand; you couldn't just walk away.

Quite suddenly she wanted to tell him about Eric and Roy. In the desire to talk about them she imagined their bodies, as she used to in the past, soon after they'd been killed. They lay on desert sand, desert birds swooped down on them. Their four eyes were gone. She wanted to explain to the teacher that they'd been happy, a contented family in Agnes Street, until the war came and smashed everything to pieces. Nothing had been the same afterwards. It hadn't been easy to continue with nothing to continue for. Each room in the house had contained different memories of the two boys growing up. Cooking and cleaning had seemed pointless. The shop which would have been theirs would have to pass to someone else.

And yet time had soothed the awful double wound. The horror of the emptiness had been lived with, and if having the Kings in the shop now wasn't the same as having your sons there at least the Kings were kind. Forty-four years after the destruction of your family you were happy in your elderliness because time had been merciful. She wanted to tell the teacher that also, she didn't know why, except that in some way it seemed relevant. But she didn't tell him because it would have been difficult to begin, because in the effort there'd be the danger of seeming senile. Instead she said good-bye, concentrating on that. She said she was sorry, saying it just to show she was aware that she hadn't made herself clear to the children. Conversation had broken down between the children and herself: she wanted him to know she knew it had.

He nodded vaguely, not listening to her. He was trying to make the world a better place, he said. 'For kids like that, Mrs Malby. Victims of broken homes.'

J. G. BALLARD
Venus Smiles

Low notes on a high afternoon.

As we drove away after the unveiling my secretary said, 'Mr Hamilton, I suppose you realize what a fool you've made of yourself?'

'Don't sound so prim,' I told her. 'How was I to know Lorraine Drexel would produce something like that?'

'Five thousand dollars,' she said reflectively. 'It's nothing but a piece of old scrap iron. And the noise! Didn't you look at her sketches? What's the Fine Arts Committee for?'

My secretaries have always talked to me like this, and just then I could understand why. I stopped the car under the trees at the end of the square and looked back. The chairs had been cleared away and already a small crowd had gathered around the statue, staring up at it curiously. A couple of tourists were banging one of the struts, and the thin metal skeleton shuddered weakly. Despite this, a monotonous and high-pitched wailing sounded from the statue across the pleasant morning air, grating the teeth of passers-by.

'Raymond Mayo is having it dismantled this afternoon,' I said. 'If it hasn't already been done for us. I wonder where Miss Drexel is?'

'Don't worry, you won't see her in Vermilion Sands again. I bet she's half way to Red Beach by now.'

I patted Carol on the shoulder. 'Relax. You looked beautiful in your new skirt. The Medicis probably felt like this about Michelangelo. Who are we to judge?'

'*You* are,' she said. 'You were on the committee, weren't you?'

'Darling,' I explained patiently. 'Sonic sculpture is the thing. You're trying to fight a battle the public lost thirty years ago.'

We drove back to my office in a thin silence. Carol was annoyed because she had been forced to sit beside me on the platform when the audience began to heckle my speech at the unveiling, but even so the morning had been disastrous on every count. What might be perfectly acceptable at Expo 75 or the Venice Biennale was all too obviously passé at Vermilion Sands.

When we had decided to commission a sonic sculpture for the square in the centre of Vermilion Sands, Raymond Mayo and I had agreed that we should patronize a local artist. There were dozens of professional sculptors in Vermilion Sands, but only three had deigned to present themselves before the committee. The first two we saw were large, bearded men with enormous fists and impossible schemes—one for a hundred-foot-high vibrating aluminium pylon, and the other for a vast booming family group that involved over fifteen tons of basalt mounted on a megalithic step-pyramid. Each had taken an hour to be argued out of the committee room.

The third was a woman: Lorraine Drexel. This elegant and autocratic creature in a cartwheel hat, with her eyes like black orchids, was a sometime model and intimate of Giacometti and John Cage. Wearing a blue crêpe de Chine dress ornamented with lace serpents and other art nouveau emblems, she sat before us like some fugitive Salome from the world of Aubrey Beardsley. Her immense eyes regarded us with an almost hypnotic calm, as if she had discovered that very moment some unique quality in these two amiable dilettantes of the Fine Arts Committee.

She had lived in Vermilion Sands for only three months, arriving via Berlin, Calcutta and the Chicago New Arts Centre. Most of her sculpture to date had been scored for various Tantric and Hindu hymns, and I remembered her brief affair with a world-famous pop-singer, later killed in a car crash, who had been an enthusiastic devotee of the sitar. At the time, however, we had given no thought to the whining quarter-tones of this infernal instrument, so grating on the Western ear. She had shown us an album of her sculptures, interesting chromium constructions that compared favourably with the run of illustrations in the latest art magazines. Within half an hour we had drawn up a contract.

I saw the statue for the first time that afternoon thirty seconds before I started my speech to the specially selected assembly of Vermilion Sands notables. Why none of us had bothered to look at it beforehand I fail to understand. The title printed on the invitation cards – 'Sound and Quantum: Generative Synthesis 3' – had seemed a little odd, and the general shape of the shrouded statue even more suspicious. I was expecting a stylized human figure but the structure under the acoustic drapes had the proportions of a medium-sized radar aerial. However, Lorraine Drexel sat beside me on the stand, her bland eyes surveying the crowd below. A dream-like smile gave her the look of a tamed Mona Lisa.

What we saw after Raymond Mayo pulled the tape I tried not to think about. With its pedestal the statue was twelve feet high. Three spindly metal legs, ornamented with spikes and crosspieces, reached up from the plinth to a triangular apex. Clamped on to this was a jagged structure that at first sight seemed to be an old Buick radiator grille. It had been bent into a rough U five feet across, and the two arms jutted out horizontally, a single row of sonic cores, each about a foot long, poking up like the teeth of an enormous comb. Welded on apparently at random all over the statue were twenty or thirty filigree vanes.

That was all. The whole structure of scratched chromium had a blighted look like a derelict antenna. Startled a little by the first shrill whoops emitted by the statue, I began my speech and was about half way through when I noticed that Lorraine Drexel had left her seat beside me. People in the audience were beginning to stand up and cover their ears, shouting to Raymond to replace the acoustic drape. A hat sailed through the air over my head and landed neatly on one of the sonic cores. The statue was now giving out an intermittent high-pitched whine, a sitar-like caterwauling that seemed to pull apart the sutures of my skull. Responding to the boos and protests, it suddenly began to whoop erratically, the horn-like sounds confusing the traffic on the far side of the square.

As the audience began to leave their seats *en masse* I stuttered inaudibly to the end of my speech, the wailing of the statue interrupted by shouts and jeers. Then Carol tugged me sharply by the arm, her eyes flashing. Raymond Mayo pointed with a nervous hand.

The three of us were alone on the platform, the rows of overturned chairs reaching across the square. Standing twenty yards from the statue, which had now begun to whimper plaintively, was Lorraine Drexel. I expected to see a look of fury and outrage on her face, but instead her unmoving eyes showed the calm and implacable contempt of a grieving widow insulted at her husband's funeral. As we waited awkwardly, watching the wind carry away the torn programme cards, she turned on a diamond heel and walked across the square.

No one else wanted anything to do with the statue, so I was finally presented with it. Lorraine Drexel left Vermilion Sands the day it was dismantled. Raymond spoke briefly to her on the telephone before she went. I presumed she would be rather unpleasant and didn't bother to listen in on the extension.

'Well?' I asked. 'Does she want it back?'

'No.' Raymond seemed slightly preoccupied. 'She said it belonged to us.'

'You and me?'

'Everybody.' Raymond helped himself to the decanter of Scotch on the veranda table. 'Then she started laughing.'

'Good. What at?'

'I don't know. She just said that we'd grow to like it.'

There was nowhere else to put the statue so I planted it out in the garden. Without the stone pedestal it was only six feet high. Shielded by the shrubbery, it had quietened down and now emitted a pleasant melodic harmony, its soft rondos warbling across the afternoon heat. The sitar-like twangs, which the statue had broadcast in the square like some pathetic love-call from Lorraine Drexel to her dead lover, had vanished completely, almost as if the statue had been rescored. I had been so stampeded by the disastrous unveiling that I had had little chance to see it and I thought it looked a lot better in the garden than it had done in Vermilion Sands, the chromium struts and abstract shapes standing out against the desert like something in a vodka advertisement. After a few days I could almost ignore it.

A week or so later we were out on the terrace after lunch, lounging back in the deck chairs. I was nearly asleep when Carol said, 'Mr Hamilton, I think it's moving.'

'What's moving?'

Carol was sitting up, head cocked to one side. 'The statue. It looks different.'

I focused my eyes on the statue twenty feet away. The radiator grille at the top had canted around slightly but the three stems still seemed more or less upright.

'The rain last night must have softened the ground,' I said. I listened to the quiet melodies carried on the warm eddies of air, and then lay back drowsily. I heard Carol light a cigarette with four matches and walk across the veranda.

When I woke in an hour's time she was sitting straight up in the deck chair, a frown creasing her forehead.

'Swallowed a bee?' I asked. 'You look worried.'

Then something caught my eye.

I watched the statue for a moment. 'You're right. It is moving.'

Carol nodded. The statue's shape had altered perceptibly.

The grill had spread into an open gondola whose sonic cores seemed to feel at the sky, and the three stem-pieces were wider apart. All the angles seemed different.

'I thought you'd notice it eventually,' Carol said as we walked over to it. 'What's it made of?'

'Wrought iron – I think. There must be a lot of copper or lead in it. The heat is making it sag.'

'Then why is it sagging upwards instead of down?'

I touched one of the shoulder struts. It was springing elastically as the air moved across the vanes and went on vibrating against my palm. I gripped it in both hands and tried to keep it rigid. A low but discernible pulse pumped steadily against me.

I backed away from it, wiping the flaking chrome off my hands. The Mozartian harmonies had gone, and the statue was now producing a series of low Mahler-like chords. As Carol stood there in her bare feet I remembered that the height specification we had given to Lorraine Drexel had been exactly two metres. But the statue was a good three feet higher than Carol, the gondola at least six or seven across. The spars and struts looked thicker and stronger.

'Carol,' I said. 'Get me a file, would you? There are some in the garage.'

She came back with two files and a hacksaw.

'Are you going to cut it down?' she asked hopefully.

'Darling, this is an original Drexel.' I took one of the files. 'I just want to convince myself that I'm not going insane.'

I started cutting a series of small notches all over the statue, making sure they were exactly the width of the file apart. The metal was soft and worked easily; on the surface there was a lot of rust but underneath it had a bright sappy glint.

'All right,' I said when I had finished. 'Let's go and have a drink.'

We sat on the veranda and waited. I fixed my eyes on the statue and could have sworn that it didn't move. But when we went back an hour later the gondola had swung right round again, hanging down over us like an immense metal mouth.

There was no need to check the notch intervals against the file. They were all at least double the original distance apart.

'Mr Hamilton,' Carol said. 'Look at this.'

She pointed to one of the spikes. Poking through the outer scale of chrome were a series of sharp little nipples. One or two were already beginning to hollow themselves. Unmistakably they were incipient sonic cores.

Carefully I examined the rest of the statue. All over it new shoots of metal were coming through: arches, barbs, sharp double helixes, twisting the original statue into a thicker and more elaborate construction. A medley of half-familiar sounds, fragments of a dozen overtures and symphonies, murmured all over it. The statue was well over twelve feet high. I felt one of the heavy struts and the pulse was stronger, beating steadily through the metal, as if it was thrusting itself on to the sound of its own music.

Carol was watching me with a pinched and worried look.

'Take it easy,' I said. 'It's only growing.'

We went back to the veranda and watched.

By six o'clock that evening it was the size of a small tree. A spirited simultaneous rendering of Brahms's Academic Festival Overture and Rachmaninoff's First Piano Concerto trumpeted across the garden.

'The strangest thing about it,' Raymond said the next morning, raising his voice above the din, 'is that it's still a Drexel.'

'Still a piece of sculpture, you mean?'

'More than that. Take any section of it and you'll find the original motifs being repeated. Each vane, each helix has all the authentic Drexel mannerisms, almost as if she herself were shaping it. Admittedly, this penchant for the late Romantic composers is a little out of keeping with all that sitar twanging, but that's rather a good thing, if you ask me. You can probably expect to hear some Beethoven any moment now – the Pastoral Symphony, I would guess.'

'Not to mention all five piano concertos – played at once,' I said sourly. Raymond's loquacious delight in this musical monster out in the garden annoyed me. I closed the veranda windows, wishing that he himself had installed the statue in the living room of his downtown apartment. 'I take it that it won't go on growing for ever?'

Carol handed Raymond another Scotch. 'What do you think we ought to do?'

Raymond shrugged. 'Why worry?' he said airily. 'When it starts tearing the house down cut it back. Thank God we had it dismantled. If this had happened in Vermilion Sands . . .'

Carol touched my arm. 'Mr Hamilton, perhaps that's what Lorraine Drexel expected. She wanted it to start spreading all over the town, the music driving everyone crazy –'

'Careful,' I warned her. 'You're running away with yourself. As Raymond says, we can chop it up any time we want to and melt the whole thing down.'

'Why don't you, then?'

'I want to see how far it'll go,' I said. In fact my motives were more mixed. Clearly, before she left, Lorraine Drexel had set some perverse jinx at work within the statue, a bizarre revenge on us all for deriding her handiwork. As Raymond had said, the present babel of symphonic music had no connection with the melancholy cries the statue had first emitted. Had those forlorn chords been intended to be a requiem for her dead lover – or even, conceivably, the beckoning calls of a still unsurrendered heart? Whatever her motives, they had now vanished into this strange travesty lying across my garden.

I watched the statue reaching slowly across the lawn. It had collapsed under its own weight and lay on its side in a huge angular spiral, twenty feet long and about fifteen feet high, like the skeleton of a futuristic whale. Fragments of the Nutcracker Suite and Mendelssohn's Italian Symphony sounded from it, overlaid by sudden blaring excerpts from the closing movements of Grieg's Piano Concerto. The selection of these hack classics seemed deliberately designed to get on my nerves.

I had been up with the statue most of the night. After Carol went to bed I drove my car on to the strip of lawn next to the house and turned on the headlamps. The statue stood out almost luminously in the darkness, booming away to itself, more and more of the sonic cores budding out in the yellow glare of the lights. Gradually it lost its original shape; the toothed grill enveloped itself and then put out new struts and barbs that spiralled upwards, each throwing off secondary and tertiary shoots in its turn. Shortly after midnight it began to lean and then suddenly toppled over.

By now its movement was corkscrew. The plinth had been carried into the air and hung somewhere in the middle of the tangle, revolving slowly, and the main foci of activity were at either end. The growth rate was accelerating. We watched a new shoot emerge. As one of the struts curved round a small knob poked through the flaking chrome. Within a minute it grew into a spur an inch long, thickened, began to curve and five minutes later had developed into a full-throated sonic core twelve inches long.

Raymond pointed to two of my neighbours standing on the roofs of their houses a hundred yards away, alerted by the music carried across to them. 'You'll soon have everyone in Vermilion Sands out here. If I were you, I'd throw an acoustic drape over it.'

'If I could find one the size of a tennis court. It's time we did something, anyway. See if you can trace Lorraine Drexel. I'm going to find out what makes this statue go.'

Using the hacksaw, I cut off a two-foot limb and handed it to Dr Blackett, an eccentric but amiable neighbour who sometimes dabbled in sculpture himself. We walked back to the comparative quiet of the veranda. The single sonic core emitted a few random notes, fragments from a quartet by Webern.

'What do you make of it?'

'Remarkable,' Blackett said. He bent the bar between his hands. 'Almost plastic.' He looked back at the statue. 'Definite circumnutation there. Probably phototropic as well. Hmm, almost like a plant.'

'Is it alive?'

Blackett laughed. 'My dear Hamilton, of course not. How can it be?'

'Well, where is it getting its new material? From the ground?'

'From the air. I don't know yet, but I imagine it's rapidly synthesizing an allotropic form of ferrous oxide. In other words, a purely physical rearrangement of the constituents of rust.' Blackett stroked his heavy brush moustache and stared at the statue with a dream-like eye. 'Musically, it's rather curious – an appalling conglomeration of almost every bad note ever composed. Somewhere the statue must have suffered some severe sonic trauma. It's behaving as if it had been left for a week in a railroad shunting yard. Any idea what happened?'

'Not really.' I avoided his glance as we walked back to the statue. It seemed to sense us coming and began to trumpet out the opening bars of Elgar's Pomp and Circumstance march. Deliberately breaking step, I said to Blackett: 'So in fact all I have to do to silence the thing is chop it up into two-foot lengths?'

'If it worries you. However, it would be interesting to leave it, assuming you can stand the noise. There's absolutely no danger of it going on indefinitely.' He reached up and felt one of the spars. 'Still firm, but I'd say it was almost there. It will soon start getting pulpy like an over-ripe fruit and begin to shred off and disintegrate, playing itself out, one hopes, with Mozart's Requiem and the finale of the Götterdämmerung.' He smiled at me, showing his strange teeth. 'Die, if you prefer it.'

However, he had reckoned completely without Lorraine Drexel.

At six o'clock the next morning I was woken by the noise. The statue was now fifty feet long and crossing the flower beds on either side of the garden. It sounded as if a complete orchestra were performing some Mad Hatter's symphony out in the centre of the lawn. At the far end, by the rockery, the sonic cores were still working their way through the Romantic catalogue, a babel of Mendelssohn, Schubert and Grieg, but near the veranda the cores were beginning to emit the jarring and syncopated rhythms of Stravinsky and Stockhausen.

I woke Carol and we ate a nervous breakfast.

'Mr Hamilton!' she shouted. 'You've got to stop it!' The nearest tendrils were only five feet from the glass doors of the veranda. The largest limbs were over three inches in diameter and the pulse thudded through them like water under pressure in a fire hose.

When the first police cars cruised past down the road I went into the garage and found the hacksaw.

The metal was soft and the blade sank through it quickly. I left the pieces I cut off in a heap to one side, random notes sounding out into the air. Separated from the main body of the statue, the fragments were almost inactive, as Dr Black-ett had stated. By two o'clock that afternoon I had cut back about half the statue and got it down to manageable proportions.

'That should hold it,' I said to Carol. I walked round and lopped off a few of the noisier spars. 'Tomorrow I'll finish it off altogether.'

I wasn't in the least surprised when Raymond called and said that there was no trace anywhere of Lorraine Drexel.

At two o'clock that night I woke as a window burst across the floor of my bedroom. A huge metal helix hovered like a claw through the fractured pane, its sonic core screaming down at me.

A half-moon was up, throwing a thin grey light over the garden. The statue had sprung back and was twice as large as it had been at its peak the previous morning. It lay all over the garden in a tangled mesh, like the skeleton of a crushed building. Already the advance tendrils had reached the bedroom windows, while others had climbed over the garage and were sprouting downwards through the roof, tearing away the galvanized metal sheets.

All over the statue thousands of sonic cores gleamed in the light thrown down from the window. At last in unison, they hymned out the finale of Bruckner's Apocalyptic Symphony.

I went into Carol's bedroom, fortunately on the other side of the house, and made her promise to stay in bed. Then I telephoned Raymond Mayo. He came around within an hour, an oxyacetylene torch and cylinders he had begged from a local contractor in the back seat of his car.

The statue was growing almost as fast as we could cut it back, but by the time the first light came up at a quarter to six we had beaten it.

Dr Blackett watched us slice through the last fragments of the statue. 'There's a section down in the rockery that might just be audible. I think it would be worth saving.'

I wiped the rust-stained sweat from my face and shook my head. 'No. I'm sorry, but believe me, once is enough.'

Blackett nodded in sympathy, and stared gloomily across the heaps of scrap iron which were all that remained of the statue.

Carol, looking a little stunned by everything, was pouring coffee and brandy. As we slumped back in two of the deck chairs, arms and faces black with rust and metal filings, I reflected wryly that no one could accuse the Fine Arts Committee of not devoting itself wholeheartedly to its projects.

I went off on a final tour of the garden, collecting the section Blackett had mentioned, then guided in the local contractor who had arrived with his truck. It took him and his two men an hour to load the scrap – an estimated ton and a half – into the vehicle.

'What do I do with it?' he asked as he climbed into the cab. 'Take it to the museum?'

'No!' I almost screamed. 'Get rid of it. Bury it somewhere, or better still, have it melted down. As soon as possible.'

When they had gone Blackett and I walked around the garden together. It looked as if a shrapnel shell had exploded over it. Huge divots were strewn all over the place, and what grass had not been ripped up by the statue had been trampled away by us. Iron filings lay on the lawn like dust, a faint ripple of lost notes carried away on the steepening sunlight.

Blackett bent down and scooped up a handful of grains. 'Dragon's teeth. You'll look out of the window tomorrow and see the B Minor Mass coming up.' He let it run out between his fingers. 'However, I suppose that's the end of it.'

He couldn't have been more wrong.

Lorraine Drexel sued us. She must have come across the newspaper reports and realized her opportunity. I don't know where she had been hiding, but her lawyers materialized quickly enough, waving the original contract and pointing to the clause in which we guaranteed to protect the statue from any damage that might be done to it by vandals, livestock or other public nuisance. Her main accusation concerned the damage we had done to her reputation – if we had decided not to exhibit the statue we should have supervised its removal to some place of safekeeping, not openly dismembered it and then sold off the fragments to a scrap dealer. This deliberate affront had, her lawyers insisted, cost her commissions to a total of at least fifty thousand dollars.

At the preliminary hearings we soon realized that, absurdly, our one big difficulty was going to be proving to anyone who had not been there that the statue had actually started growing. With luck we managed to get several postponements, and Raymond and I tried to trace what we could of the statue. All we found were three small struts, now completely inert, rusting in the sand on the edge of one of the junkyards in Red Beach. Apparently taking me at my word, the contractor had shipped the rest of the statue to a steel mill to be melted down.

Our only case now rested on what amounted to a plea of self-defence. Raymond and myself testified that the statue had started to grow, and then Blackett delivered a long homily to the judge on what he believed to be the musical shortcomings of the statue. The judge, a crusty and short-tempered old man of the hanging school, immediately decided that we were trying to pull his leg. We were finished from the start.

The final judgment was not delivered until ten months after we had first unveiled the statue in the centre of Vermilion Sands, and the verdict, when it came, was no surprise.

Lorraine Drexel was awarded thirty thousand dollars.

'It looks as if we should have taken the pylon after all,' I said to Carol as we left the courtroom. 'Even the step-pyramid would have been less trouble.'

Raymond joined us and we went out on to the balcony at the end of the corridor for some air.

'Never mind,' Carol said bravely. 'At least it's all over with.'

I looked out over the rooftops of Vermilion Sands, thinking about the thirty thousand dollars and wondering whether we would have to pay it ourselves.

The court building was a new one and by an unpleasant irony ours had been the first case to be heard there. Much of the floor and plasterwork had still to be completed, and the balcony was untiled. I was standing on an exposed steel cross-beam; one or two floors down someone must have been driving a rivet into one of the girders, and the beam under my feet vibrated soothingly.

Then I noticed that there were no sounds of riveting going on anywhere, and that the movement under my feet was not so much a vibration as a low rhythmic pulse.

I bent down and pressed my hands against the beam.

Raymond and Carol watched me curiously. 'Mr Hamilton, what is it?' Carol asked when I stood up.

'Raymond,' I said. 'How long ago did they first start on this building? The steel framework, anyway.'

'Four months, I think. Why?'

'Four.' I nodded slowly. 'Tell me, how long would you say it took any random piece of scrap iron to be reprocessed through a steel mill and get back into circulation?'

'Years, if it lay around in the wrong junkyards.'

'But if it had actually arrived at the steel mill?'

'A month or so. Less.'

I started to laugh, pointing to the girder. 'Feel that! Go on, feel it!'

Frowning at me, they knelt down and pressed their hands to the girder. Then Raymond looked up at me sharply.

I stopped laughing. 'Did you feel it?'

'Feel it?' Raymond repeated. 'I can *hear* it. Lorraine Drexel – the statue. It's here!'

Carol was patting the girder and listening to it. 'I think it's humming,' she said, puzzled. 'It sounds like the statue.'

When I started to laugh again Raymond held my arm. 'Snap out of it, the whole building will be singing soon!'

'I know,' I said weakly. 'And it won't be just this building either.' I took Carol by the arm. 'Come on, let's see if it's started.'

We went up to the top floor. The plasterers were about to move in and there were trestles and laths all over the place. The walls were still bare brick, girders at fifteen-foot intervals between them.

We didn't have to look very far.

Jutting out from one of the steel joists below the roof was a long metal helix, hollowing itself slowly into a delicate sonic core. Without moving, we counted a dozen others. A faint twanging sound came from them, like early arrivals at a rehearsal of some vast orchestra of sitar-players, seated on every plain and hilltop of the earth. I remembered when we had last heard the music, as Lorraine Drexel sat beside me at the unveiling in Vermilion Sands. The statue had made its call to her dead lover, and now the refrain was to be taken up again.

'An authentic Drexel,' I said. 'All the mannerisms. Nothing much to look at yet, but wait till it really gets going.'

Raymond wandered round, his mouth open. 'It'll tear the building apart. Just think of the noise.'

Carol was staring up at one of the shoots. 'Mr Hamilton, you said they'd melted it all down.'

'They did, angel. So it got back into circulation, touching off all the other metal it came into contact with. Lorraine Drexel's statue is here, in this building, in a dozen other buildings, in ships and planes and a million new automobiles. Even if it's only one screw or ball-bearing, that'll be enough to trigger the rest off.'

'They'll stop it,' Carol said.

'They might,' I admitted. 'But it'll probably get back again somehow. A few pieces always will.' I put my arm round her waist and began to dance to the strange abstracted music, for some reason as beautiful now as Lorraine Drexel's wistful eyes. 'Did you say it was all over? Carol, it's only just beginning. The whole world will be singing.'

JOHN MCGAHERN
Lavin

When I knew Lavin he was close to the poorhouse but he'd still down mallet and cold chisel to limp after the young girls, crooked finger beckoning, calling, 'Come, give us a peep, there must be a few little hairs beginning,' and that strange inlooking smile coming over the white stubbled face while the girls, shrieking with laughter, kept backing just fast enough to stay outside his reach.

When I heard them speak of Lavin it was in puzzlement that when young and handsome he had worked such cruel hours at his trade, though he had no need because his uncle had left him Willowfield, the richest farm around, and had taken no interest in girls though he could have had his pick; and at a threshing or in a wheatfield he'd be found at nightfall gathering carelessly abandoned tools or closing gaps after the others had gone drinking or to dress for the dances. Neither could they understand his sudden heavy drinking in Billy Burns's: if before he had to enter a pub he'd accept nothing but lemonade. Burns was blamed for giving him credit when his money ran out; and after he seized and held in the house the gipsy girl who sold him paper flowers with wire stems, it was the same Burns who gave him the money to buy the gipsies off in return for Willowfield. The gipsies had told him that if he didn't pay what they wanted they'd come and cut him with rusted iron. What money he was able to earn afterwards was from his trade, and that steadily dwindled as machinery replaced the horse. All of his roof had fallen in except the kitchen, where oats and green weeds grew out of the thatch. Whatever work he had he did outside on the long hacked bench except when it was too cold or wet. The first time I stopped to watch him it was because of the attraction of what's forbidden. He was shaping a section of a cart wheel but put down mallet and chisel to say, that strange smile I'll always remember coming over his face, 'Those sisters of yours are growing into fine sprigs. Have you looked to see if any of them have started a little thatch?'

'No,' his smile frightened me.

'It should be soft, light, a shading,' his voice lingered on the words, I felt his eyes did not see past their smiling.

'I haven't seen,' I said and started to watch the roads for anybody coming.

'You should keep your eyes skinned then. All you have to do is to keep your eyes skinned, man,' the voice was harder.

'I don't sleep in their rooms.'

'No need to sleep in the same room, man. Just keep your eyes skinned. Wait till you hear them go to the pot and walk in by mistake. It'll be cocked enough to see if it has started to thatch,' the voice had grown rhythmical and hard.

It was more desire to see into this hot dark I glimpsed behind the smile than his constant pestering for the information made me begin to watch.

'The two eldest have hair but the others haven't,' I told him.

'The others have just a bald ridge with the slit,' he pursued fiercely.

'Yes.' I'd have escaped but he seized me by the lapels.

'The hair is fairer than on their heads?'

'Yes.'

'Fair and soft? A shade?'

'Yes, but let me go.'

'Soft and fair. The young ivy covering the slit,' he let me go as the voice grew caressing and the smile flooded over the face.

'So fair you can see the skin through it yet. A shading,' he gloated and then, 'Will you come with me a minute inside?'

'I have to go.'

He turned as if I no longer was there and limped, the boot

tongueless and unlaced, to the door, and though I hurried frightened away I heard the bolt scrape shut before I was out of earshot.

I avoided Lavin all that winter, I'd heard his foot was worse though and that he was unlikely to see another winter outside the poorhouse, it should have assuaged my fear but it did not, and besides I'd fallen in love with Charley Casey.

Charley Casey was dull in school; but he was good at games, and popular, with a confident laugh and white teeth and blue dark hair: he had two dark-haired sisters of seven-teen and nineteen, who were both beautiful, and a young widowed mother, and there hung about him that glamour of a house of ripe women. I helped him at his exercises, and in return he partnered me in handball. We started to skate in the evenings together on the shallow pond and to go to the river when the days grew warmer. I was often sick with anxiety, days he was absent – able to concentrate on nothing but the bell that would set me free to race to his house to see what had kept him away.

I tried to get him to read *David Copperfield* at that time so that we could share its world but he had always excuses. When the school closed and I had to go with my family to the sea he promised the day I left that he'd have it read by the time I got back: and instead of playing or swimming that week I spent most time alone among the sandhills imagining the conversations about *David Copperfield* on the riverbank in so many days when the slow week at the sea would be over.

'I read a good deal of it,' he answered to my first impatient question. The morning we got back I'd rushed to his house without waiting to eat, but as I pursued him with questions it grew depressingly clear that he'd not read a word and he admitted, 'I did my best to read it but I fell asleep. It's too hot to read. I'll read it when it rains.'

'You promised,' I accused bitterly; it broke me he could fall asleep over the beloved book.

'Honest, I'll read it when it rains. Why can't we go to the river same as before!'

'I don't want to go to the river. Why don't we go to see Lavin?' I said in thirst for some perversity or desire to degrade.

'That's a great idea,' I was taken aback by his enthusiasm. 'Why don't we see old John?'

I walked slowly and sullenly to Lavin's, resentful that he had fallen so easily in with my proposal.

Tools beginning to rust were outside on the old bench and the door was open. Lavin sat inside, his foot upon a footrest. The foot was wrapped in multicoloured rags that included red flannel and stank in the heat. Casey crossed the shaving-littered floor to go up to where Lavin sat at the empty fireplace to ask gaily, 'How's the old foot, John?'

'Playing me up, Charley Boy, but Himself was never in better order.'

'I've no doubt,' Charley laughed loudly.

I stood close to the door in smouldering anger and outrage.

'How are the two beauties of sisters? The thatch must be good and black and thick, eh? Brimmin' with juice inside, or have they shaved?' The smile came instantly, the repetitious fondling voice.

'No. They didn't shave it, John. It's as thick as thatch. Not that thatch is going to be all that thick above your head for long,' Casey laughed.

'Never mind the roof now. How is little John Charles coming along? Sprouting nicely?' he touched Casey's fly gently with his fingertips.

'You have to show me yours first. You never saw such a weapon as old John has,' Casey laughed and winked towards me at the door.

'No sooner said than done,' Lavin at once opened his trousers, what he took out looked to me enormous and brutal, it was stiff.

'A fair weapon and as stiff as a stake,' Casey gripped it in his fist.

'Know the only place the stiffs get in: the cunt and the

grave,' Lavin joked and I noticed his mouth full of the black stumps of teeth as he laughed.

'I bet you put it stiff and hard into the gipsy, old Johnny Balls,' Casey teased.

'Yeah, and what about seeing little John Charles now?'

'Fire ahead,' Casey laughed and I wanted to shout but wasn't able as Lavin unbuttoned Casey's fly and gently started to play with it in his fingers.

'Sprouting along royal, fit for milking any day.'

He fondled it until it was erect and then stretched to take a heavy carpenter's rule from the mantel.

'An increase of a good inch since the last time upon my soul,' he said. 'Why don't you come up from the door to see which little John Charles is farthest advanced?'

'No,' I had to fight back tears of rage and humiliation.

'Come on,' Casey said challengingly. 'Let old John compare them.'

'I don't want.'

'Have it your own way so,' he said, and as he took the rule to measure Lavin I left and waited in a fury outside. Either he grew scared alone or had enough because he soon followed.

'Why did you do it?' I attacked immediately he came.

'Oh, I like to take a hand at old John every now and then and get him all worked up,' he said casually.

'What did you let him fool around with you for?'

'What does it matter? It gets him all worked up.'

'I think it's disgusting,' I said with puritanical bitterness disturbed by feelings that had never touched me so fiercely before.

'Oh, what does it matter? He'll soon be in the poorhouse. Why don't we go for a swim?'

I walked in sullen silence by his side across the bridge. I wanted to swim with him, but I wanted to reject him, and in my heart I hated him. I calmed as we walked and at the boathouse helped him lift someone's night line, it had no fish though the hooks had been cleaned of bait. We started to talk again as we went to where the high whitethorns shielded the river from the road. We stripped on the bank and swam and afterwards lay on the warm moss watching the bream shoal out beyond the reeds, their black fins moving sluggish above the calm surface, white gleam of the bellies as they slowly rolled, until harness bells sounded on the road behind the whitethorns, and at the iron gate where the whitethorns ended two gipsy caravans and a spring cart came into our view. The little round curtained window in the back glittered in the sun, and two dogs roped to the axle trotted head low mechanically between the red wheels. Now and then a whip cracked above the horses' heads into the jingling of the harness bells.

'Do you think Lavin did what he was supposed to do to the gipsy girl?' I asked.

'He'd hardly have to pay with the farm if he didn't,' Casey answered with quiet logic. The image of the monstrous penis being driven deep in the guts of the struggling gipsy girl made me shiver with excitement on the moss.

'It'd be good if we had two caravans, you and me, like the caravans gone past. You and me would live in one caravan. We'd keep four women in the other. We'd ride around Ireland. We'd make them do anything we'd want to,' if Casey had been more forward with Lavin I was leading now.

'It'd be great,' he answered.

'They'd strip the minute we said strip. If they didn't we'd whip them. We'd whip them with those whips that have bits of metal on the ends. We'd whip them until the blood came and they'd to put arms round our knees for mercy.'

'Yes. We'd make them get down on their hands and knees naked and do them from behind the way the bull does,' Casey said and dived sideways to seize a frog in the grass, he took a dried stem of reed and began to insert it in the frog, 'That's what'll tickle him, I'm telling you.'

'Why couldn't we do it together?' I tentatively asked stiff with excitement, and he understood without me having to say more.

'I'll do it to you first,' he said, the dead reed sticking out of the frog in his hand, 'and then you'll do it to me.'

'Why don't you let me do it to you first and then you can have as long as you like on me?'

'No.'

The fear was unspoken: whoever took his pleasure first would have the other in his power and then might not surrender his own body. We avoided each other's eyes. I watched the dead reed being moved in and out of the frog.

'They say it hurts,' I said and there was the relief of the escape now from having to go through with it.

'It'd probably hurt too much,' Charley Casey was eager to agree. 'It'd be better to get two women and hurt them. They say a frog can only live so long under water.'

'Why don't we see?'

I found a stone along the bank and we tied one of the frog's legs with fishing line to the stone. We took it some hundred yards up the bank to where a shallow stream joined the river. We dropped the stone and watched the frog claw upwards but each time dragged back by the line, until it weakened, and it drowned.

We went silent across the Bridge, already changing. I helped him at school for sometime afterward but in the evenings we avoided each other, as if we vaguely glimpsed some shameful truth we were afraid to come to know together.

I never saw Lavin again, they took him to the poorhouse that October when the low hedges were blue with sloes, though by then the authorities, in their kindness, referred to it as the Resthome for Senior Citizens.

Casey is now married with children and runs a pub called the *Crown and Anchor* somewhere in Manchester but I've never had any wish to look him up, he seldom in fact enters my mind: but as I grow older hardly a day passes but this picture of Lavin comes to trouble me, it is of him when he was young, and they said handsome, gathering the scattered tools at nightfall in a clean wheatfield after the others had gone drinking or to change for the dances.

Notes on the Contributors

The following biographical and bibliographical information is, obviously, highly selective for reasons of space. For each author represented in the book brief biographical details are provided, including an indication of the kind of writing mainly done in addition to stories. The lists of short story collections are the main titles by individual authors. Publication, unless otherwise indicated, is London and usually represents first publication of the collection: individual stories in the volume may well have been written and published in periodicals years before. However, in the case of a few Commonwealth and non-British authors – including Morley Callaghan and Frank Sargeson – whose primary publishers have not been in London, this can be deceptive as collections may have been published in their own countries some years before British publication.

SYLVIA TOWNSEND WARNER was born in Harrow in 1893. Despite her father being a teacher at Harrow School, she claimed: 'I wasn't educated, I was very lucky'. After a period in a First World War munitions factory, she became involved in music scholarship and spent ten years at the Oxford University Press as a co-editor of the ten volume *Tudor Church Music*. In the 1930s she was active against General Franco. She was an expert on parapsychology. She wrote a biography of T. H. White (1967) as well as poetry. She won the Katherine Mansfield Prize in 1968; and died in 1978. She published seven novels.

STORIES

Some World Far from Ours, and Stay, Corydon, Thou Swain
  (Mathews, 1929)
Elinor Barley (Cresset, 1930)
Moral Ending (Joiner & Steele, 1931)
The Salutation (Chatto and Windus, 1932)
More Joy in Heaven (Cresset, 1935)
A Garland of Straw (Chatto and Windus, 1943)
The Museum of Cheats (Chatto and Windus, 1947)
Winter in the Air (Chatto and Windus, 1955)
The Cat's Cradle Book (Chatto and Windus, 1960)
A Spirit Rises (Chatto and Windus, 1962)
A Stranger with a Bag (Chatto and Windus, 1966)
The Innocent and the Guilty (Chatto and Windus, 1971)
Kingdoms of Elfin (Chatto and Windus, 1977)
Scenes of Childhood (Chatto and Windus, 1981)

JEAN RHYS was born in Dominica, West Indies in 1894. She
came to England when she was sixteen, and spent one term
at the Royal Academy of Dramatic Art, having to leave when
her father died. She drifted into a series of hopeless jobs –
chorus girl, mannequin, artist's model – and began to write
when the first of her three marriages broke up. She was
living in Paris at the time, and was taken up by Ford Madox
Ford, who wrote an enthusiastic introduction to her first
book, published in 1927. With the outbreak of the Second
World War, her work went out of print and Jean Rhys
dropped from sight. Nearly twenty years later she was
rediscovered. In 1966 her fifth and last novel, *Wide Sargasso
Sea*, won the W. H. Smith Award. She was made a CBE in
1978 and died the following year, aged eighty-four.

STORIES

The Left Bank (Cape, 1927)
Tigers Are Better-Looking (Deutsch, 1968)
Sleep it Off Lady (Deutsch, 1976)

LESLIE POLES HARTLEY was born in Cambridgeshire in 1895 and educated at Harrow School and Balliol College, Oxford. For many years he reviewed fiction for a wide range of periodicals. He wrote eighteen novels, the third in the *Eustace and Hilda* trilogy winning the James Tait Black Memorial Prize in 1946. He died in 1972.

STORIES

Night Fears (Putnam, 1924)
The Killing Bottle (Putnam, 1932)
The Travelling Grave (Barrie, 1951)
A White Wand (Hamish Hamilton, 1954)
Two for the River (Hamish Hamilton, 1961)
Mrs Carteret Receives (Hamish Hamilton, 1971)
The Complete Short Stories of L. P. Hartley (Hamish Hamilton, 1973)

ELIZABETH BOWEN was born into a landed Anglo-Irish family in 1899. She lived in England for most of her life and was married to an ex-Army officer, Alan Cameron. She died in 1973. Her best work memorialized the life and world of the Anglo-Irish gentry, and London during the Second World War. She wrote ten novels, almost eighty short stories, a history of her family and several other non-fiction books.

STORIES

Encounters (Sidgwick & Jackson, 1923)
Ann Lee's (Sidgwick & Jackson, 1926)
Joining Charles (Constable, 1929)
The Cat Jumps (Gollancz, 1934)
Look At All Those Roses (Gollancz, 1941)
The Demon Lover (Cape, 1945)
A Day in the Dark (Cape, 1965)

SEAN O'FAOLAIN was born in Cork in 1900, the son of a policeman. He studied at University College, Cork and in his early twenties joined the Irish Republican Army. In 1926 he went to Harvard, and remained in America for three years before returning to Europe, to London, to teach, by which time he was married and a father. One of his three children is the writer Julia O'Faolain. When his first book was published in 1932 and banned in Ireland that did not deter him from returning to live there. He has remained ever since, making his living mostly as a journalist and publishing more than twenty books: collections of stories, four novels, travel, biography, criticism as well as his autobiography, *Vive moi!* He lives in Dunlaoire.

STORIES
Midsummer Night's Madness (Cape, 1932)
There's a Birdie in the Cage (Grayson, 1935)
A Purse of Coppers (Cape, 1937)
Teresa (Cape, 1947)
I Remember, I Remember (Hart Davis, 1962)
The Heat of the Day (Hart Davis, 1966)
The Talking Trees (Cape, 1971)
Foreign Affairs (Constable, 1976)
The Collected Stories of Sean O'Faolain, Volumes 1, 2 and 3 (Constable, 1980, 1981 and 1982)
A Nest of Simple Folk (Constable 1989)

FRANK SARGESON was born in Hamilton, New Zealand in 1903 where his father kept a shop. He was educated at Hamilton West primary school, and then at the High School where he distinguished himself at games. As an extra-mural student of Auckland University he qualified in 1926 as a solicitor but he didn't practise. In the same year he went to Europe where he travelled. He returned to New Zealand in 1928 and lived at Takapuna, Auckland from 1932. He worked as a farm hand, market gardener, milkman and pantryman; and, for longer, as a journalist. He began publishing short stories in 1935. Since 1949 he wrote plays, six novels and three volumes of memoirs. He died in 1982.

STORIES
Conversation with my Uncle (Auckland: Unicorn, 1936)
A Man and his Wife (Christchurch: Caxton, 1940)
That Summer (Lehmann, 1946)
Man of England Now (Martin Brian and O'Keefe, 1972)
Collected Stories (MacGibbon & Kee, 1965)

MORLEY CALLAGHAN was born in Toronto, Canada, in 1903. He was educated at St Michael's College, University of Toronto. He worked for much of his life as a newspaperman. A Roman Catholic, he was married and had two children. He published eleven novels. He died in 1990

STORIES
Native Argosy (Toronto: Macmillan, 1929)
Now That April's Here (Toronto: Macmillan, 1936)
The Short Stories of Morley Callaghan, Volumes 1 and 2 (Macgibbon & Kee, 1963 and 1964)

RHYS DAVIES was born in the Rhondda Valley in 1903, and educated at Porth County School. He published seventeen novels before he died in 1978.

STORIES
The Song of Songs (Archer, 1927)
Aaron (privately printed, 1927)
A Bed of Feathers (Mandrake, 1929)
Tale (E. Lahr, 1930)
The Stars, the World and the Women (Joiner and Steele, 1930)
A Pig in a Poke (Joiner and Steele, 1931)
A Woman (Capell, 1931)
Arfon (Foyle, 1931)
Daisy Matthews (Waltham St Lawrence: Golden Cockerel, 1932)
Love Provoked (Putnam, 1933)

One of Norah's Early Days (Grayson, 1935)
The Things Men Do (Heinemann, 1936)
A Finger in Every Pie (Heinemann, 1942)
The Trip to London (Heinemann, 1946)
Boy with a Trumpet (Heinemann, 1949)
The Darling of Her Heart (Heinemann, 1958)
The Chosen One (Heinemann, 1967)
Collected Stories (Heinemann, 1955)

GRAHAM GREENE was born in 1904 and educated at Berkhamsted School, where his father was headmaster. On coming down from Balliol College, Oxford, where he published a collection of verse, he worked for four years as a sub-editor on *The Times*. In 1926 he was received into the Roman Catholic church; and established his reputation with his fourth novel, *Stamboul Train*. He became film critic of the *Spectator*, and in 1940 literary editor. In 1941 he served in the Foreign Office. He was made a Companion of Honour in 1966. He has written some thirty novels, 'entertainments', plays, children's and travel books, collections of essays and short stories, his autobiography and a biography of Rochester. Many of his novels and two of his stories have been filmed.

STORIES
The Basement Room (Cresset, 1935)
The Bear Fell Free (Grayson, 1935)
Twenty-one Stories (Heinemann, 1954)
A Sense of Reality (Bodley Head, 1963)
May We Borrow Your Husband? (Bodley Head, 1967)
Collected Stories (Bodley Head/Heinemann, 1972)
Collected Short Stories (Penguin, 1986)
The Last Word and Other Stories (Rheinhardt Books, 1990)

SAMUEL BECKETT was born near Dublin in 1906 and educated at Portora Royal School, County Fermanagh and Trinity College, Dublin. He was brought up a Protestant. He worked with James Joyce, and began publishing in 1929 but went almost unrecognized by the reading public until the international success of his play *Waiting for Godot* (1953). Married in 1948, he lived in Paris since 1938. He wrote principally in French, and usually translated his work into English himself. He published many plays, novels and shorter prose fictions as well as criticism and poetry. He was awarded the Nobel Prize for Literature in 1969. He died in 1989.

STORIES

More Pricks than Kicks (Chatto and Windus, 1934)
From an Abandoned Work (Faber, 1958)
Imagination Dead Imagine (Calder and Boyars, 1965)
No's Knife (Calder and Boyars, 1967)
Lessness (Calder and Boyars, 1971)
The Lost Ones (Calder and Boyars, 1972)
First Love (Calder and Boyars, 1973)
For To End Yet Again and other Fizzles (John Calder, 1976)
Collected Shorter Prose (John Calder, 1984)
Knowhow On (John Calder, 1989)
As the Story was Told (John Calder, 1990)

R. K. NARAYAN was born in Madras, India, in 1907 and educated at Maharaja's College, Mysore, whence he graduated in 1930. In 1964 Prime Minister Nehru awarded him the Padma Bhushan, one of four honours given annually in India for distinguished service. He has also won the National Prize of the Indian Literary Academy, the country's highest literary honour. He lives in Mysore but frequently visits Europe and the USA. In addition to his eleven novels, he is the author of a memoir and two works dealing with Indian legend as well as of numerous short stories.

STORIES

Cyclone (Mysore: Indian Thought Publications, no date)
Malgudi Days (Mysore: Indian Thought Publications, 1943)
An Astrologer's Day (Eyre & Spottiswoode, 1947)
Dodu (Mysore: Indian Thought Publications, no date)
Lawley Road (Mysore: Indian Thought Publications, 1956)
A Horse and Two Goats (Bodley Head, 1970)

WILLIAM SANSOM was born in London in 1912 and educated at Uppingham School. He then went to Bonn to study German, and later travelled and lived in various European countries including Spain, France, Austria and Italy. He started a commercial career in a London merchant bank but after some years joined an advertising agency as a copy-writer. Although he had been writing since childhood, he remained unpublished in any serious way until he was thirty, when he began contributing to leading literary journals such as *Horizon* and *New Writing*. He published over thirty books, including eight novels, and travel books. Married, with one son and a step-son, he died in 1976.

STORIES
Fireman Flower (Hogarth, 1944)
Three (Hogarth, 1946)
Something Terrible, Something Lovely (Hogarth, 1948)
South (Hodder and Stoughton, 1948)
Equilibriad (Hogarth, 1948)
The Passionate North (Hogarth, 1950)
A Touch of the Sun (Hogarth, 1952)
Lord Love Us (Hogarth, 1954)
A Contest of Ladies (Hogarth, 1956)
Among the Dahlias (Hogarth, 1957)
The Ulcerated Milkman (Hogarth, 1966)
The Vertical Ladder (Chatto and Windus, 1969)
Penguin Modern Stories 1 with other authors (Penguin, 1969)
The Marmalade Bird (Hogarth, 1973)
The Stories of William Sansom (Hogarth, 1963)

PATRICK WHITE was born in London in 1912, when his parents were in Europe for two years. His great-grandfather went from England to Australia in 1826, and the family remained there. At six months he was taken back to Australia, where his father owned a sheep station. When he was thirteen he was sent to school in England, to

Cheltenham, after which he studied languages at King's College, Cambridge. When he left university he settled in London, determined to become a writer. During the Second World War he was an RAF Intelligence officer in the Middle East and Greece, and only thereafter returned permanently to Australia. In 1973 he was awarded the Nobel Prize for Literature. He published eleven novels, and plays, poetry and a volume of autobiography. He died in 1990.

STORIES

The Burnt Ones (Eyre and Spottiswoode, 1964)
The Cockatoos (Cape, 1974)

MARY LAVIN was born in Massachusetts in 1912, and came to live in Ireland when she was ten. She has remained there ever since, and married an Irish lawyer. After his death she lived with her three daughters on their farm in County Meath. She remarried in 1969. She was awarded a D.Litt. by University College, Dublin, of which institution she was already a graduate. She has received two Guggenheim fellowships and has won many prizes including the James Tait Black and the Katherine Mansfield. She has published three novels.

STORIES

Tales from Bective Bridge (Michael Joseph, 1943)
The Long Ago (Michael Joseph, 1944)
The Becker Wives (Michael Joseph, 1946)
A Single Lady (Michael Joseph, 1951)
The Likely Story (Macmillan, 1957)
The Patriot Son (Michael Joseph, 1957)
The Great Wave (Macmillan, 1961)
Happiness (Constable, 1969)
A Memory (Constable, 1972)
The Shrine (Constable, 1977)
The Stories of Mary Lavin, Volumes 1, 2 and 3 (Constable, 1964, 1974 and 1978)
A Family Likeness and Other Stories (Constable, 1985)

NOTES ON THE CONTRIBUTORS

ELIZABETH TAYLOR was born in Reading, Berkshire in 1912. She was educated at the Abbey School, Reading until 1930, then lived at her home near High Wycombe working as a governess. Later she worked as a librarian. She married in 1936, and had two children. She and her husband lived in Penn, Buckinghamshire until her death in 1975. She published twelve novels.

STORIES
Hester Lilly (Peter Davies, 1954)
The Blush (Peter Davies, 1958)
A Dedicated Man (Chatto and Windus, 1965)
Penguin Modern Stories 6 with other authors (Penguin, 1970)
The Devastating Boys (Chatto and Windus, 1972)

FRED URQUHART, born in Edinburgh in 1912, spent most of his childhood in Fife, Perthshire and Wigtonshire and was educated at local schools. He worked in an Edinburgh bookshop from 1927 to 1935. His first published story was in the *Adelphi* in 1936. He has worked for a literary agency, as a reader for MGM, as London 'scout' for Walt Disney Productions, and from 1951 to 1974 was reader and editor for Cassell. He has reviewed fiction for various periodicals, and published four novels. He has lived in Sussex for twenty-five years.

STORIES
I Fell for a Sailor (Duckworth, 1940)
The Clouds Are Big With Mercy (Glasgow: Maclellan, 1946)
Selected Stories (Fridberg, 1946)
The Last GI Bride Wore Tartan (Edinburgh: Serif, 1947)
The Year of the Short Corn (Methuen, 1949)
The Last Sister (Methuen, 1950)
The Laundry Girl and The Pole (Arco, 1955)
Proud Lady in a Cage (Edinburgh: Paul Harris, 1980)
A Diver in China Seas (Quartet, 1980)
Collected Stories, Volume 1: *The Dying Stallion* (Hart Davis, 1967); Volume 2: *The Ploughing Match* (Hart Davis, 1968)

ANGUS WILSON was born in Bexhill, Sussex in 1913. A South African childhood was followed by education at Westminster School, then three years at Merton College, Oxford. In 1936 he joined the staff of the British Museum Library, and after the Second World War – during which he worked for the Foreign Office – he became Deputy Superintendent of the Reading Room. His first book was published when he was thirty-five. In 1955 he resigned from the Museum. He lives in Suffolk, and from 1963 has been associated with the University of East Anglia, where he was Professor of English Literature. He has published eight novels, biographies of Dickens and Kipling, much criticism and a play.

STORIES
The Wrong Set (Secker & Warburg, 1949)
Such Darling Dodos (Secker & Warburg, 1950)
A Bit Off the Map (Secker & Warburg, 1957)

ROALD DAHL was born in Llandaff, Glamorgan, in 1916 of Norwegian parents, and educated at Repton School. After taking part in an expedition to explore the interior of Newfoundland, he joined Shell in London. Four years later he was sent to Dar-es-Salaam but the next year, on the outbreak of the Second World War, he enlisted with the RAF in Nairobi. He was severely wounded in Libya, but later saw service as a fighter pilot in Greece and Syria. In 1942 he went to Washington as Assistant Air Attaché and it was there he began writing stories, about his RAF experiences. He ended the war as a Wing Commander. Many of his stories have been dramatized for television (*Tales of the Unexpected*) and he has written successful children's books as well as two novels. He died in 1990.

STORIES
Over to You (Hamish Hamilton, 1946)

NOTES ON THE CONTRIBUTORS

Someone Like You (Secker and Warburg, 1954)
Kiss Kiss (Michael Joseph, 1960)
Twenty-nine Kisses (Michael Joseph, 1969)
Switch Bitch (Michael Joseph, 1974)
The Wonderful Story of Henry Sugar (Jonathan Cape, 1977)

MURIEL SPARK was born in Edinburgh in 1918 and educated at James Gillespie's School for Girls there. She then spent some years in Central Africa but returned to Britain during the Second World War. She worked in the Political Intelligence Department of the Foreign Office. She subsequently edited two poetry magazines, and published poetry, criticism and biography. In 1951 she won an *Observer* short story competition, since when she has won many awards including the James Tait Black and an Italia Prize. She became a Roman Catholic in 1954, and was awarded an OBE in 1967. Divorced, with one child, she lives in Rome. She has published sixteen novels, one, *The Prime of Miss Jean Brodie*, having been filmed.

STORIES
The Go-Away Bird (Macmillan, 1958)
Voices at Play (Macmillan, 1961)
Collected Stories, I (Macmillan, 1967)

DORIS LESSING was born in Persia in 1919 but moved at the age of five to Southern Rhodesia, where her father went to farm. In 1949 she came to London, where she still lives. She has been married twice, and has three children. Her first novel was published in 1950, and her first collection of stories the following year. 1956 saw her last visit to the country where she grew up, the Southern Rhodesian authorities declaring her a prohibited immigrant after her return to England. She is interested in left-wing activism (she was a Communist but became disillusioned), female psychology and mysticism. She has published more than a dozen novels, including *The Golden Notebook* and the 'Children of Violence' sequence, a play and three volumes of non-fiction.

STORIES
This was the Old Chief's Country (Michael Joseph, 1951)
Five (Michael Joseph, 1953)
The Habit of Loving (MacGibbon & Kee, 1957)
A Man and Two Women (MacGibbon & Kee, 1963)
African Stories (Michael Joseph, 1964)
The Story of a Non-Marrying Man (Cape, 1972)
Collected African Stories, Volume 1: *This was the Old Chief's Country* (Michael Joseph, 1973)
Collected African Stories, Volume 2: *The Sun Between Their Feet* (Michael Joseph, 1973)
Collected Stories, Volume 1: *To Room Nineteen* (Cape, 1978)
Collected Stories, Volume 2: *The Temptation of Jack Orkney* (Cape, 1978)

ELSPETH DAVIE was born in Ayrshire in 1920. Her father was Scottish and her mother Canadian. She went to school in Edinburgh, trained at the University there, and at the College of Art. For some years thereafter she taught painting. She lived for a while in Ireland before returning to Edinburgh. She is married, with one daughter. She has published three novels, and in 1978 was awarded the Katherine Mansfield Prize.

STORIES
The Spark (Calder & Boyars, 1968)
The High Tide Talker (Hamish Hamilton, 1976)
The Night of the Funny Hats (Hamish Hamilton, 1980)

EDMUND CRISPIN was the pseudonym of Bruce Montgomery, born in Buckinghamshire in 1921. He was educated at Merchant Taylors' School and St John's College, Oxford, graduating in Modern Languages. He became organist and choirmaster at his local church when fifteen, and was organist and choirmaster at St John's for two of his undergraduate years. He taught for three years at Shrewsbury School, after which time he was able to earn a living as writer and composer. He edited detective and science fiction anthologies, reviewed regularly, and published nine detective stories. Most of his published music was for chorus and orchestra. He composed the background music for more than forty films. Married, he died in 1978.

GEOFFREY BUSH, born in 1920, is a composer and invented the plot of 'Who Killed Baker?'. Edmund Crispin completed the story, introducing his own detective, Gervase Fen.

STORIES
Beware of the Trains (Gollancz, 1953)
Fen Country (Gollancz, 1979)

GEORGE MACKAY BROWN was born in Stromness, Orkney in 1921 and still lives and works there. He was educated at Stromness Academy and Newbattle Abbey College – when the poet Edwin Muir was warden – then read English at Edinburgh University, where he did post-graduate work on Gerard Manley Hopkins. The composer Peter Maxwell Davies has set several of his texts, prose and poetry, to music. Being an unenthusiastic traveller, he has only once been out of Scotland: to Ireland in 1968, on a Society of Authors Travel Award. He was made an OBE in 1974. He has published much poetry, two books about Orkney, two novels, and plays. In 1971 he won the Katherine Mansfield Prize.

STORIES
A Calendar of Love (Hogarth, 1967)
A Time to Keep (Hogarth, 1969)
Hawkfall (Hogarth, 1974)
The Sun's Net (Hogarth, 1976)
The Golden Bird: Two Orkney Stories (John Murray, 1987)
The Masked Fisherman and Other Stories (John Murray, 1990)

FRANCIS KING was born in Adelboden, Switzerland in 1923, his childhood being spent in that country and in India. He visited England for the first time at the age of nine, when sent home to school. He was educated at Shrewsbury School and at Balliol College, Oxford having won classical scholarships to both places. He spent the Second World War working on the land as a conscientious objector. In 1949 he joined the British Council and until 1964 served in Italy, Greece, Egypt, Finland and Japan. He then lived in Brighton before moving to London. He has worked as a publisher's reader, is drama critic of a national newspaper and regularly reviews fiction. He has published poetry and seventeen novels, including one under a pseudonym. He has won the Katherine Mansfield and Somerset Maugham Awards.

STORIES
So Hurt and Humiliated (Longman, 1959)
The Japanese Umbrella (Longman, 1964)
The Brighton Belle (Longman, 1968)
Penguin Modern Stories 12 with other authors (Penguin, 1972)
Hard Feelings (Hutchinson, 1976)
Indirect Method (Hutchinson, 1981)

NADINE GORDIMER was born in Springs, a gold mining town on the East Rand in South Africa in 1923, and was educated at Witwatersrand University. She started writing when a child and published stories in the children's supplement of Johannesburg's biggest newspaper. She has been married twice, and has two children. She has published eight novels, won the W. H. Smith Award in 1961 for *Friday's Footprint* and the Booker Prize in 1974 for *The Conservationist*.

STORIES
Face to Face (Johannesburg: Silver Leaf, 1949)
The Soft Voice of the Serpent (Gollancz, 1952)

Six Feet of the Country (Gollancz, 1956)
Friday's Footprint (Gollancz, 1960)
Not for Publication (Gollancz, 1965)
Penguin Modern Stories 4 with other writers (Penguin, 1970)
Livingston's Companions (Cape, 1972)
Selected Stories (Cape, 1975)
Some Monday for Sure (Heinemann African Writers Series, 1976)
A Soldier's Embrace (Cape, 1980)
Something Out There (Cape, 1984)

GEORGE MACDONALD FRASER was born in Carlisle in 1925 and educated at Carlisle Grammar School and Glasgow Academy. In the army he was reduced to the ranks for losing a tea-urn, served as an infantry scout in Burma, and was commissioned in the Gordon Highlanders. He was deputy editor of the *Glasgow Herald*, 1964–69. He is married and has three children. He has published half-a-dozen novels about Harry Flashman, the bully of *Tom Brown's Schooldays* (*The Flashman Papers*), and written screenplays. He lives in the Isle of Man.

STORIES
The General Danced at Dawn (Barrie & Jenkins, 1970)
McAuslan in the Rough (Barrie & Jenkins, 1974)

RUTH PRAWER JHABVALA was born in Cologne in 1927 of Polish parents and came to England with them when she was twelve. She was educated in England, took her degree at London University, and married an Indian architect with whom she lived in Delhi for many years. She has three daughters. With the director James Ivory she has written the scripts for several films, and has written television plays. In 1975 her novel *Heat and Dust* won the Booker Prize. She has published eight novels.

STORIES
Like Birds, Like Fishes (Murray, 1963)
A Stronger Climate (Murray, 1968)
An Experience of India (Murray, 1971)
Penguin Modern Stories 11 with other writers (Penguin, 1972)
How I Became a Holy Mother (Murray, 1976)

ALAN SILLITOE was born in Nottingham in 1928. Having failed the 11+ examination twice he worked from the age of fourteen in factories, then as an air traffic control assistant with the Ministry of Aircraft Production. In May 1946 he enlisted in the RAF and served as a wireless operator in Malaya. He was discharged as medically unfit in November 1949, then lived in France and Spain from 1952–58. He now lives in Kent and in London with his wife, the writer Ruth Fainlight. They have two children. He has published poetry and plays in addition to eleven novels.

STORIES
The Loneliness of the Long Distance Runner (W. H. Allen, 1959)
The Ragman's Daughter (W. H. Allen, 1963)
Guzman, Go Home (Macmillan, 1968)
Men, Women and Children (W. H. Allen, 1973)
The Second Chance (Cape, 1981)

WILLIAM TREVOR was born in County Cork in 1928 and spent his childhood in provincial Ireland, being educated at St Columba's College and Trinity College, Dublin. For a while he worked as a sculptor, then won the Hawthornden Prize with his novel *The Old Boys*. He is married, has two sons and lives in Devon. He previously lived in London, working in an advertising agency. He has published nine novels, and written television, stage and radio plays. He was made a CBE in 1977.

STORIES

The Day We Got Drunk on Cake (Bodley Head, 1967)
Penguin Modern Stories 8 with other writers (Penguin, 1971)
The Ballroom of Romance (Bodley Head, 1972)
Angels at the Ritz (Bodley Head, 1975)
Lovers of Their Time (Bodley Head, 1978)
Beyond the Pale (Bodley Head, 1981)
Fools of Fortune (Bodley Head, 1983)
The News From Ireland (Bodley Head, 1986)
Family Sins (Bodley Head, 1990)

JAMES GRAHAM BALLARD was born in Shanghai of English parents in 1930, and lived there until he was fifteen. During the war he was interned for two and a half years by the Japanese in a civilian prison camp. He was repatriated in 1946 and after leaving school read medicine at King's College, Cambridge. He then became a copywriter, a Covent Garden porter and an RAF pilot. He began to write seriously in 1957. He is a widower, with three children. He has contributed to all the leading science fiction magazines. He has published nine novels.

STORIES

The Voices of Time (New York: Berkley, 1962)
Billenium (New York: Berkley, 1962)
The 4-Dimensional Nightmare (Gollancz, 1963)
Passport to Eternity (New York: Berkley, 1963)
The Disaster Area (Cape, 1967)
The Day of Forever (Panther, 1968)
The Atrocity Exhibition (Cape, 1970)
Vermilion Sands (Cape, 1973)
The Terminal Beach (Gollancz, 1974)
Low-Flying Aircraft (Cape, 1976)
The Best Short Stories (Cape, 1978)
The Venus Hunters (Panther, 1981)

Myth of the Near Future (Cape, 1982)
The Day Of Forever (Gollancz, 1986)
War Fever (Harper Collins, 1990)

JOHN MCGAHERN was born in Dublin in 1934. He was educated at University College, Dublin and later became a Fellow of the University of Reading. He has been Professor of Literature at Colgate University, Hamilton, New York. He has written plays and published four novels.

STORIES

Nightlines (Faber and Faber, 1970)
Getting Through (Faber and Faber, 1978)

NOTES